# TEAMWORK AND THE BOTTOM LINE:

## GROUPS MAKE A DIFFERENCE

# SERIES IN APPLIED PSYCHOLOGY

**Edwin A. Fleishman,** George Mason University
*Series Editor*

# TEAMWORK AND THE BOTTOM LINE:

## GROUPS MAKE A DIFFERENCE

### BY

### NED ROSEN

### THE TEAMWORKERS, INC.

**LAWRENCE ERLBAUM ASSOCIATES, PUBLISHERS**
1989   Hillsdale, New Jersey                    Hove and London

Lawrence Erlbaum Associates, Inc., Publishers
365 Broadway
Hillsdale, New Jersey 07642

Library of Congress Cataloging-in-Publication Data

Rosen, Ned A.
    Teamwork and the bottom line : groups make a difference / by Ned
  Rosen.
        p.       cm.
  Bibliography: p.
  Includes index.
  ISBN 0-8058-0459-5. -- ISBN 0-8058-0461-7 (pbk.)
  1. Work groups.   I. Title.
HD66.R66   1989
658.4´02--dc19                                              88-32458
                                                                CIP

**Printed in the United States of America**
**10  9  8  7  6  5  4  3  2  1**

This book is dedicated to the memory of

Douglas McGregor

and

I. R. Knickerbocker,

a small but dedicated team

# CONTENTS

# FOREWORD

There is a compelling need for innovative approaches to the solution of many pressing problems involving human relationships in today's society. Such approaches are more likely to be successful when they are based on sound research and applications. This Series in Applied Psychology offers publications which emphasize state of the art research and its application to important issues of human behavior in a variety of societal settings. The objective is to bridge both academic and applied interests.

This volume, TEAMWORK AND THE BOTTOM LINE, fits in with this objective. In the context of strengthening this country's economy and competitive position, teambuilding, alternative work designs, self-managed work groups, and new approaches to motivation and organizational effectiveness are being discussed with increasing frequency in both academic and business publications. At the same time, a great deal of research from social and organizational psychology has been concerned with studies of group processes, leadership, social interaction and motivational mechanisms. This book shows how this research is relevant to the development of highly motivated and productive work groups in organizations.

The author, Ned Rosen, draws on his unique experience as a researcher and practitioner concerned with these issues. During his twenty-one year career as a professor at Cornell University he conducted research on many of the core topics covered in this book. He also was able, in his role as a management consultant during this period, to apply many of these concepts. Several years ago he left his faculty position to found the Teamworkers, Inc. In this role he has continued testing many of the concepts covered in this book with a number of the world's best known corporations and international agencies. His writing reflects his career - a blend of substantive conceptual interests and insistence upon practical application.

The book, which is very readable, is designed for organizational psychologists and students of organizational behavior, and for managers concerned with improving their own effectiveness as well as that of their organizations.

Edwin A. Fleishman, Editor
Series in Applied Psychology

# PREFACE

This is a book about the development and management of team-work in task groups, a concept over which the Japanese have no monopoly. It has grown out of almost three decades of university teaching and extensive consulting and research experience with many varied organizations. It is based on my observation that successful managers are people who understand the dynamics of group interaction, and can use that understanding effectively to motivate members of their work group to achieve important goals.

No extensive effort to increase productivity, employee committment to customer service, quality and excellence, or to encourage innovation, competitiveness, and greater risk taking behavior is likely to achieve its potential in the absence of serious attention to group factors. Groups make a difference to productivity, the bottom line, and organizational survival. The following chapters show how and why this is so.

Indeed, many observers believe that properly nurtured and led, a group becomes synergistic and achieves at a higher level than might be expected of the individuals involved. In other words, the total often appears to be larger than the sum of its parts. This concept and the principles involved are relevant at all organizational levels. From first line supervisor to Chief Executive Officer, from task force chairman to Chairman of the Board, most managers are responsible for making things happen through groups, not just through people.

I have heard many hearty guffaws from men and women of practical affairs when one or another public speaker proclaimed that "a camel is a horse created by a committee!" The fact is, if a committee really did create the camel, it was a very effective committee. (The camel is remarkably adapted to its environment.) The laughter seems to come primarily from those who strongly value individual effort and achievement. They apparently believe that groups are to be avoided, or at least disdained, possibly because of their conformity producing influences and "time wasting" nature.

On the other hand, it is clear that group effort not only is unavoidable in most task settings, but frequently is highly desirable. One needs only a brief tour of any hospital, government agency, insurance company, department store, university, army barrack or factory to observe group formats. It also is clear that people often are thrown together and expected to perform without any special attention to what is known about groups and their unique needs for composition, leadership, reward systems, and procedures in relation to task requirements. While the state of our research-based knowledge about task groups in work organizations is limited, we do know enough to help avoid major errors and to enhance the probabilities of effectiveness in many cases.

My intended audience is the manager or aspiring manager of people at work, and students of organization and groups. The book is appropriate for readers having applied interests and who want to know more about how and why things happen as they do. Those looking for easy answers and quick fixes on how to build and manage for teamwork will not find them in these pages; there simply aren't any. The reader will become acquainted, however, with ways of thinking about groups, and the many ways in which they may be influenced. This should be helpful to those looking for new strategies to improve both productivity and quality of work, to say nothing of quality of life.

The manuscript's lengthy developmental history makes it difficult for me to acknowledge all of those who have contributed in some significant way. My interest in groups began at Antioch College where I was among the several students who were strongly influenced by Douglas McGregor during his Presidency there. My first course in organizational psychology was taken as a tutorial with him. While the field has grown far beyond the concepts of Theory X and Y, he obviously struck a chord having lasting appeal. The chapters that follow owe his influence a great deal.

Several others who have influenced my thinking about organizational and leadership processes or who otherwise have been instrumental in the development of the book include: William F. Whyte, Hermann H. Remmers, Ross Stagner, Hjalmar Rosen, Lauren Wispe, Carroll Shartle, Nick Georgiades, Felician Foltman, Jack Stewart, Bob Johnson, Jerry Abarbanel, Hank Bertram, Harlan Reynolds, Bob Dawson, James Reeder, Bob Henderson, Jim Etherington, Dunston Chicanot, Larry Armstrong, Gautum Kaji, Anthony Williams, Martijn Paijmans, and Lee Roberts. Some of the above people are former professors of mine; others were professional colleagues in academia. Still others were particularly supportive clients for one or another of my applied research, management development, or consulting projects over the years. All of them provided many opportunities for me to learn.

Conceptually the book's content also owes a lot to the writings of Kurt Lewin, Alvin Zander, Norman R. F. Maier, Dorwin Cartwright, Robert Kahn, Daniel Katz, Bernard Bass, and Fred Fiedler. Any student of groups has been influenced heavily by these scholar-researchers. I have borrowed freely of their thinking while translating their work into terminology and applications that I hope many readers will find useful. My apologies are offered for any errors of translation. My apologies also are extended to the many additional scholars whose important works are not cited here. My purpose is to "tell a story" and raise consciousness levels within a strict page limit, not to provide a comprehensive textbook.

I also am indebted to the students in my leadership and group dynamics seminars during my prior career at Cornell University. They wrestled with early versions of draft materials and provided useful feedback. The recent bibliographic support of Tim Buckley and Tove Hammer are especially appreciated.

Ed Fleishman has my gratitude for his encouragement and interest in the manuscript, and his persistence in making things happen. It seems only fitting that at this stage of his distinguished career he should renew his interest in the topic at hand.

Valuable suggestions and criticisms of the manuscript at various stages of its development came from Bernard Indik, Steve Kerr, Herb Meyer, Len Greenhalgh, Mary Scott, Barbara Daugherty, and several anonymous reviewers. They are gratefully acknowledged for their suggestions, and for stimulating harder thinking. They also are absolved of responsibility for the book's shortcomings.

Elsie Cole did much of the typing on early draft materials and provided the protection an author needs from one's environment to get such a job started. The early writing often was accomplished at the expense of Lawrence K. Williams who picked up the administrative slack in our office on numerous occasions while also providing good ideas and a sense of humor.

My greatest debt is to my patient wife, Phyllis, whose supportiveness is unmatched. Her many hours at the word processor keyboard and unflagging attention to the endless details of proofreading also are gratefully acknowledged.

Acknowledgement also is due all those responsible for the remarkable technology associated with microcomputers. Without it this manuscript never would have been completed.

Finally, my thanks are extended to USA TODAY, the NEW YORKER MAGAZINE, and the King Features Syndicate, Inc. for their permission to reproduce cartoons that make a point.

Ned Rosen
Lighthouse Point, Florida
November 19, 1988

# CHAPTER 1

## INTRODUCTION

Most of us are brought into this world with the aid of a group in the maternity ward of a hospital. We also, in most cases, will be phased out of this world with support from a group organized by a funeral home. In between we:

- are raised in a group called a family.

- go to school in something called classes.

- play games as members of teams.

- worship in groups called congregations.

- receive help, in some cases, from therapy groups.

- live in homes built by construction groups.

- even have our garbage picked up by groups.

If we travel in a large aircraft, it is operated by a flight crew. Should we be foolish enough to commit a serious crime, quite likely we will be tried by jury. If we require appendectomies or open heart surgery the operations are performed by teams, not by individual doctors working alone. And, until recent years, if invited by Uncle Sam to serve in the Army, the decision was made by a group of our neighbors called the local draft board.

Indeed, we are influenced by countless additional decision making groups. Examples include the Federal and 50 State Supreme Courts, key committees in legislatures, the National Security Council, the National Labor Relations Board, the Civil Aeronautics Board, and the Nuclear Energy Commission. For many people crucial decisions are made by a college admission committee; even if such a committee is assisted by a computer, you may be sure that the computer was both designed and built by groups.

Most of us also work in groups once we enter the labor force. In short, groups are found everywhere. Many of them are task groups. They exist to organize some level of collective effort in pursuit of a parent organization's goals, while simultaneously satisfying needs of their individual members.

Task groups in work organizations differ from each other, as do individuals, along many dimensions:

- Their goals may be more or less clear, may be long term or short term, may or may not be socially significant, and their tasks may be more or less challenging;

- They differ in their functions - some exist purely to make decisions, others build things, some are designed to control processes or coordinate complex activities, and so on;

- Groups vary in size;

- They vary in the complexity of their internal structure and requirements for specialization among members;

- Some last longer than others (life span);

- They differ in the attitudes and prejudices shared by their members;

- Different groups employ different kinds of communications systems, and vary in their requirements for unique vocabulary;

- They differ in the extent to which they have internal harmony, in their effects on their members, in their decision making processes, and in their selection standards; and

- Finally, they differ in their methods and effectiveness at getting things done.

The above and other task group dimensions, and the context in which they operate, are what this book is about. Effective task groups, like effective people, usually don't just happen...

## TASK GROUPS AND THE SOCIAL SYSTEM AT WORK: A DISASTER CASE COMPARED WITH A SUCCESS STORY

The nation's productivity and labor problems and achievements discussed periodically in magazines and newspapers are strongly influenced by group dynamics in work organizations. The enthusiasm displayed by space workers after a successful rocket launch reflects a common form of team spirit. Alternatively, chronic absenteeism, sub-standard productivity, negative attitudes, poor service, and shoddy workmanship are at least partly a function of inadequate attention to social organization in general and group dynamics in particular.

**Disaster case** - Perhaps a brief case history will illustrate my point. A major organization I once worked in had within it a packaging and shipping department staffed by approximately 120 people (almost all female) when the plant was busy. For many years the personnel worked in teams of 8 to 10 members. The teams were of fairly stable membership and became viable social units. Each team worked at a separate, mechanically paced conveyor belt. The teams' function was to pack different products into boxes of various sizes, pack these boxes and various printed matter into larger shipping cartons and apply appropriate sealing tape and labels. The physical layout of each short conveyor and related tables and stools enabled easy, face-to-face interaction among the employees who, by-and-large, seemed to enjoy each other's company. Indeed, some of the women were there for more than their pay; they liked being with their friends. Thus, the department evolved into a cultural unit comprised of several teams, and the social relationships seemed perfectly healthy. Relationships between workers and supervisors also were friendly.

*Then came the computer.* The production planning department, staffed by engineers, converted the entire plant to a computerized production scheduling system. Disregarding group dynamics, the engineers designed their computer program in a way that destroyed the long-established social structure of the department. The new system required that stable groups not be used; at the beginning of each shift and after lunch, the individuals were re-shuffled into different combinations.

In other words, *group composition was changed twice every day!* As a result the attitudes and behaviors in this formerly viable department deteriorated badly. Supervisors found that they didn't know the names of their frequently changed group members -- they began calling some of them, "Hey you." Absenteeism increased dramatically; numerous grievances arose; the employees became agitated with peers, and excessive rest breaks were taken during working hours. To combat the latter, female supervisors were ordered by higher level managers into the ladies' rooms to take down the names of violators. Eventually many people resigned and this became a very difficult department for which to recruit new people because its increasingly bad reputation spread throughout the community.

The above series of events illustrates that groups can be powerful and constructive forces in the work organization. The computer could have been programmed to capitalize on the existing group structure; instead it destroyed that structure and produced many of the same problems that plague work forces and organizations the world over. Please note that computerization is not the only threat to viable groups and teamwork in the work place. The extensive "re-structuring and downsizing" of many American corporations in recent years also has been highly damaging to group structure and effectiveness. I shall return to this point in Chapter Eleven.

**Success story** - Let me now compare the above account with a totally different experience reported in the professional research literature. A major textile manufacturer was experiencing disappointment with performance after introducing new and expensive automatic looms to replace obsolete nonautomatic machines at its mill in India. While labor-management relations reportedly were amicable, neither the quality nor quantity improvements expected of the new machines materialized. In this case, the workers were "organized" primarily as a collection of individuals, each being responsible for one of several specialized tasks in this mill, which operated more than 200 automatic looms. There were 12 specialties represented among 29 workers, covering such tasks as supplying new thread to the machines, minor repairs to work in process, correcting major machine breakdowns, removal of finished product, routine maintenance, floor cleaning and so on.

To increase productivity and quality to levels appropriate to the machines' potential, the management had to chose between two strategies. They could keep the existing specialized staffing pattern while increasing "supervision" (meaning closer observation and prodding), or, re-organize the 29 men into teams, giving each team total responsibility for the operation and maintenance of several machines. The team strategy was chosen, and implemented with the aid of a behavioral science research group.

The action researcher reported that for more than two years after the changes were introduced, productivity improved and was maintained at ninety-five percent of potential. It was eighty percent prior to the reorganization into teams. There also was a substantial reduction in the amount of damaged cloth - a quality measure. The researcher described unusually strong worker motivation under the new system. Weavers <u>ran,</u> rather than walked, to their machines to repair breakdowns. Because of government labor law restrictions on work during mealtime, supervisors had to stay in the work area during lunch breaks to restrain enthusiastic team members from returning to their looms before the end of their lunch. The improved motivation and team spirit enabled the company to implement a third shift, something previously deemed impossible because of the difficult climatic conditions there. The researcher summarized as follows:

> "Despite the great difference in culture between India and western societies, the same ... findings in worker motivation are apparent. When people have a meaningful task and membership in a satisfactory primary work group organized meaningfully for task accomplishment they work harder and are more satisfied with their work."[1]

## GROUP LIFE CYCLE MAKES A DIFFERENCE

Some task groups are more effective than others, in part because they are at different phases of development. Effective leaders need to be aware of what phase of life cycle development their group is in and to use that knowledge to help the group achieve its goals.

Take the Philadelphia Flyers 1979-80 hockey team, for example. Supposedly in a "rebuilding" phase following a decline of their previous dynasty, the Flyers unexpectedly went on a record - breaking 35-game undefeated streak in late 1979 and early 1980; they became, at least temporarily, the toast of professional hockey. The Montreal Canadiens, on the other hand, winners of several consecutive hockey championships in the seasons immediately preceding 1979-80, got off to an unexpectedly slow start that year. They played lethargically and lost several early games to teams they had previously dominated. Their new coach, somehow sensing that he could not turn this decline around, resigned early in the new season. (Later in the season this team regained its form and took first place in its division.)

Direct observation and comparison of these two teams, both engaged in the same task against the same level of competition under similar economic conditions, probably would have revealed many differences. While both teams were staffed by highly talented players, the motivation levels may well have been different since one team was not expected to be a big winner while the other was. Coaching skills and style, interpersonal relations among the players, the system of maintaining internal discipline, and hometown crowd behavior also may have been much different. (Indeed, special "team building" techniques were used by the Flyer's new coach. These techniques, which also have been used in many business organizations, are described in a later chapter.)

## THE MANAGER OFTEN IS THE KEY

While many factors are important, at this point there is overwhelming evidence that one of the most important elements of task group viability is the manager. Whether a coach, first line supervisor, committee chairperson, middle level manager, or senior executive, the individual known as the group's "manager" is a key figure. Let us move on, then, to the business at hand.

## ENDNOTES

1   Katz, D. and Kahn, R., THE SOCIAL PSYCHOLOGY OF WORK ORGANIZA-TIONS, 1966, New York: Wiley, 443-446. The original research was conducted and reported by Rice, A. K., PRODUCTIVITY AND SOCIAL ORGANIZATION: THE AHMEDABAD EXPERIMENT, 1958, London: Tavistock Publications. The reader may also want to read some other, more recent accounts of teamwork in the work place. For an American example see Bassin, M., "Teamwork at General Foods: new and improved," PERSONNEL JOURNAL, May 1988, 62-70. For an account of teamwork in Volvo automobile manufacturing plants, see Gyllenhammar, P., PEOPLE AT WORK, 1977, Reading, MA: Addison-Wesley. Gyllenhammar, now the chairman of the Volvo Board, believes that a team approach represents a cost-effective alternative to traditional assembly lines. Finally, a recent movie made in Hollywood, California called STAND AND DELIVER, depicts a true and engaging story of a high school teacher who applied team building tactics in his calculus class with great effectiveness. The high school is located in a working class Los Angeles neighborhood whose population includes large percentages of Hispanics and blacks.

# CHAPTER 2

# THE MANAGER'S PART IN GROUP PROCESS

"Believe me, gang. Just because I've been given my own cubicle
doesn't mean I'm going to forget my old friends."

Drawing by H. Martin; ©️ 1973

The New Yorker Magazine, Inc.

Many managers fail to realize that if they are accepted by
their subordinates they also are considered by them to be part of
their group. And, in circumstances where a manager does not lead
a group or unit toward its goals, an informal leader is likely to
arise from the ranks to fill the gap. In other words, the manager
or supervisor, although appointed by higher managers, "vested" with
authority to do the job, and usually selected on the basis of long
experience and task-relevant accomplishments, nonetheless is considered by subordinates to be an integral part of their work group or

team only after proving his or her value as a leader to subordinates. Until accomplishing this, the manager is merely an appointed "head," not a leader. This is true for academic administrators, industrial supervisors, executives, military officers, athletic coaches, and all other leader-follower combinations.)[1] (Actor Gene Hackman's motion picture portrayal of a new coach taking over a basketball team in a small Indiana high school offers rich insights into this process. See Hoosiers.)

In addition, the manager or supervisor, like an elected public office holder, must maintain legitimacy in the eyes of subordinates on a continuing basis. One cannot remain the unchallenged leader strictly on the basis of past accomplishments. As new members replace or supplement old ones, they, too, must be shown that the appointed manager is "their leader." After building an effective team a manager must continually maintain it just as the local union president or leader of a boys' neighborhood gang must do.

## HOW MANAGERS GAIN ACCEPTANCE BY THEIR GROUPS

The appointed manager becomes a leader rather than a "head" by showing an ability to help the group members achieve their goal(s). Of course, there are many factors that influence the chances of demonstrating this to subordinates. "Heads" will be accepted as leaders and have enough power to act effectively if:

- they have superior knowledge about the group's task and how it ties in with the larger organization;

- group members feel the manager has a right to tell them what to do;

- the group members think the manager is just like them, only better; and

- group members find acceptable both the manager's apparent personal motives for being in the job and the process by which he or she was selected.

These sensitive matters are likely to be affected by the appointed "head's" personal traits, past task-related accomplishments, technical expertise, leadership style, and length of service with the organization. Beginning with the manager's personal motives for being in the job, let us see how these and other factors come into play.

**The manager's will to manage** - It often has been observed that many managers, task force, and special project chairpersons serve unwillingly or at least reluctantly. Such people may not wish to spend the extra time required or may not like the idea of being responsible for other people. They are pushed into leadership roles because they are the "obvious" choice, because "there is no one else," or because they are the least of several mediocre alternatives. Appointing (or electing) authorities appeal to their sense of organizational loyalty and citizenship to get them to accept a position. Other individuals eagerly seek leadership positions through which they can exercise power, or to enhance their visibility for career mobility and further advancement purposes. Still others thrive on being the center of attention and seek or remain in leadership positions, accordingly. Some accept leadership positions as a means of achieving worthwhile professional or organizational goals - or even for ideological reasons. Thus, a medical doctor may leave a private practice to head up a new hospital at a modest salary, believing that more people will derive health benefits. Finally, various managers sometimes are beholden in a political sense to one or another person or sub-group who may have "helped" him or her get the job.

It is reasonable to assume that managers' motivational reasons for being in a position will affect their focus, energy levels, and strategies. For example, a reluctant candidate may be able to exact resource concessions from superiors as a condition for accepting an undesirable assignment, or may strike a bargain that will require him or her to remain in the unwanted position for only a short time. The extra resource may be an increase in the group's staff or budget, while the negotiated short term will probably result in something less than full personal effort in the new job. The group will like the first outcome but may feel cheated about the latter.

**Some managers look out only for "number one"** - A candidate who takes on a specific managerial assignment to gain visibility and a stepping stone to a higher level position is likely to approach the new job with considerable vigor, thereby producing new burdens for the group. To capitalize on this stepping stone position, she or he also may spend too much time initiating and attending meetings outside the assigned work group. While generating a personal spotlight and building a reputation for the next career move, an absent manager may be leaving the group leaderless much of the time. This usually will be resented...

**Others are too eager to change things** - This type of person, who may take the job for "ideological" reasons, has a "vision" for the group and its future, and probably will try hard to bend the group's efforts in that direction. This may be good or bad from the group's point of view. A vivid example of this is provided by the case of a 23 year old emergency medical service coordinator who once worked for a small city fire department. Seven months after being hired to help the department's several paramedics (rescue vehicle crews) pass difficult advanced cardiac life support courses needed to renew their licenses, he was fired. Apparently he alienated many of the paramedics by reviewing their rescue reports for procedural errors and by riding rescue vehicles with them to observe their performance. Some of the men complained about this to higher management, claiming the new young coordinator was "trying to make doctors out of us." Convinced that the paramedical rescue workers' standards of care were not up to par, the coordinator eventually complained to the local press about it. His boss, the fire chief, subsequently fired him, citing the young man's "impatience and inability to work within the department's limitations." The chief said, "He's a brilliant young man. Maybe because he's so good at it, any person who is not up to his own standards was viewed as incompetent." [2] This apparently was a classic case of an individual having the right idea but the wrong methods for implementation. While the young man in fact had support from medical authorities, he lacked the interpersonal skills and strategy needed to introduce change.

**Still others are beholden to another master** - The candidate who had a special sponsor may manage the group according to what he believes the sponsor would like to have done. This may or may not be good for the group as a whole. One manager I know was once told, upon being selected by a more senior one to take over a certain unit, "I'm giving you chicken shit; I want you to make it into chicken soup." This perspective did not endear the new manager to his new group; his attitude, shaped by his more senior sponsor, was apparent to the group and deeply resented. The group's morale in a company-wide attitude survey became one of the lowest in the entire organization.

Group members frequently are aware of the reasons why a candidate is selected. The grapevine usually tells them. They may or may not be receptive to the rationale, and the new manager, therefore, may or may not be warmly received. If a manager is not warmly received, his or her potential influence on the group may be limited or negative.[3,4]

**Sources of potential power** - Managers can derive *potential* influence over their groups from several sources:

- From the mere fact that they have been appointed by higher level management, *provided* that the group members trust higher management and respect their judgment;

- From the rewards and punishments that the organization places at their disposal to influence subordinates, e.g., bonus decision authority, freedom to promote, fire, transfer, or demote subordinates;

- From the warm feelings and respect the group members have for the manager as a person, because of his or her past accomplishments or personality;

- From the group's need for the manager's task knowledge and abilities that nobody else in the group has; and

- From the manager's support in external organizations which can affect such matters as professional licensing decisions and professional practice standards.

Reward and punishment power stems from the availability to leaders of specific rewards and sanctions that are valued or feared by subordinates and which leaders are free to utilize without constraints.  The development of trade unions, protective legislation, personnel departments, and budgetary control systems have sharply diminished this source of power for most managers, especially those in lower level supervisory positions.  But the experienced or inventive supervisor finds ways to work within these constraints.  For example, a supervisor will not necessarily treat every subordinate alike when assigning work, determining vacation schedules, recording "down time" in incentive operations, enforcing lunch and rest break schedules, and so on.  In other words, although the system of policies sets guidelines, the manager still is able to maneuver within limits.  This must be done, however, in ways that are perceived to be fair if group cohesion and teamwork are to be developed and maintained.

**Reputation counts** - The extent to which managers can aggrandize and use reward and punishment power is influenced by their own personalities and by their groups' needs. Some amount of power is granted by the group to its manager simply because they may like the leader, or because of his or her reputation. The extent of this power (called "referent power" in the literature) depends a lot on the manager's personality, leadership style (described below), what trusted peers have told the group about him or her, and whether there is an informal leader in the group whom the group members feel should have been appointed instead.

**"Knowing the job" often is valued** - Expert power stems from the perceived and demonstrated competence of a manager to do, analyze, evaluate or understand, and control the task that the group performs. This source of power differs from referent power -- a leader can have considerable expert power and little referent power, or the opposite pattern, or can be high or low on both. Different groups of course, have different ways to assess and ascribe expert power. Boys' gangs engage in fisticuffs to test the leader; professionals may examine academic credentials first and later look at achievements such as books written and patent disclosures. Typically work groups like to have a manager who "knows the job." Therefore, people tend to be skeptical of managers not promoted from within their own ranks. The manager brought in from a different function, or worse yet, from another company, normally has an uphill struggle to gain acceptance. Of course, sometimes a group welcomes an outsider knowing that it needs an infusion of new ideas and methods, or knowing that the outsider has influence in important places.

**"External political power" can be significant** - Both managers and rank and file group members can be affiliated with powerful professional or political organizations outside the work place. For example, a nursing supervisor I once knew in a hospital was an influential figure in a state-wide professional association. She used this external base as a power source to influence behavior and policy within the hospital where she was employed. Such connections can strongly influence career mobility, among other things. One executive I know in a large company also happens to be a member of his nation's parliament!

It seems to me that the growing distrust of leadership and authority among Americans in recent years has greatly reduced the degree of legitimate power enjoyed by supervisors and managers in all kinds of work organizations. Moreover, the apparent evolutionary progress of industrial man appears to be blunting reward--punishment power. For better or worse, earned referent and expert power seem to be the most effective bases of influence today. In any event, managers who do not have the power to effect changes needed by their groups are unlikely to be effective leaders of team building efforts.

**Leader or follower; a matter of balance** - As previously pointed out, group members' goals are not necessarily the same as the organization's goals for the group. The most typical situation is the mixed case where both the organization's and the group members' goals can be pursued with reasonable sacrifice on either side. Some leadership approaches offer more potential for such accommodation than others.

The major point here is that a supervisor or manager can actually perform such a two-way function, even in the eyes of subordinates, without having to "sell-out" the employer and becoming "one of the gang." In fact, the existing evidence suggests that group members frequently want their manager to act like a leader, not like one of them, despite the fact that the manager is part of the group. For example, many work group rank-and-file members have reported in corporate attitude studies that their supervisors spend appreciable amounts of time doing the same kinds of work as they do themselves. The evidence indicates that such groups tend to be less productive and less satisfied with their leaders than groups who report that their supervisors spend very little time "doing the chores" with their subordinates.[5]

**To be a manager, one must act like one** - Managers who roll up their sleeves to help with the chores, often without realizing it, are defining their role too narrowly and ignore many important leadership functions. As a consequence, in spite of technical ability, such managers are seen as ineffective by many subordinates; in effect, they do not even attempt to lead by any means other than setting an example, which is not enough. Such managers may help their subordinates get the work done (which employees typically feel is their own, not the supervisor's, job), but they fail to attend to other important managerial functions. (This often is what happens when managers are promoted from the ranks and take over the same group from which they were promoted.)

In one study, for example, factory foremen who were unpopular with their groups, as compared with much more popular foremen, were described as follows by their men:[6]

- Highly knowledgeable about the work their men do;

- Highly skilled in doing the work their men do;

- Unenthusiastic and low on drive;

- Take life too lightly;

- Easy to push around;

- Do not act better than their men; and

- Do not stick to company rules.

Popular leaders were seen in opposite terms.  It is clear that in this case a manager cannot be a leader in the eyes either of superiors or subordinates without acting like one.  However, sometimes it is necessary to "help with the chores," even if clumsily from lack of practice, to demonstrate to your group that you still know how to do their job!

Managers who remain too far apart from the group and overplay their role and status difference may create as much trouble as they would by remaining too close.  It is a delicate balance.

**How power is used is the issue** - The issue here is not potential sources of power and influence, but rather how they are used.  Some managers make a great show of demonstrating their power, to make sure the group knows who is boss.  For example, an R & D manager may feel it necessary to remind a troublesome junior scientist about the difference between their respective professional credentials and experience levels.  Others, at the opposite extreme, seem reluctant to use the powers they have.  Still others are too quick to invoke support from higher levels to solve all challenges to their authority.  The way in which a manager uses power, the frequency with which it is done, and the pattern of power resources relied upon are observed and reacted to by group members.

People do expect their managers to try and get their way; *how they do it*, however, can either motivate or demotivate.  One research study revealed varied individual strategies for exercising interpersonal influence.  Included are:  making loud assertions, bargaining, use of deceit, playing on emotions, claiming expertise, reasoning, threat, thought manipulation, compromise, fait accompli, hinting, persistence, and making simple statements. These interpersonal influence strategies were interpreted from numerous written essays. Thought manipulation, for example, is the strategy inferred from the statement, "I usually try to get my way by making the other person feel that it is his idea." An example of playing on emotions is found in the statement, "I try to put him in a good mood." [7] Overall, it's quite an arsenal...

During a consulting assignment in a hospital, I was once asked by a young physician for some advice. He recently had been promoted from number two to number one in one of the hospital's largest laboratories. His predecessor, who had retired, was an internationally renowned expert who had dominated the lab for many years. Upon being promoted, the new chief inherited his predecessor's administrative assistant, a woman old enough to be his mother who greatly admired and identified with the retired chief. Unfortunately, the administrative assistant continued to look upon the new chief as if he were still number two, and behaved accordingly. I advised him to start conducting traditional medical "rounds" of the lab every Monday morning, making sure that his assistant accompanied him to take notes. During these rounds he asked questions and made various technical suggestions. The strategy worked; his administrative assistant found out that the young doctor had "taken charge." He did it by exercising his "expert power" in a visible but culturally appropriate way.

**Being nice vs. being helpful** - Gaining and maintaining acceptance by your group does not require a "be nice to people at any cost" approach. Helping a group reach its goals in a work organization in the long run usually requires much more than that. Time schedules, quality control, task procedures, information flow, availability of equipment and raw materials, liaison with other groups, proper instructions, and related matters normally require at least as much attention from the manager, and sometimes more. Such technological and administrative factors have important influences on the ability of a group to function smoothly both from the members' and from the organization's point of view. Being nice to people and observing the Golden Rule is neither necessary nor sufficient for effective leadership; sometimes a manager has to take an unpopular course and make it stick. It goes with the territory.

## ASSESSING MANAGERS AND THEIR PERFORMANCE

**There are no universal performance standards** - Managers frequently debate the question, "What is the best way to tell an effective supervisor or manager from an ineffective one?" They usually disagree on such possible effectiveness criteria as productivity records, market share, return on investment, profitability, growth rate, cost-control, ratio of new customers to old, employee attitudes, turnover, absenteeism and others. Actually, *the best way to judge managerial performance depends upon the operation being managed.* Managerial effectiveness is intimately bound up with group or unit effectiveness, and different groups within organizations may very well have different, and even conflicting, objectives. One cannot apply the same yardstick to two managers whose groups or units are striving for different goals without misjudging the effectiveness of one of them.

For example, many managers direct operations where productivity (output per man hour) is entirely controlled by machine pacing (assembly lines, for instance) or inventory availability factors; therefore, they have little opportunity to influence productivity. In such cases, the manager may stress minimum turnover, absenteeism, and favorable employee attitudes. In other operations, accuracy, quality or creativity, rather than high output, may be the goal. In some cases a work group, department, or even an entire organization may be geared to meet unpredictable emergencies rather than having a goal of steady, high productivity. Group cohesion then may become a consideration of greater importance than productivity. This is true of armies, fire stations, hospitals, and many industrial, clerical, shipping and duplicating (printing) functions. Research and development groups also are special cases where high output per hour or year frequently is a less relevant goal than others. And, a manager of managers (who comprise a group) may find that inducing change and developing individuals for the future are more important goals than Return on Investment during a specified period of time.

**The managerial team needs to be treated like a winning sports team** - After the National Basketball Association playoffs in 1980, the coach of the winning Los Angeles Lakers explained in a nationally televised interview how his team won it. He maintained that the (informal) team leader Abdul Jabbar, an outstanding veteran player on the team, accepted him - thus making it possible for him to coach (an observation that fits with accumulated research evidence in work organizations). He added that Magic Johnson, another player, inspired the rest of the team with his outstanding effort and willingness to endure pain; he "picked up" the team during lulls. Another player named Chones made key baskets, and was considered especially helpful because he was willing to play at positions (forward) different from the one he preferred (guard). Another was called "Silk" for his smooth-as-silk play making, while a fifth was known as "Steady Eddie."

This interview with a winning coach illustrates that different team members contribute in different ways - they should not all be judged by the same standard, points scored. The same is true of the managerial team members in work organizations; *different managers have different strengths and are responsible for different kinds of work units at different stages of development.* For these and other reasons, it is extremely difficult to measure the effectiveness of managers and supervisors. The factors responsible for this difficulty are closely intertwined with the related problems of identifying leadership potential, selecting leaders, and training them. The same factors also create difficulties in explaining to current managers how they can analyze their jobs systematically and improve their performance.

**There are no universal leadership traits** - Just as there are no universal performance standards for managers, there are no universal personality traits (e.g., dominance, extroversion) that all effective managers have and ineffective ones lack.

Many studies of personality and other characteristics have provided evidence on why some persons and not others get to be leaders. However, the factors that help an individual get selected to fill a leadership position are not necessarily the same as the factors that influence someone's performance of leadership responsibilities once on the job. In addition, it now is generally agreed that the qualities which make a good manager are different for different situations.[8] This explains why first-rate executive recruiters try hard to obtain insight into the corporate cultures and job demands of their clients.

**The importance of personality** - Regardless of the largely inconsistent and insignificant findings from a large number of "trait" studies over the years,[9] some people nevertheless hold strongly to the belief that the qualities that make a good manager are largely a matter of personality. Indeed, there has long been general agreement among managers on the importance of personality characteristics to managerial performance.[10]

There also is some scientific evidence that personality traits do influence leader effectiveness. One research group, for example, has demonstrated with an impressive multi-study program over a long period of years that Machiavellian tendencies (deceitful manipulation of others) can be measured, and that this personality dimension predicts behavior and leader effectiveness in a variety of tasks.[11]

Another study produced some further sensible findings. The authors report that "dominance" as a personality characteristic in group leaders predicts group performance *provided* that the appointed leader is the most dominant member of the group. In groups where a highly dominant leader was accompanied by a dominant subordinate, things didn't turn out so well.[12]

Still other and often overlooked evidence that has been in the literature for a long time involves a concept called "interaction potential." Interaction potential reflects an individual's tendency to seek and engage in face-to-face interpersonal communication. Early research showed significant relationships between this personality dimension and both leader emergence and effectiveness.[13]

**The "well-rounded" generalist notion** - Many people believe that individuals having the ability to analyze and adapt can mold themselves into many different kinds of leadership roles, given a little time and some appropriate staff assistance. One can hardly rebut the argument that there may be an occasional outstanding candidate around who is the "right person for every managerial job." However, such people do not appear on the scene frequently. Most organizations do not count on finding candidates having unlimited ability to analyze and adapt when filling a managerial vacancy.

General ability and intelligence alone will carry a person in some managerial positions, but not in others. Beyond general ability and intelligence, many leadership assignments require extensive technical knowledge and interpersonal skills.

**Managers are, as a group, brighter than average** - Many studies have shown that higher level managers tend to have above average intelligence. This suggests that people who become organizational leaders are more intelligent than those who do not. Such evidence from the industrial world agrees with what is known about leadership more generally; that is, people who become leaders in almost all settings tend to be more intelligent than those who do not.[14]

**But intelligence is not enough** - There is much less evidence as to whether intelligence, in and of itself, has any direct effect on the performance or effectiveness of leaders after they become leaders. Other variables must be taken into account. For example, an often overlooked study shows that measured leader intelligence predicts military task group effectiveness, in bomber and tank crews where the leader is accepted by the members.[15] Such acceptance is influenced by leader (and follower) personality.

Leadership trait theory was in disrepute among scholars for a long time, but it seems to be enjoying a rejuvenated career in a more sophisticated form. New measures and more useful, situational models are available and are being developed from what is now known.[16] One business implication of all this lies in performance appraisal. I have seen numerous corporate performance appraisal forms that include either non-systematic lists of personality traits, or lists based upon outdated models. While some companies have made major changes in their performance appraisal forms to reflect more modern thinking, there are many others that have not.

**There is no one best leadership style** - The term "leadership style" refers to the characteristic behavior pattern exhibited by a manager in the process of making decisions and exercising authority. While there is no consensus on how many style dimensions exist, the concept has been the subject of much research and a large amount of expensive training activity in American industry for more than 30 years. Let us see why.

*Style dimension I: authoritarian vs. democratic:* The behaviors referred to as authoritarian or autocratic are so named because the way a work group is managed under an authoritarian leader has many similarities to the way dictatorships are run. At any choice point where the leader can either share some leadership tasks with the group members or centralize all the decision making and order giving in his own hands, the extremely authoritarian leader usually chooses the latter. The democratic leader has as much power as the authoritarian leader, but chooses to exercise it differently during the policy-making and work-role assignment phases of group action. Democratic style has also been referred to as "permissive," "participative," or "consultative management," and as "general supervision," although these are not fully interchangeable terms.

The way a democratic manager deals with a work group contrasts sharply with the way an authoritarian leader operates. The democratic leader permits more individual freedom among subordinates, permits more requests for information that is "nonessential" to the individual"s specific work assignment, permits more questioning of work orders, and permits more constructive nonconformity. The democratic leader also encourages subordinate participation in policy making and goal setting and consults subordinates for ideas in a full two-way communication flow. When democratic leaders decide on a "best way" or "best goal," they attempt to persuade subordinates of the worth of the decision rather than issuing commands or unexplained orders. Obviously this approach to management has sound potential for helping people to learn, and for developing self-sufficiency and a sense of teamwork.

Finally, democratic leaders use general supervision "by objectives"; i.e., they do not try to oversee each move made by group members, but rather insure that they understand the result that is to be achieved and then allow them to work without looking over their shoulders. The authoritarian leader, on the other hand, maintains direct control over every action by group members and writes the "book" that must be followed.

*Style dimension II: employee centered vs. work centered*: The "employee centered" manager believes that the most important leadership functions are motivational, i.e., maintaining internal group harmony and member satisfaction. A completely employee centered manager spends much daily effort in analyzing and satisfying employee needs, to the relative neglect of technological concerns. The "work centered" manager considers as most important planning ways and means for accomplishing the goals of the group, and organizing the activities of the members. Work-centered managers think of individual subordinates mainly in terms of the task. Many do not relate well to people; they are "all business."

*Style dimension III: rewarding vs. punishing*: This dimension, which overlaps Dimension I considerably, refers to the manager's basic assumptions about human motivation. The punishing manager assumes that subordinates are basically lazy, unwilling to take responsibility, unimaginative, and unlikely to act in a required way or stop acting in an undesired way unless they are threatened with punishment. (Some readers may have read descriptions of this style where it was named "Theory X" and contrasted with the rewarding style labeled "Theory Y.")[17]

Rewarding managers assume that the carrot is always better than the stick. Further, they believe that the carrot does not have to be a traditional reward like money or leisure time. They also believe that non-managerial employees will expend effort to obtain rewards similar to the ones that motivate managers, such as variety in work, opportunity to take responsibility and initiative, and recognition.

**"Style," personality, and the exercise of power are part of the same package** - By comparing the above "style" descriptions with the earlier "How I Get My Way" discussion, you will see considerable overlap. Decision making style, personality, methods of influencing others, and the ways in which managers exercise authority are inseparable phenomena. They reflect an individual's beliefs about human nature, basic interest patterns (e.g., does one enjoy working with people, things, or ideas), reactions to parents' and other important leaders' practices, and so on. Style also can be a reflection of self-confidence. Young managers, like young teachers having limited experience, often rely on a highly task-oriented, or even an autocratic style, to make sure that their subordinates (or students) know who is in charge. In many instances this can be counterproductive for team building purposes, although it does maintain the manager's personal comfort level.

Just as there is no personal quality that automatically guarantees success in any and every managerial situation, there is no known managerial style that represents a "one best way." The democratic style probably produces good results in more situations than does the authoritarian style, but the fact remains that there are some situations where a manager whose style is autocratic, work-centered and punishing is needed (some employees actually prefer this) and a democratic, employee centered and rewarding supervisor would be likely to fail.

**Factors influencing the appropriateness of a style** - Many managers have expressed the view that the choice of style should be determined only by the kind of group (or its life cycle phase), the kind of task it does, and its members' competency, and that the leader should adapt to these demands. But most of us find that there are some leadership styles which are more or less compatible with our personality characteristics. Attempts to use a leadership style that is not compatible with one's personality will likely place some amount of strain on the manager, other group members, and possibly the manager's boss, as well.

Everyone concerned may prefer the manager to be a relaxed, predictable and believable autocrat rather than a nervous, unpredictable or unconvincing democrat. Moreover, there may well be certain styles which a person of a particular personality type is incapable of acquiring, even with extensive "therapy" or management training. You may have observed the same phenomenon among professional actors and actresses. Many are "type cast" because they seem unable to act comfortably and convincingly in roles other than their best fit, e.g., tough guy or sex siren. People differ in their flexibility and adaptability.

Group member characteristics and the tasks they perform also have a bearing on the choice of appropriate leadership style. An authoritarian leadership style often will cause difficulty, for example, if applied to a group of persons who value freedom of choice and free expression of ideas, or who are highly experienced in the task at hand. This normally would be especially true of academic, research, and other professional groups. On the other hand, football players who have come to expect a very directive, work centered quarterback may be unnerved by a new one who tries a participative style which can be interpreted as a sign of incompetence. I have known many professional level employees who react very negatively to a manager who turns their questions back to them and says, "What do *you* think we should do?" They misinterpret the manager's attempt to involve them in the decision process as a sign of inadequate knowledge of the task. A quick and noticeable change from one style of leadership to another requires time for adjustments to be made.

**Some well-known examples in the sports world** - The task of playing winning football is not always amenable to general supervision, except in the case of a highly experienced, skillful and cohesive team at an advanced stage of development. It was in such a case that Paul Brown, for example, founder and former coach of the champion Cleveland Browns, learned the hard way that permissive, general supervision had become *over a period of years* the appropriate style in his players' eyes. His team, which won many championships, became irritated with his very structured approach to coaching.

Paul Brown eventually left the Cleveland organization and joined the newly formed Cincinnati Bengals. In both cases his skillful organizing and strategic coaching eventually led to winning ball teams. *He is known as a calm organizer and systematic builder of new teams who achieved long-term results.* (It is no accident that an unusually large percentage of Brown's former players have become coaches throughout the National Football League.)

Billy Martin, a much travelled professional baseball manager, offers an interesting contrast. He has taken charge of five different lackluster teams over the last several years and is given credit for quick and vast improvements in all of them, including divisional championships and even a national championship. One of his veteran players on the Oakland A's team once said of Martin, "Billy not only has us doing things we never thought we could, he's taught us things we never even heard of." (This view of leadership was applied by actress Shelley Duvall in an interview about her leader, movie and play director Stanley Kubrick, in a different article in the same magazine.)[18] *Quite unlike the calm master strategist and organizer coach Brown, Martin is known as an inspirational, fiery and outspoken leader.* On several occasions he has settled arguments with his own and opposing players (not to mention spectators) by using his fists!

**My point here is that two very different leadership styles (Brown's vs. Martin's) can "work."** However, each obviously is appropriate for a different situation. Martin's represents a "quick fix," often needed by a stagnant group or one slipping below its potential. Brown's approach is the more suitable for a long-term building and developmental program.

This argument also applies to many different operations in the work world. Thus, when two groups are at different developmental stages, have different average expectations about how a good leader should act, different "typical" personalities, different skill mixes, and different task requirements, they will respond differently to the same leadership style. The style which is optimum for one group may not be appropriate for another.

**Senior management sets the tone** - Although it is clear that a manager's personality, the kind of group involved and the nature of the task to be performed all have a bearing on the choice of the most appropriate leadership style, there is another point worthy of re-emphasis here. That is, regardless of what the most appropriate or logical leadership style might be in a given situation, the style that actually develops is strongly influenced by the example provided by higher managers. Autocratic or work centered management at higher organization levels is likely to beget similar management at middle and lower levels because lower and middle level managers know that their performance will be judged by their superiors not only on the basis of what they accomplish, but also on the basis of how they go about it (style). Note that despite the winning ways of his several baseball teams, Billy Martin was fired from all of them at least in part for his inability to get along with higher level executives in the parent organizations. He gets "bottom-line" results on the playing field and at the box-office, but is not seen as an organization man. While viable in the short run, his motivational methods often irritate highly paid, talented team members.

## MANAGERIAL FUNCTIONS - THE CONTENT OF THE JOB

While many writers have classified the manager's leadership responsibilities into two categories, the task and people management components,[19] I propose eight, as follows:

- *The manager as strategist and task expert* -includes input to strategy formation, planning and budgeting, goal setting, work methods, coordination, analyzing performance indicators, and providing expertise;

- *The manager as team builder* - includes the definition of who does what, managing internal conflict, dispensing rewards and punishments, providing career guidance and developing subordinates, and encouraging internal cohesion and morale;

- *The manager as ideologist* - providing members with a "vision," that is, a set of beliefs, values, information and behavior standards, serving as an exemplar or model, and generally shaping the group's (or organization's) culture;

- *The manager as link-pin* - acting as the representative and spokesperson for the group, initiating and receiving messages both within and outside the chain of command, and bargaining with representatives of other groups;

- *The manager as change agent* - developer of internal climate and group process to encourage appropriate level of trial and error, constructive non-conformity, and the generation or importation of new ideas and methods;

- *The manager as resource generator* - includes activities ranging from recruitment and assignment of new members to budget acquisition, fund raising, and acquisition of space, equipment, and other forms of support;

- *Customer or client and community relations* - Direct contact with the external environment through the media (TV, radio, press), participating in community affairs, and face-to-face meetings with customers or clients; and

- *Administrative details* - Documentation, reading/writing memos, processing forms, proofreading reports, and related.

**The job dimensions combine in many different ways** - Two points should be made about these functions. First, different management positions require different emphases on them - that is, they have different priorities or profiles. Second, the same position may change its priorities on these functions over time because of environmental or internal group developments.

The first point may be illustrated by contrasting a foreman's position in an auto factory with a head-nurse's position in a hospital emergency room. The foreman's leadership role is likely to be highly circumscribed by a collective bargaining agreement, personnel policies and regulations, production quotas determined by top management, and methods constraints dictated by fixed assembly line technology and formal engineering standards. Consequently, the foreman often has limited freedom to plan, make policy, offer expertise, control member relations, or offer rewards and punishments. The head nurse, on the other hand, normally will find that role much less constrained, even though both the nurse and the foreman may appear at the same level in their respective organizational charts.

**The job changes** - The second point, that a given manager's requirements may change over time, also is easily illustrated. I once observed a brand new thoracic surgical team being installed in a hospital. The surgeon (leader) building this team was heavily challenged in the team's formative stages with planning, goal setting, providing technical expertise, and selecting, training and properly integrating new team members. Once the surgeon built a viable team, other members developed expertise and knowledge which permitted them to assume partial if not substantial responsibility for these functions. The surgeon's role requirements then changed, demanding, for example, less expertise and more administration and external relations as the team's activities, new functions, and growing case load *increasingly impinged upon other units in the hospital and created controversy.* There was a very real question at the time as to whether the highly dedicated surgeon would be able to modify his interest pattern and behavioral habits sufficiently to meet these new role demands.

Such individuals have not necessarily "risen to their level of incompetence," as some popular management literature claims. Rather, in some cases the new role requirements conflict with their talent levels and are not sufficiently challenging. To pursue them diligently would require a sacrifice of other expertise that would atrophy from disuse. The surgeon in this case chose to accept the administrative responsibilities for the good of his new unit. It may not have survived otherwise. Eventually he became chief of surgery. Along the way he shared his knowledge with many young physicians from all over the world, and in effect reproduced himself many times.

A well-known example in American professional athletics is Paul Brown. As mentioned earlier, he appears to have been better fit as a builder of new teams than as a coach or general manager of a going, mature team. Relatedly, in a later chapter I point out that the experienced auto workers in one of Volvo's autonomous group experiments voted to eliminate the role of foreman because they didn't need one. An interesting job enrichment experiment in the USA produced a similar phenomenon; enlargement of some machine operators' jobs left supervisors with too little to do, so they developed a pattern of "over supervising" the operators. Such behavior proved to be irritating to their subordinates.[20] *The inference to be drawn from all of these experiences is that the stage of evolutionary development in a work units' history influences the kind of management the group should receive.*

Similar leadership role requirement changes occur in many organizations and groups as they evolve through different stages of development. Other cases in point are trade unions whose local leadership requirements change after their initial organizational drives, nation-states, whose leadership needs change with the fortunes of war and economics, and corporations, which also are susceptible to external pressures. The replacement of Winston Churchill as Prime Minister of Great Britain following his effective leadership during World War II, provides still another example. Though he was widely respected and had provided inspirational leadership during the War, he was not seen as the best person to lead the rebuilding of his nation's economy.[21]

## THE CHIEF EXECUTIVE OFFICER

Many observers of the corporate world in recent years seem to agree that the role demands on the CEO are changing. One writer maintains that the CEOs in the 21st century will need a "double dollop of moxie and charisma" to guide their corporations through change and difficult times. Citing others, the same writer suggests that the CEO will *also* have to be less a "commander" and more like a coach who leads through persuasion, as discussed earlier in this chapter. Acknowledging that applying team management concepts to senior management groups is difficult because of strong egos at that level, he concludes that "whether through teamwork or by personal fiat, business leaders must manage large-scale rapid change, envision business conditions 5 or 10 years down the road, and muster the courage to steer a firm in radical new directions."[22] He also emphasizes special demands on the future executive to be a "consummate politician" capable of dealing with multi-national circumstances on a global scale.

**Shared leadership is not necessarily a good idea** - Different people in a work group sometimes divide the labor on task and maintenance functions. This normally appears to be an informal development; occasionally it is a deliberate strategy designed to overcome personality or technical-task shortcomings, or to compensate for work overload on a manager. While such a division of leadership responsibility can work, groups characterized by above average performance and employee satisfaction are more often than not managed by someone who initiates structure and clearly states what needs to be done and who, at the same time, is sensitive to the emotional side of group life.[23] Jury-rigged leadership sharing arrangements, often observed in professional and office clerical settings, will not maximize teamwork.

## OFFICE AUTOMATION IMPACT ON MANAGERIAL WORK

A new dimension is emerging in the way many managers do their work. An increasing number are using microcomputers for a variety of purposes including internal communications (electronic mail and word processing), project scheduling, decision making analysis (spreadsheets), monitoring external events and activities (data base access), enhancing meetings (presentation graphics), and others.[24] Even if not computer users personally, managers increasingly are finding it necessary to understand how to apply information technology to business problems and strategies. Specifically, they need knowledge of:

- different applications and their costs;

- quality control issues;

- how to evaluate the performance of information technology users and their helpers;

- issues associated with the deployment of relevant training resources;

- implications of technology for hiring decisions; and

- organizational structure and authority issues that are likely to be impacted by electronic technology.

It is not yet clear just how the growth of office technology will re-define the nature of managerial work. However, it will have an impact. The resultant changes in managerial behavior patterns may also have a profound impact on teamwork at all organization levels, for better or worse, depending on how executives decide to use the technology. Since executive style has a strong bearing on how participative an organizational climate is likely to be, and since maximum benefit from electronic technology requires widespread access to information throughout an organization, some autocratic executives may actually retard the benefits available from the new technology.[25]

## TAKING STOCK

The stage is now set to examine a variety of ways that individual managers can influence the development, cohesion, level of teamwork, attitudes, and performance of their work groups. As I stated in the Preface, from first line supervisor to Chief Executive Officer, and from task force chairman to Chairman of the Board, managers are responsible for making things happen through *groups*. They will happen more effectively when ways are found to apply what follows.

## ENDNOTES

1   Al McNeil, former coach of the Montreal Canadiens, offers an exception to this generalization.  He was dismissed from his job shortly after his team won the coveted Stanley Cup as the best professional hockey team in 1971.  Here we have a case where a group accomplished its major goal in spite of perceived leadership deficiencies and then forced out its formal leader. Newspaper accounts suggest that a personality clash was involved. Apparently the team was unwilling to absorb this source of tension in the long run.

2   Goldstein, A. and Mooney, Carolyn, "Hallandale rescue service caught up in controversy," MIAMI HERALD, Broward Edition, April 1, 1984, 1A.

3   For empirical evidence of how follower consensus on the supervisor relates to work group productivity and cohesion, see Rosen, N., LEADERSHIP CHANGE AND WORK GROUP DYNAMICS, 1969, Ithaca, N.Y.: Cornell University Press, and Pryer, Margaret, Flint, A., and Bass, B., "Group Effectiveness and Consistency of Leadership," SOCIOMETRY, 1962, 25 (4), 391-397

4   Gordon, G. and Rosen, N., "Some critical factors in leadership succession," JOURNAL OF ORGANIZATIONAL BEHAVIOR AND HUMAN PERFORMANCE, 1981, 27, 227-254.

5   See Kahn, R.L. and Katz, D., "Leadership practices in relation to productivity and morale," in Cartwright, D., and  Zander, A., (Eds.), GROUP DYNAMICS, 1960, (2nd Ed.), New York: Harper, 554-570.

6   Rosen, N., cited above, 94-96.

7   Falbo, Toni. "Multi-dimensional scaling of power strategies," JOURNAL OF PERSONALITY AND SOCIAL PSYCHOLOGY, 1977, 35 (8), 537-547; see, also, Schmidt, S. and Kipnis, D., "The perils of persistence," PSYCHOLOGY TODAY, November 1987, 32-34.

8   The most explicit case for this argument is made by Fiedler, F., THEORY OF LEADERSHIP EFFECTIVENESS, 1967, New York: McGraw-Hill.

## 30  The Manager

9   Guion, R. and Gottier, R., "Validity of personality measures in personnel selection," PERSONNEL PSYCHOLOGY, 1965, 18, 135-164.

10  See Rosen, Doris, "Personality testing in industry," Industrial and Labor Relations Library Technical Reports Series, Ithaca, N.Y.: NYSSILR, Cornell University, 1966.

11  Christie, R. and Geis, F. (Eds.), STUDIES IN MACHIAVELLIANISM, 1970, New York: Academic Press.

12  Ghiselli, E. and Lodahl, T., "Patterns of managerial traits and group effectiveness," JOURNAL OF ABNORMAL AND SOCIAL PSYCHOLOGY, 1958, 57, 61-66.

13  See, for example, Bass, B., LEADERSHIP, PSYCHOLOGY AND ORGANIZA-TIONAL BEHAVIOR, 1960, New York: Harper, Chapter 5. See, also Sorrentino, R. and Boutillier, R. "The effect of quantity and quality of verbal interaction on ratings of leadership ability", JOURNAL OF EXPERIMENTAL SOCIAL PSYCH-OLOGY, 1975, 11, 403-411.

14  Gibb, C., "Leadership." In Linzey, G. and Aronson, E. (Eds.), HANDBOOK OF SOCIAL PSYCHOLOGY, second edition, Vol 4, 1969.

15  Fiedler, F. and Meuwese, W., "The leader's contribution to task performance in cohesive and uncohesive groups," JOURNAL OF ABNORMAL AND SOCIAL PSY-CHOLOGY, 1963, 67, 83-87.

16  See Yukl, G., LEADERSHIP IN ORGANIZATIONS, 1981, Englewood Cliffs, NJ: Prentice-Hall, esp. Chapters 4 and 5, for a more extensive discussion of leadership traits and relevant theory.

17  McGregor, D., THE HUMAN SIDE OF ENTERPRISE, 1960, New York: McGraw, 33-57. See, also, Curtis, W., Smith, R. and Smoll, F., "Scrutinizing the skipper: a study of leadership behaviors in the dugout." JOURNAL OF APPLIED PSY-CHOLOGY, 1979, 64 (4), 391-400.

18  See Shah, Diane, "Billy's back - so are the A's," NEWSWEEK, May 26, 1980, 64. The Duvall-Kubrick story is on page 99.

19  See Krech, D., Crutchfield, R. and Ballachey, E., THE INDIVIDUAL IN SOCIETY, 1962, New York: McGraw-Hill, 428-430 for the original list from which this list was adapted. See, also Likert, R., NEW PATTERNS OF MANAGEMENT, 1961, New York: McGraw-Hill for extensive discussion of the manager as a "link-pin" among work groups.

20  Lawler, E., Hackman, R. and Kaufman, S. "Effects of job redesign: a field experiment," JOURNAL OF APPLIED SOCIAL PSYCHOLOGY, 1973, 3, 46-62.

21  The reader who has seen the movie THE GODFATHER may recall that the organization's leadership, in anticipation of gang warfare, requested its trusted and effective legal counselor to step aside for a period in favor of a "wartime consigliere."

22  Work, C., "The twenty-first-century executive," EASTERN REVIEW, June 1988.

23  Research evidence supporting this statement appeared as early as the 1950s when the classic Ohio State Leadership Studies were published. See Fleishman, E., and others, LEADERSHIP AND SUPERVISION IN INDUSTRY, 1955, Bureau of Education Research, The Ohio State University, Columbus. More recent studies

have supported the same point, which has been incorporated as gospel in various systems for developing managers and organizations. See, for example, Blake, R. and Mouton, Jane, THE MANAGERIAL GRID, 1964, Houston: Gulf, Chapters 7 and 12.    For a review of the research on "Initiating Structure" and "Consideration," see Fleishman, E., "Twenty years of consideration and structure," in Fleishman, E. and Hunt, J. [Eds.], CURRENT DEVELOPMENTS IN THE STUDY OF LEADER-SHIP, 1973, Carbondale, Ill.: Southern Illinois University Press.

24    See Meyer, N. D. and Mary Boone, THE INFORMATION EDGE, 1987, New York: McGraw-Hill, Chapter 10 for several provocative examples; see, also, Bohl, D. [ED], AMA REPORT ON END-USER AND DEPARTMENTAL COMPUTING, WITH THE COOPERATION OF THE MICROCOMPUTER MANAGERS ASSOCIATION, 1988, New York, NY: American Management Association.

25    See Zuboff, Shoshana., IN THE AGE OF THE SMART MACHINE, 1988, New York, NY: Basic Books, Inc., especially Part Two.

SOME ADDITIONAL LITERATURE FOR THE INTERESTED READER:

-    House, R. and Singh, J., "Organizational behavior: some new directions for I/O psychologists," ANNUAL REVIEW OF PSYCHOLOGY, 1987, 38, 678-691.

-    Graumann, C. and Moscovici, S. [EDS.], CHANGING CONCEPTIONS OF LEADER-SHIP, New York, NY: Springer-Verlag, 1986.

-    Kotter, J., THE LEADERSHIP FACTOR, New York, NY: Free Press, 1987.

-    Carlzon, J., MOMENTS OF TRUTH, New York, NY: Ballinger, 1987.

# CHAPTER 3

## FROM BIRTH TO RESURRECTION:
## A MODEL FOR GROUP DEVELOPMENT

Group viability, to me, is a composite of cohesion, morale or esprit-de-corps, a shared sense of challenge among members, and smooth, well-coordinated internal functioning. Effective work groups do not develop overnight. Instead, they must evolve, over time, from the primitive collection stage at which they begin to a point where they become viable, cohesive social units.

In the beginning most industrial work groups are collections of individual members whom the employer expects to carry out various goal-oriented tasks. Members of an *established* work group, on the other hand, normally interact with one another regularly, share certain traits, work together toward a common goal, and agree (within limits) on beliefs and values which concern matters of common interest. They may also have norms, or standard ways for their members to behave, both on and off the job. They also define themselves and are defined by others as "belonging to 'the group'" and share the feeling of having a common destiny with other members of the group.[1] Groups that are fully developed are described in more detail later.

## WHY A LIFE CYCLE MODEL IS IMPORTANT

The evolutionary process for a newly formed group is depicted in Figure 1. A reader might now ask, "How will this model be of any use to me?" It is clear that task groups in work organizations have life cycles. If change is needed in a given group, or if a new manager is to be appointed, an understanding of the group's history is crucial to *effective planning*. Such insight also can help *avoid unnecessary conflict*. The manager who understands what stage of development the group currently is in, how or why it got that way, and what factors are currently operating to keep the group in its present state, can make *better informed decisions* than the manager who lacks such understanding. Different types of problems and different levels of group member receptivity to change and help exist during the various stages of a group's life cycle. Consequently, alternative management strategies and tactics have to be considered in relation to these different needs. Therefore, I encourage you to take a deep breath, turn up the lights, lock your door, disconnect your telephone, have an extra cup of coffee, and delve into the following explanation of Figure 1.

**Early and middle stages** - Stages 1-4 in the model reflect the beginnings of group development. They include pre-assembly, assembly, organizing and learning activities. In stages 5 and 6 the group begins to perform effectively. It is a time of readiness, after intensive trial and error, training, practice, decision-making, personnel shifting and goal setting activities have occurred and the dust has settled. The group begins to function on a regularized basis and displays substantial evidence of teamwork.

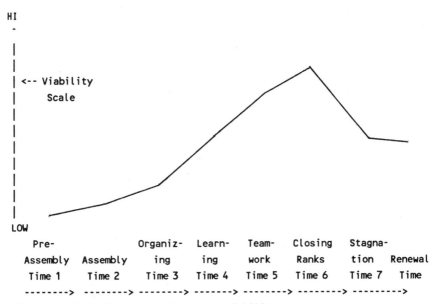

Fig. 1. An Evolutionary model of group viability
(Adapted, with modifications, from Rosen, N.,
SUPERVISION: A BEHAVIORAL VIEW, Grid, Inc., 1973.

Throughout the development and performance phases, maintenance is essential. Maintenance involves, among other things, "repair" work on interpersonal relations problems. Some of these problems grow out of the early development activities and others evolve later. Job changes are occasionally made, machinery or equipment may be modified, and procedural tinkering occurs, along with counselling and outright member replacements from time to time. Members are helped both with their on-the-job problems and any problems off-the-job that may be affecting the group. The idea is to keep the group well-oiled as a social machine.

**Maturity and renewal phases** - Time periods 6 and 7 remind us that no group can stay at peak performance indefinitely, and that measures must be taken to prevent stagnation. Attending to the group's <u>maintenance</u> needs on a continual basis can postpone this decline, but eventually renewal becomes necessary. Group renewal is a process that occurs when the maintenance process proves inadequate, or when management simply tries to squeeze too much out of a group for too long a period of time without any maintenance at all. Time Period 7 (stagnation) indicates that some things can happen to disrupt the group to such an extent that re-building must be started. Rebuilding may become necessary because too many members get complacent, too old, obsolete, quit, retire or develop other competing interests. Or, the group's goal(s) or basic assignment may change because of the needs of the parent organ-ization, and the existing members may not fit the new require-ments, e.g., computerization of a payroll department.[2]

The renewal process, at least in its early stages, differs from the initial development process because it requires mixing estab-lished members (who often are older and more experienced) and procedures with newer (often younger, less experienced) members having different backgrounds and different ideas about what should be done, why, how and by whom. This process is often accom-panied by intense conflict. The development phase, on the other hand, often is characterized by challenge, problem solving and growing optimism.[3]

The general process depicted in Figure 1 is a model--it doesn't always work out so neatly. For example, the evolutionary process for a group can break down at several points in time, or the steady acceleration of the development curve may never materialize. In addition, the time periods for the different stages are unlikely to be of equal durations, and certain phases may repeat themselves.

But the general model is useful in analyzing groups in or-ganizational settings. It can be applied to a technical task force established on a temporary basis to conduct a research project, a steering committee, an assembly team in a factory, an office ac-counting group carrying out regularized clerical functions, profes-sional athletic teams, and so on.

## APPLYING THE MODEL TO A HYPOTHETICAL CASE

Everyone at some time or another has been a member of at least one task group from the time of its initial formation through and including much later stages of the group's development. Your group may have been an athletic team, a task-force or management committee formed to solve a problem or draft a new policy statement, an amateur group convened to put on a play, or a sailboat racing crew. You might find it useful to keep such experiences in mind as you read the following example, namely the processes involved as a brand new management team is put together to manage a newly acquired corporate division. Imagine the choices the CEO of this new division must make in order to develop a viable management team.

**Pre-assembly stage** - The first consideration to be resolved, prior to group formation, is a policy matter. Leaders must ask: "Should we recruit experienced, skillful people to staff this group, thereby hastening development of the group, and reducing the related demands on us? Or, should we recruit less experienced but highly trainable individuals and settle for limited short-run accomplishments while building for the future?" This decision often is made when an organization plans to open a new branch, a new department or new division in government or industry. Expansion teams in professional athletics also make such decisions.

The policy decision on what level of initial competence to recruit for a new group in a work organization is influenced by several considerations. Some of them are:

- The "labor market," e.g., what is the potential supply?

- The financial resource situation, e.g., do we have the money to pay higher priced, experienced people?

- The timetable for group achievement, e.g., how quickly must this new group jell and become viable?

For example, a freshly promoted and still fairly junior level manager of this new corporate division may have to "take what s/he can get" for lieutenants, just to get started in a new job. An established, more senior executive may be able to pursue a highly selective strategy in order to insure a high quality cast of characters for a new team.

*what about, should this be a team job?*

**Practical implications** - There are several implications of the above policy decision for subsequent group development, because people tend to join groups on the basis of anticipated rewards. The nature of the recruiting campaign conveys cues to prospective members as to "how tough" it will be to get into the group; this, in turn, provides cues of motivational import. "Can I compete or do my full share in such a group (crew, team or whatever), or should I look for something easier?" is a question likely to be considered by some prospective members before the first meeting is even held!   Or, individuals characterized by high self-confidence and prior relevant experience may say to themselves, "That new divisional management group sounds better to me than most others because my fellow managers will be competent, skillful and probably well motivated."  Or some may think, "This sounds like an opportunity to gain substantial visibility with a senior executive who can influence my career progress."

**Early expectations are critical** - The recruiting techniques and sources utilized to attract potential members also create expectations having implications for subsequent motivation, group development and performance.  You might compare the expectations created by the national TV ads used for recruiting by the US Army and the Marine Corps.  The Army ads stress two themes - "teamwork" and "Be all you can be."  The Marine Corp ad says, "We are looking for a *few good* men with the mettle [sword displayed] to be Marines." (Emphasis mine)

It can make quite a difference if the recruiting for our hypothetical management team is routinely handled through casual contact as contrasted with a vigorous national search process.  The latter strategy can convey a sense of something new and different which may attract more attention than will the less formal, routine strategy.

A group recruited informally may well turn out to be highly congenial and internally cohesive, but the vigorous national search probably would provide more diversity and quite possibly a more exciting corporate experience.  Thus, groups that are formed on the basis of personal friendships and informal contacts may meet their needs for warm bodies, but they will not necessarily turn out to be viable, high performance units in the long run.

Recruiting policy and activities produce applicants or prospective group members.  The next step involves screening, on the assumption that not all applicants can be accommodated. The selection or screening strategies used at this stage have implications for the reputation of the division and the motivational and developmental dynamics that follow.

**The manager's role in the staffing process influences expectations** - Thus, if the CEO plays a key part in the process, personally conducting far-ranging, penetrating, and demanding interviews he will convey important cues to the candidates, including those eventually selected. The personal interview strategy can convey to candidates that the manager is strongly interested in picking the right combination of people, not just warm bodies.

Regardless of how carefully and systematically the recruiting and selection methods are applied, the group members do not come in with the same motives, interests and abilities. Most may be appropriate, but some misfits may find their way in because all selection systems make mistakes. Thus, while many members may be eager from the start, others may use the new division simply as a short term stepping stone. Still others are there because of a friend. Some are between jobs or just looking for something to do until their regular or a more desirable job becomes available again. Others are eager to join because of what they know about the new operation, and some are administratively assigned. Indeed, until recent years the United States Army was staffed by two categories of personnel - volunteers and draftees.

*The sources from which applicants are recruited, the philosophy governing the recruiting campaign, and the selection system used all combine to create preliminary expectations among those ultimately brought into the group.* The same mechanisms and related experience create preliminary expectations on the part of the manager regarding what kind of group it is to be, what disciplinary and other control techniques are needed, and how to motivate the group for task accomplishment. These expectations are then carried over into the first management meeting or two, when the members are first brought together in one place at the same time. Prior to that time there may very well be some interpersonal sharing of information and viewpoints, but probably only among various pairs or threesomes.

**Other resources also have an impact** - Another set of factors also influence the expectations of potential members, namely, the resources that they perceive to be available to the group. Many people have options when it comes to choosing which group to join; their choice can be influenced at least partly by the resources involved. For example, the same experienced racing sailor may be the recruiting objective of two boat owners who both need crew. If one of the boats is of a more advanced and exciting design than the other, the prospective crew member may be influenced accordingly. This, of course, is only one consideration, but an important one. In the case of our new division, the prospective managerial recruit may have a choice between two organizational units, one of which has a brighter budget picture than the other. In other words, advance perceptions, even if not fully accurate, of the new group's likely physical environment and control over resources also affects the recruiting process. A major resource, by the way, is the manager (or racing boat captain). That individual's reputation can have a profound effect on the pre-assembly outcome.

**Assembly stage** - Once most or all of the members have been recruited and selected for a new management team, it is typical for a meeting, or even a 3-4 day retreat, to be held, which everyone is expected to attend. Of course, not everyone who shows up is necessarily committed. Some who are there because of an administrative requirement may even be involved in behind the scenes efforts to escape!

What goes on at this first meeting will depend a lot on the leader and the nature of the task, time constraints and other factors. It is likely that the first meeting will be used by all the parties concerned for some preliminary work, equipment examination, stock taking, planning, and further assessment of skills, attitudes and goals, and so on. In short, both the leader and many of the members are still "testing" for goodness of fit. Here are some of the things likely to happen at this meeting:

- The group's mission is explained and possibly discussed at some length;

- Members exchange information with each other about their backgrounds;

- While sharing background information and doing some preliminary task-related activities, the members begin to observe each others' abilities, personalities and attitudes - including those of the CEO;

- Equipment, printed matter (and even uniforms in the case of sports teams) are distributed. Administrative ground rules are discussed and interpreted; and

- The reward system is discussed, e.g., basis of salary increases and bonus payments.

The prospective members are exposed to a number of stimuli in this first meeting that will help them sharpen or modify the preliminary expectations they developed during the pre-assembly stage. They may not be aware of all of these stimuli, but the combined effects have implications for the subsequent development of the group.[4]

As a function of what goes on and how it is interpreted in this first meeting, at least some prospective members and the leader usually will begin informal assessments of the group's chances of success, potential problems that may be encountered, how much personal time and energy will be required and whether it will be worth it. Discussion among those present occurs and other relevant individuals (such as others who have worked with the CEO previously) are likely to be consulted. As a result, some members may drop out, and additional recruiting may occur through those who like the prospects of the group and therefore attempt to bring in a friend. If some or all of the members are present because of administrative requirements, i.e., the parent organization ordered them to move in, and therefore have no choice in the matter, they may be especially sensitive to any cues they think are negative and a grumbling pattern may begin immediately. A group including too many involuntary members is likely to have an uphill development struggle in front of it.

**In summary** - *The perceptions that develop during the pre-assembly and the early assembly stages lay the ground work or context for the group's future.* The quality of interpersonal relationships, reactions to the leader, the extent of structure in the task and administrative rules, the perceived abilities of the members and a host of other variables begin to converge and influence the further development of group goals, effort, task procedures and process.

**Organizing stage** - The preliminaries, by and large, are now over. The group membership, at least for the immediate future, is known, and the process of group development and goal seeking can get underway. However, the organizing stage also is a fluid situation; several things can occur during this period, most of which benefit from active influence by the leader or manager. Some of the process is described below:

- The group is named, its formal mission and goal(s) discussed, and alternative or subsidiary goals are contemplated;

- Task definitions begin to emerge;

- Individuals are assigned or assign themselves to specific tasks;

- Status competition begins among the members; competition also develops over task assignments;

- Tentative schedules are developed for the achievement of intermediate objectives;

- Procedures are proposed, developed, experimented with and possibly debated;

- Further self-assessments and assessments of others are made. "Can I do it?" "Can s/he do it?" "Can we (as a group) do it?" All of these questions are likely to be considered during this stage;

- Regularized communications and interpersonal influence patterns begin to emerge;

- Time-schedule conflicts begin to develop. Some members may ask such questions of the leader as, "Can I come 15 minutes late?" "Can I leave early?" Or someone may say, "I can't make all the meetings or planning sessions because..." Such cases can occur despite efforts made in the pre-assembly and assembly stages to prevent them. Policy decisions are then required; Can the group live with irregular attenders or not? and,

- In the light of the above paragraph, further recruiting may be necessary to replace some members.

The above list is illustrative, not exhaustive, and some of the activities may occur at other times or not at all. It can be applied to the staffing of a task force or committee, in addition to our new divisional management.

**Freedom from administrative constraints can help** - Finally during this (and earlier) stages of group development, it is likely that the group enjoys a certain amount of freedom from administrative restriction by the larger organization of which it is a part. Thus, even though the larger organization has well-developed policies governing recruiting, selection and assignment of members, and even though formal systems exist in the larger organization for obtaining and allocating material resources and even space (rooms), new groups just getting underway often can take some license in these regards simply because they are new and need encouragement. Thus, the corporate accounting office or personnel department may not have very much impact on the procedures of a new divisional management team in its formative stages.

**Learning stage** - While pursuing group goals, practicing and performing tasks, doing limited preparatory assignments and socializing as the schedule permits (e.g., lunch and coffee breaks), the members interact with and observe each other, and exert (often unequal) influences on one another. From these observational and influence processes, more shared impressions and evaluations among and about members emerge.

In addition, interpersonal ties develop, involving pairs or more people as informal sub-groups. Overall camaraderie and group identity strengthen. *Unique vocabulary* required for effective task performance is developed and learned. Specialized roles become structured through trial and error, volunteering, bargaining and arbitrary assignment. The group's status hierarchy (see next chapter) begins to stabilize. Goal commitment increases; when necessary, some or all members resolve personal schedule and energy conflicts on the outside in favor of the group. Personal sacrifices in behalf of the group become easier to secure, if required. Processes and procedures begin to emerge for the allocation of resources, resolving interpersonal conflict, dealing with the larger organization (e.g., schedule conflicts) and disciplining members for unacceptable behavior. Marginal performing members either leave, get pushed out and replaced, or are worked into limited but functional roles. (Personality considerations have a lot to do with the treatment of marginal members.) And, the larger organization (e.g., Personnel, Legal, and Accounting Departments) begins to catch up with the group on administrative paper work and systems requirements related to organization policy, government regulations, and the like.

**Teamwork stage** - The teamwork stage describes a group's condition when it "jells." Teamwork reflects the group's early task successes and the development of positive interpersonal relationships, which encourage the group and build its confidence. All of this provides reinforcement or reward value, and enhances the group's desire for further success if the experience was challenging. The same processes that were getting underway in the prior learning stage gain momentum in this stage. To list a few:

- Performance standards continue to develop and probably increase

- Group shared norms and attitudes solidify and a unique vocabulary characteristic of the group becomes evident;

- Individual and coordinated task expertise approach a peak, and the task-role structure stabilizes;

- Teamwork and willingness to help each other are characteristic patterns;

- Group processes experimented with and developed earlier for allocating resources, resolving interpersonal conflict, disciplining members and dealing with the larger organizational environment, function smoothly with the full support of most group members; and

- A clear, group-shared idea emerges on "who we are and where we are going."

*This is the stage in a group's life cycle where the members have everything put together; the people, the systems and the technology are all working in concert.* However, while structure has emerged, sufficient flexibility remains within the group to permit more experimentation with members' assignments, role relationships, alternative methods and higher goals.

Teamwork is a combination of behaviors and a shared mind state. A group exhibiting substantial teamwork is characterized by:

- Shared beliefs that what we do as members influences the group as a whole, and what the total group achieves as a whole influences each member.

- Mutual anticipation and coordinated task performance, both of which require coaching and practice.

- A lot of shared knowledge and acquired skill that permit members to routinely and unhesitatingly do things for each other at critical points which makes the overall job less difficult, or possibly less dangerous, and enhances the group's performance.

- An absence of dysfunctional factionalism and infighting, and a good deal of coaching and support by senior group members for their junior colleagues; and

- Very rapid and functional responses to unexpected problems or opportunities.

One example of teamwork response to a problem is a member of a mountain climbing group immediately taking the proper action with rope and spikes when another team member slips and falls. Or an office worker might quickly take corrective action upon finding an error made in a document going through a sequence of processing operations.

An example of a teamwork response to an unexpected opportunity is provided by the Boston Celtics dramatic playoff victory over the Detroit Pistons in 1987. With seven seconds remaining in the sixth game, and the Celtics losing by one point, their star player Larry Bird intercepted a Piston player's pass. He *instantly* spun around and passed the ball in one fluid action several feet to a teammate, Dennis Johnson, who *already was running* between defensive players toward the Piston's basket. Johnson took the ball in mid-stride and made a driving layup shot that won the game for Boston. The point is, Bird knew where Johnson was going to be without even looking, and Johnson knew what Bird would do the instant he saw that Bird was going to steal the pass. *Mutual anticipation in task performance is part of teamwork.* It takes practice and experience to acquire.

**Closing ranks stage** - While the prior, jell stage is characterized by some amount of flexibility, the closing ranks stage is not. A group that goes into this stage of its life cycle, and many do not, becomes very strongly focused on its goal(s). Maximal motivation, very tight cohesion, and peak performance characterize the group. Strong conformity pressures develop and deviant members, if any, are disciplined or even expelled if the group has power; if not, they are socially rejected because the group wants to succeed. Personal sacrifices in the group's behalf are not only evident in this phase, but are expected by the members. Interpersonal rivalries are sub-merged or set aside; bickering and factionalism are not tolerated, although they may resurface at a later time. New members are not integrated easily into groups during such periods, unless they can contribute immediately to the group's efforts.

Finally, bureaucratic administrative rules and policies often are ignored or circumvented as the group attempts to reach its goal. For example, task groups in an advanced college seminar may dis-regard reserve book regulations in the library, or find illicit ways to get documents copied or typed in contravention of school policies on the use of copying machines and allocation of secretarial time. A sales district competing for a prize might violate government and corporate equal opportunity hiring policy during such a period when filling an important territory vacancy. A senior executive group under comparable pressure might skin some rules about com-petitive bidding. The group in this stage becomes preoccupied with getting the job done, or with winning, under time pressure or other adverse conditions.[5]

These behaviors tend to arise in groups competing with others, or in groups initially created to accomplish some specific objective by a certain deadline. As the deadline approaches, and if the previous stages of development have been worked through reason-ably well or better by the group, the highly motivated, closing ranks stage is likely to occur. Since most task groups in organizations operate on a more continuous and non-competitive basis, this phase is not observed often. However, if the motiva-tional conditions are right, many task groups can move part way into such a peak performance stage, but it is not a state that is easily maintained for long periods of time.

**Stagnation stage** - Stagnation, as shown in Figure 1, occurs for various reasons, one being *over-conformity* within the group--a dysfunctional condition that arises after the closing ranks stage or earlier. Because of overconformity the group becomes inflexible and unresponsive to its environment. Typically in such periods some members rebel, others leave, internal bickering increases and performance declines. Alternatively, a viable group that achieves repeated success often experiences *reduced challenge* in its activities after a period of time. Members of such groups become complacent; some pursue other interests. As a result the group loses its "edge" or momentum.

There are numerous other possible reasons why a previously viable group deteriorates. Several are listed below:

- Long term adverse effects accumulate from an overdose of autocratic management;

- A key member gets hurt or sick, dies or leaves for some other reason;

- The group's mission loses significance in the larger organization;

- The entire group comes to believe it is not being adequately rewarded for its efforts and achievements;

- Some individual members come to believe that they are not being adequately rewarded for their contributions to the group;

- One or more new members are brought into the group and disturb the status equilibrium previously established;[6]

- The larger organization, a manager or some governmental agency imposes rules changes viewed as unfair or unreasonable;

- Age-related skill decrements occur; or

- Previously planted seeds of factionalism find time or impetus to develop, especially if in the closing ranks stage the group lost in competition, or failed to meet its goal.

## WHY THE MANAGER MUST UNDERSTAND A WORK GROUP'S HISTORY

This chapter began by illustrating how groups can differ from each other in significant ways. Then a seven stage life cycle model of task group development was proposed and described in some detail. The model forms a useful way to organize one's thinking about how groups operate and why. The presentation should serve as a reminder that motivational, attitudinal, and behavioral processes in groups begin to form even before the group has its first meeting, and continue to develop and change over a protracted period of time.

The model used herein is based on an intentionally drawn "success" story; however, *many, perhaps most, groups get bogged down in the sequential process somewhere between the organizing and the jell stage and never really approach their full potential.* And this is precisely why managers, most of whom have had little or no exposure to the academic discipline of social psychology, need to understand the evolutionary process through which task groups pass. There is great untapped potential in many such groups because most managers either are wedded to the concept of <u>individual</u> motivation, or simply don't know enough about the different group level factors that can be modified, combined in different ways, or otherwise turned to an organization's advantage. Group viability depends upon managerial actions and organizational policies. Many of the buttons to push are described in subsequent chapters.

## ENDNOTES

1    See, for additional detail, Hackman, R. and Morris, C., "Group tasks, group interaction process, and group performance effectiveness: A review and proposed integration," In Berkowitz, L., (Ed.), ADVANCES IN EXPERIMENTAL SOCIAL PSYCHOLOGY, 1975, 8, 45-99.

2    Several other "models" of group development have been proposed by various authors and are summarized by McGrath, J. E., "Theories of group development and categories for interactions analysis," SMALL GROUP BEHAVIOR, 4 (3), 1973, 259-304, and more recently by Shaw, M. E., GROUP DYNAMICS; THE PSYCHOLOGY OF SMALL GROUP BEHAVIOR, 1981 (3rd Ed), New York: McGraw Hill, 98-107. Unfortunately, all the models were developed by researchers or theorists interested in therapy groups or contrived groups in experimental laboratories rather than task groups embedded in work organizations. For that reason, I have developed my own descriptive model, although it overlaps others to some extent. See, also, Butzer, K. W., "Civilizations: Organisms or systems?," AMERICAN SCIENTIST, Sept-Oct, 1980, 517-522, Quinn, R. E. and Cameron, Kim, "Organizational life cycles and the criteria of effectiveness," unpublished ms, Graduate School of Public Affairs, SUNY Albany, and Kimberly, J., Miles, R. and Associates, THE ORGANIZATIONAL LIFE CYCLE "Issues in the creation, transformation and decline of organizations," 1980, San Francisco: Jossey-Bass, Inc.

3    Tuckman, as early as 1965, proposed a somewhat different conceptual model of group development that encompasses four stages; "forming, storming, norming and performing." He pointed out that the initial formative stage may include or be followed by considerable conflict and emotional behavior before the group "settles down." See Tuckman, B. W., "Developmental sequence in small groups," PSYCHOLOGICAL BULLETIN, 1965, 63, 384-399.

4    Hackman refers to these as "ambient stimuli" and proposes several interesting hypotheses about how they operate. Orne, in an earlier publication, referred to some functionally related stimuli in the context of laboratory social psychological experiments and called them "demand characteristics." See Hackman, R., "Group

influences on individuals," in Dunnette, M.D., (Ed.), HANDBOOK OF INDUSTRIAL AND ORGANIZATIONAL PSYCHOLOGY, 1976, Chicago: Rand McNally College Publishing Company; and Orne, M., "On the social psychology of the psychological experiment: with particular reference to demand characteristics and their implications," AMERICAN PSYCHOLOGIST, 1962, 17, 776-783.

5    For numerous examples of coping and circumvention behavior under pressure, see Dalton, M., MEN WHO MANAGE, 1959, New York: Wiley.

6    See Ziller, R. C., "Toward a theory of open and closed groups," PSYCHOLOGICAL BULLETIN, 1965, 64 (3), 164-182 for a provocative discussion of dynamic membership change and related phenomena.

# CHAPTER 4

## HOW GROUPS AFFECT THEIR MEMBERS

Groups can be strong, binding agents that help to hold a labor force together. They also can be reservoirs of potential energy which, if properly harnessed, can be of great benefit to any organization. But if they are improperly treated or left entirely to their own devices, they can develop organizationally damaging behavior patterns and attitudes.

People think and act differently as group members than as individuals. Because groups influence the behavior, attitudes, and motives of their members, it's important for managers to understand how and why that happens.

## COHESION AS THE HUMAN GLUE

Cohesion can be defined as: "The degree to which group members feel attracted to their group and desire to remain members of it." Cohesive groups that are attractive to their members (and usually to nonmembers too) have many important related characteristics. For example, most highly cohesive groups also seem to carry out their activities and interpersonal relations with "vim, vigor and enthusiasm."[1] These features often are referred to as indicators of high "morale." Morale, in other words, is a group phenomenon.[2]

Just as societal groups have cultural traditions, task groups also have patterns of collective feelings and beliefs that are passed along to new members. Task groups become points of reference, strongly influencing the way their members view themselves in relation to the organization or society at large. The members use the group's standards or comparison points when making judgments and evaluations.[3]

## CONFORMITY PRESSURES - GOOD OR BAD?

Such group pressures for uniformity serve valuable functions. They help the group to accomplish its goals and to maintain itself, and help the members develop a source of reinforcement of their opinions -- to create for them a social reality. By helping members to define their relations to their social surroundings, the group makes it easier to coordinate members' actions.

Group pressures on their members help to stabilize behavior, thereby easing the organization's control problems. Without the stabilizing, self-controlling influence of groups, most managers would find themselves facing anarchy. No formal organization, not even a university or a research laboratory, can afford the luxury of completely independent and individualistic thinking among its employees all of the time. Within limits, conformity pressures are necessary for the survival of any group, organization, or society.

**Conformity is a mixed blessing** - Overdoses of conformity, on the other hand, can be harmful to industrial, military, government, educational and voluntary organizations alike. For example, when the task to be performed requires creativity or problem solving, or during periods of rapid administrative or technological change, group tendencies to silence or cut off outspoken or otherwise deviant members can produce serious losses of good ideas. Strong conformity pressures within cohesive groups also can produce inbreeding, stifle individual initiative, and encourage resistance to change.[4] Thus group cohesion is a mixed blessing and requires continual leadership attention.

## GROUP INFLUENCES ON MEMBER ATTITUDES AND BELIEFS START EARLY

A person who is a member of a group already is distinguished in certain ways from a person who is simply one individual employee in a collection of employees who happen to be in the same place at the same time. One can be considered a member of a "work group" when one personally has a feeling of belonging to this group, shares the group's beliefs, attitudes, and norms of behavior, or at least is motivated to learn and adopt these beliefs, attitudes and norms.

Because belonging to a group makes a person sensitive to relations with others, one becomes especially responsive to the judgments expressed by other members. Members come to perceive and do things in a similar fashion because they are receiving similar information and similar environmental stimuli.

How does an employee develop these feelings and perceptions in the first place? A "new hire" is often put into a vacancy in a work unit which developed into a group long before he or she came on the scene. The newcomer soon learns that there is an ongoing group life surrounding the task that goes beyond the requirements of the work. If the appearance and activities of the group members look attractive, the new employee may make the effort necessary to gain acceptance. This decision may reflect a great deal of thought, or it may reflect a largely previously learned process that draws on the new member's past experiences in gaining and maintaining good standing in other groups (i.e., family, groups of classmates, neighborhood groups, other work groups on previous jobs and so on).

Gaining membership in a social group involves learning the things that make the group different from other groups, e.g., specialized language or slang that non-group members cannot understand, the rules for social games invented by the group, specific attitudes toward non-group members or specific things (like the cafeteria, the air conditioning and even "the boss"), or general standards to use in making judgments about new events and administrative policy.

*In brief, groups exert strong potential influences on how their members will interpret and react to all major managerial proposals related to the conduct of their work. Motivational strategies introduced to the employees by management will be interpreted and reacted to not only in terms of individual differences, but also in terms of group pressures.*

**New members are special targets** - Groups impose high uniformity pressures on new members. The established members direct efforts at new members to educate them, and to produce "appropriate" values and behavior. A central objective of such messages when directed at new members is to influence their beliefs about the group and its administrative/organizational environment. In particular, groups typically try to "educate" their new members (and remind other members) regarding what rewards and costs are present in the group, who controls them, and what behaviors by group members lead to these rewards and avoid the costs. The new member may actually seek these stimuli to improve his or her self-understanding, enhance personal progress and contributions to the group, or to test reality in order to "fit in" as quickly as possible.[5] In fact, many newly appointed managers brought into a group from "outside" will experience serious difficulties if they fail to recognize that this socialization process also applies to them. (See Chapter 2.)

**Territory pressures begin early** - Some "messages" from established members to newer ones are intended to produce *diversity* rather than uniformity. For example, as the members develop a role-status-task structure, they send messages to individuals perceived as encroaching on others' role boundaries (e.g., "You stick to your job and I'll do mine."). Similarly, the group may encourage a newcomer to adopt a unique role for himself or herself in the group that nobody else is filling. The motive behind this "be unique" message is not necessarily in the overall group's best interest; often it represents the protection of the sender's personal "territory" and as such reflects that individual's insecurity, fear of change, or competitive nature. Group process and leadership influence need to be directed at the members' differentiation tendencies to assure that the resulting role structure is task-relevant and flexible when the need arises.

**Group influences become permanent individual baggage** - The learning that occurs in the process of gaining and maintaining membership in a work group becomes an integral part of the person that is not necessarily turned on when one is in the group and turned off when other members are not present. Persons who see themselves as members of a group and identify with it tend to keep the attitudes they express while in the group. In fact, they may feel guilty whenever their behavior contradicts these attitudes. Thus shared attitudes that develop among work group members frequently affect a person's behavior when other group members are not present if the group really functions as a reference for the individual. This influence can be observed, for example when an employee is being interviewed in a supervisor's office, bowling with employees from another department, discussing the employer with strangers, or refusing to cross a rival union's picket line in front of a restaurant. The same process applies to managers as they represent their organizational functions in different meetings.

## HOW AND WHY GROUP PERFORMANCE STANDARDS EVOLVE

Aside from their influence on attitudes, conformity pressures also produce effects on performance standards. For example, even under financial incentive conditions, members of work groups do not necessarily maximize their performance. They make tradeoffs, instead, and therefore establish performance "norms" (behavior standards) above which and below which members are not supposed

to deviate, except in special cases. (Professors in academic departments do this, too, by pressing for specific teaching load norms.
Students also tend to establish standards of "reasonable" output.)

Groups often develop techniques for punishing members who
too often either overproduce (ratebusters in industry; greasy grinds
or grade grubbers in academia) or underproduce (chiselers in
industry). Punishment, however is not automatic. For example,
"rate busting" under a financial incentive system may be tolerated
by a group for a limited period in the case of an individual who
develops a sudden financial problem, such as the birth of twins.
Substandard performance may be tolerated in the case of an
individual who is ill or is having a personal problem off the job.

The establishment and maintenance of performance standards
is a vital matter in all serious task groups. The process begins in
the pre-assembly stage and continues throughout the group's life.
The qualitative and quantitative aspects of performance standards,
moreover, are an almost continuous source of debate and frequently
give rise to serious conflict. A task group's manager can have an
almost continual role to play in this regard if the group is inadequately or inappropriately staffed, or is badly motivated.

## HOW GROUPS INFLUENCE WORK-RELATED HABITS

Our discussion, thus far, of conformity pressures and norms
has focused primarily on the development of performance standards.
However, there are additional important matters that groups develop
norms about, such as :

- Coffee and rest break frequency, duration and timing;

- The length of the "lunch hour;"

- The interpretation of "sick leave" policy and frequency of its use (known as "sick and tired" leave among
  U.S. Government workers);[6]

- Willingness to work overtime hours and restriction
  of output to insure overtime opportunities;

- Arrival and departure times;

- dress code; and

- Safety.

These matters are frequently discussed by managers in all types of organizations because they believe that widespread abuses exist. Normally the employer tries to control these matters on an organization-wide basis through the establishment of overall policies which are then enforced, through punishment, on an individual basis. Actually, individual behavior on such matters is influenced highly by group norms--both the norms of the formal work group and those of the informal groups that exist in the organization. If the norms are dysfunctional, the change strategy that is based on a group model probably has a better chance of success than an individual approach has. The trick is to encourage the formation of appropriate norms during the group's developmental phase, and then maintain them.

Note that six out of the eight "problems" listed above involve the dimension of time and its allocation. This may explain why new forms of work scheduling such as the four-day week and flexitime work schedules have proved very effective in many organizations. Such arrangements greatly reduce the amount of conflict and friction within an organization. Many of the above "abuse" problems can be alleviated by these modern strategies.

**A case study: turning down bribes can pay** - An unusual example of a work group norm was reported in a study of agents employed by a government agency responsible for certain regulatory controls over business organizations.[7] An operating rule in this agency was that offers of bribes to its agents were to be reported for possible prosecution. However, there was an unofficial norm among the agents that they would not report such bribe offers; according to the researcher, the agents did not like "squealers" (thus reflecting an attitude typically found among criminals). *The researcher found that agents could exploit their own bargaining position with a businessman once a business official made a bribe offer.* Thus, upon receiving a bribe offer an agent could firmly refuse it, thereby putting the offerer in a potentially punishable position. The next step was for the agent to inform the offerer what changes had to be made in his business practices in order to comply with government regulations. Knowing that he could be prosecuted for his previously attempted bribe, according to the researcher, the businessman was likely to conform. *Thus, the norm of not reporting bribe attempts reflected both an attitude among the agents and certain functional advantages in getting their job done, even though the norm was contrary to their employer's rule.*

## HOW GROUPS INFLUENCE PREJUDICES

It should now be abundantly clear that people, in general, are "controlled" to a large degree by the groups to which they belong and feel a part of.  This widespread phenomenon has implications for a large variety of organizational problems including incentive administration, organizational renewal and the management of change.  Prejudicial attitudes and race relations are increasingly urgent problems to which group influences also apply.

**A rose by any other name** - The dynamics of racial prejudice actually are quite similar to those involved in any other prejudice.  Thus, white collar employee prejudice toward factory workers, factory worker prejudice toward managers, field staff prejudice toward headquarters, enlisted men's prejudice toward commissioned officers, young people's prejudice toward the "older generation," and "town-gown" prejudices in academic communities all involve similar social-psychological mechanisms.

**Prejudicial attitudes are learned** - According to a large body of research, most prejudiced individuals develop their negative attitude initially by being taught to do so by people who are important to them.[8]  The main support for the resistance of prejudiced individuals when other people make attempts to change their attitudes is that the "important people" usually are fellow group members.  Most of us find it disturbing to hold opinions contrary to the opinions of people or groups that we like and trust.  The "right" way to think about certain groups is learned very early by most children, long before they have any direct personal experience with members of such groups.  The same is true about our opinions of "government bureaucrats," "bosses," and labor unions.

These negative attitudes, formed early in life, lead us to avoid direct experience with members of such disliked groups whenever possible.  This prolongs the period during which corrective new information cannot be received.

**Job-related prejudice also starts early** - Employment-related prejudices (which are not always undeserved) in some cases are acquired long before the individual obtains his or her first job.  The folklore of the past is passed from one generation to the next starting with lullabies sung to children and through folksongs, family discussions, church sermons and annual celebrations of past, sometimes bloody events.  Certain images of miners and coal owners persist in central Kentucky and West Virginia just as polarized, mutually negative views of each other are maintained through several generations by Israelis and Arabs in the Middle East and Catholics and Protestants in Northern Ireland.

Other employment-related prejudices are learned by new members from their work groups. If an existing group has a long-standing competitive feud going with a neighboring department, or feels threatened by that department, the newcomer, as part of the socialization process, is likely to be taught to dislike that department's members, bad mouth the quality or quantity of its work, and question the importance of its mission in the organization. Prejudices in work organizations develop in much the same way as other social prejudices develop elsewhere.

## HOW GROUPS INFLUENCE INDIVIDUAL MEMBER WORK EFFECTIVENESS

So far I have described a variety of ways in which groups affect their members, and vice-versa. Some of these influences, group performance norms for example, bear directly on members' work effectiveness, primarily through motivational processes. Others, such as group shared beliefs and attitudes about the management, have a less direct linkage to individual work performance, but are relevant because they can affect resistance to change and organizational conflict. They also can affect effort expenditure.

**The work group is a skills teacher** - Aside from group shared attitudes and norms, groups affect members in other ways. Specifically, job knowledge and skills are learned at least in part from fellow group members. New members often are assigned temporarily to a senior member for instruction, because the group's formal leader is unavailable or lacks the detailed expertise. New members also pick up job-related knowledge and skills by simply observing and listening to their more experienced peers. They receive praise or criticism from other group members for their work and the ways they go about it. This feedback can serve to reinforce "correct" methods and punish "incorrect" methods.

Groups may withhold task knowledge and "tricks of the trade" from new members thereby allowing them to learn improper methods or to make avoidable mistakes. Sometimes this is done as part of a "hazing" process for all new members. Sometimes it is aimed at someone who is disliked either as an individual, as a member of a stereotyped minority group, or as a former member of a disliked neighboring group in the work organization. A reward system geared to individual competition among members within a group also fosters such withholding of information and skill instruction, or can result in the deliberate provision by one employee to another of erroneous information or improper task performance techniques.

**The group can be a bad teacher** - Even in the absence of internal competition, the group is not necessarily a source of accurate information or functional task techniques. Rather, the group may pass along to a new member inaccurate information without realizing it, or teach by example unsafe or inefficient work techniques simply because such techniques were incorporated by the group in its learning stage and were never challenged or corrected by its leader or by outside staff specialists.

It is true that individual differences in task knowledge and skills have more impact in some jobs and groups than others. It also is true that formal (but imperfect) recruiting and selection systems exist to try and insure the employment only of qualified individuals. Nevertheless, the group remains a significant influence on member task effectiveness. And, because of belongingness needs and conformity pressures, the group may have greater impact upon a new member's work methods than formal, highly organized training programs. The group's potential impact on a member's work methods, of course, depends upon the complexity and skill level requirements of the task, the phase of group development involved, and other factors.[9]

**Some members are more effective teachers than others** - As is the case with all member learning in a group, every member does not have equal potential influence over the task behavior, knowledge or effort level of another member, The highest status member may be, knowingly or not, the most important source or example, especially for newcomers. Some newcomers, on the other hand, may consider the high status member to be too awesome, and therefore an unrealistic model to emulate. Still others may seek out a group member of his or her same ethnic or sex category, feeling more comfortable with such an information source. If that person, chosen for non-task related reasons, happens to be socialized incompletely or inaccurately to the group's culture and task, the newcomer can be expected to make mistakes, too. *If managers want newcomers to learn the right way to do things, they must involve themselves in their training.*

## HOW GROUPS GET THEIR MEMBERS TO CONFORM

**Some examples** - An extreme case of conformity pressure was reported by an Associated Press dispatch to many American newspapers on April 10, 1972. A "punishment squad" of the Irish Republican Army, according to Belfast police, had beaten, painted, and feathered a 24-year old pregnant housewife while her three young and screaming children watched. Apparently this Catholic woman's crime had to do with drug use, which violates IRA norms. The dispatch added that the IRA, which has a strong grip on the district where this victim lived, often metes out its own punishment if its code is violated. Such are the ways of groups in conflict.

A less extreme example was reported by THE GUARDIAN on February 7, 1968. Five union stewards at Colt factory, Havant, Hampshire, where workers, "working overtime for Britain" contrary to the union's advice, were "tried" by their union for supporting the scheme to increase productivity. Four of the five stewards were found "guilty of discrediting the union and acting in a manner detrimental to it." They were dismissed from their shop steward roles by the union, but subsequently were re-elected by their constituents!

**Groups have many methods** - Aside from the rather dramatic conformity inducing tactics described above, groups usually resort to less stringent measures. Persuasion, practical jokes (stolen lunch box, air let out of tires) and subtle threats are more common. However, the cowardly and deliberate spreading of rumors about a member who deviates from a group norm, malicious lies and behind the scenes character assassination also can and do occur in the world of work, usually under conditions when the target cannot fight back.

What determines the strength of such conformity pressures? Some norms are more important to the group than others. When uniform beliefs, attitudes, values, or behavior are felt to be in the group's interest, the group may be expected to use whatever means it can to assure member compliance. But groups differ considerably in their ability to exert influence on their members. If members feel the threat of punishment does not conflict with their values, the coercive power of the group is likely to be great. If membership is very important, the mere threat of social ostracism may be sufficient to keep some members in line. Such controls may even include the use of violence.

Finally, if the group members regularly reward those who live by the norms and punish those who do not, this fact will influence every individual member who finds the group rewards valuable and the punishments threatening. For example, an individual worker may be privately inclined to work harder under a newly installed financial incentive system. However, the rest of the work group may perceive this system as the first step toward a "speed up" and eventual displacement of workers, and may be verbally or physically aggressive toward members who do not agree with the majority. The potential advantages from receiving higher than average bonuses must be balanced against the loss of social rewards which the group withholds from anyone who does not behave in accord with its norms.

**A management example** - Simiiar dynamics apply to all groups at work, regardless of the presence or absence of financial incentive systems. Indeed, such conformity pressures sometimes appear in very unlikely circumstances. For example, a budget cut of two percent was once announced by the top management of a large hospital where I served as a consultant. Several department heads were discussing how they were going to implement this. Most were complaining. One, however, said that he could absorb the cut and probably could cut even more than the prescribed two percent. Upon hearing this, another department head said, "Don't ruin it for the rest of us." (In other words, don't be a rate-buster.)

## MULTIPLE-GROUP MEMBERSHIP AND CONFLICTING LOYALTIES

The conformity-cohesion picture is complicated by the fact that most of us belong to, or identify ourselves with, more than one group. Each of these groups has its own set of conformity pressures. Usually we can manage these multiple-group membership demands with little difficulty. For example, most corporate board of directors members can handle their dual responsibilities to their company's executive team and their stock holders. However, if compensated by stock options a director may be caught in a conflict of interest situation when making a decision about declaring dividends vs. reinvesting corporate surplus in new plant and equipment.[10] There are circumstances, however, when demands arising from different groups come into direct conflict more visibly. Factory foremen, office supervisors, and academic deans recently promoted from the rank and file are classic examples. They must deal, in one way or another, with conflicting conformity pressures from the "old gang," on the one hand, and their new "managerial" group, on the other. This phenomenon is known as "role conflict." (See Chapter 2 on managerial role conflict.)

**We can have our cake and eat it, too** - A similar work-related example of potential conflict between apparently conflicting groups or organizations having competing conformity demands arises in the case of union members. However, evidence collected through several attitude surveys in industry supports the conclusion that, historically speaking, most organized employees like both their employer and their union. When asked the two questions separately, "Do you like your union?" and "Do you like your employer?" the majority replied "yes" to both questions. Most organized employees have not seen union and management as two mutually exclusive groups whose separate activities are necessarily in direct conflict with each other. Rather, they have seen the activities of the union as contributing to satisfaction of one set of their needs, and the activities of management as contributing to another set, with some amount of overlap where the activities of both are common to the same goals. The long-standing stereotype of union and management as natural enemies, with the union trying to get need satisfaction for its members and management blocking these efforts, apparently isn't heavily subscribed to by union members.[11]

Given what is known about multiple-group membership and potential role conflict, this finding is not surprising. There is no theoretical barrier to prevent a person from being attracted simultaneously to two different groups as long as the following conditions are met:

- Each group makes substantial contributions to the person's need satisfaction;

- Neither group requires the person to hold unfavorable attitudes toward the other group; and

- Neither group's actions conflict with the other's goal-seeking. Of course, a strike temporarily demands that the worker "choose sides", but when the conflict ends, most strikers seem to return to their previous state of dual allegiance.

When local rank and file and community norms define a "good union member" as one who supports the union and dislikes the employer and the "good employee" as one who supports the employer and dislikes the union, no one can fit both definitions. Knowing this principle, many U.S. Catholic southerners, according to numerous media accounts, were observed to have their children turn around and face in a different direction when groups of nuns carrying anti-segregationist placards paraded in Mississippi streets in the 1960s. The children were protected, at least temporarily, from a strong conflict between the family and its church.

**We avoid some multiple-group membership conflicts through psychological sleight of mind** - Most of us manage our multiple--group membership demands without conflict either because simultaneous pressures for competing loyalties rarely arise, or because a given set of competing pressures is easily resolved in favor of one group or the other. (In the latter case many of us would work overtime when needed by our employer in an emergency rather than take the family on a picnic that can be postponed.) On the other hand, most of us occasionally encounter serious conflicts between competing group demands. One researcher studied a pertinent example of this -- the military chaplain who has to live with the conflict between the role of warrior and the nonviolent role of minister.[12] He found that four psychological mechanisms were used by chaplains to handle the potential discomfort of this conflict:

Rationalization: "Someone has to carry the gospel to these boys"

Compartmentalization: "Render unto Caesar the things that are Caesar's and unto God the things that are His"

Repression or Denial: "I don't see any conflict" and

Withdrawal: "I'd rather not talk about it."

It is possible that some of the union members who say they like both their union and their employer are "compartmentalizing" their groups (management and union) or "repressing" their conflict to avoid painful feelings.

*The old battle cry, "You're either for me or against me, you can't be in between," does not fit the psychological facts.* (Sometimes this slogan is used by leaders -- or parents -- as a deliberate tactic to induce guilt feelings and secure conformity to group, organizational, or religious norms. A college student wishing to marry a young man of a different religious group from her own may find that her parents will say, "Him or us; you can't have both.")

**Role conflict at work; whistle-blowers** - Serious role conflict problems due to multiple-group memberships are not uncommon in the world of work. In some instances they even produce good results for employer organizations and the larger society as well. For example, there was a case in a New England furniture factory where a long-service worker who also was an active member of a conservation club incurred the wrath of management when he reported to state government authorities that his employer was dumping liquid industrial waste, which killed fish, into a small stream alongside the plant. The stream emptied into one of Vermont's finest trout rivers. While management was irritated at their internal "whistle blower," the company would have suffered substantially larger financial losses had the problem been discovered much later.

Another role conflict case known to me in a large metropolitan hospital exemplifies a typical multi-group membership problem found in all modern organizations that employ professional-technical personnel. A supervisor of a technical service unit refused to carry out an order from her superior (a physician) because she believed his order was in conflict with state legislation regulating the employment and licensing of certain medical technicians. (He wanted her to hire some foreign trained technicians who did not meet state licensing requirements.) This young woman, by acting in accordance with her occupational group's norms (and her perception of state law), badly damaged her relationship with her boss, and diminished her own career mobility in trying to do what she felt was the right thing for the larger organization, the hospital. Indeed, had she followed her doctor's orders, the hospital for which they both worked may very well have been penalized by the government. The hospital's personnel department, however, considered her to be a trouble-maker.

**Escalation is potentially serious** - Some multiple-group loyalty conflicts can escalate from the individual level into major confrontations. A classic example occurred in England some years ago when the Wolverhampton Transport Committee refused to allow bus crew members, who also were adherents to the Sikh religion, to wear turbans at work. A 23-year-old bus driver was fired for defying the ban. *Six months later he led 4,000 marchers from all over England in a public protest.* The marchers carried banners proclaiming, "Sikhs laid down their lives [during World War II] for Britain in beards and turbans." (On Jan. 6, 1974, the NEW YORK TIMES reported the pending court-martial of an American soldier for refusing to remove his beard and turban, and for not getting his hair cut. The soldier, a convert to the Sikh religion, was the fourth such court martial case within a short period of time.)

**In the end some role conflict may be good for us all** - Multiple-group memberships often provide checks and balances that can be highly functional to society and organizations alike, even though they sometimes cause pain for individuals and conflict within organizations. But individuals who have to live and work under conditions of continual role conflict may not be able to avoid experiencing considerable stress. Accordingly, research on role conflict has shown that serious health problems may result from such stress. This matter will be discussed at greater length in a later chapter. Meanwhile, the reader might consider the case of Paul Cabell, Jr., a black assistant principal at Beecher High School in Flint, Michigan. Mr. Cabell committed suicide in despair over the state of race relations among students in the school. Comments from his friends indicate that as a moderate and integrationist, he could not handle (psychologically) the conflict built into his role by extremists.[13]

## SUMMARY OF GROUP CONFORMITY PRESSURE EFFECTS

The life history of a group reflects a complex and continuous process of mutual accommodation among the members, between the members and the task requirements, and between the group and its external environment. Thus, groups, like individuals, go through different stages of development, at different rates of speed, and with different levels of pain and grace.

Cohesion is a key dimension of group life that must be developed to some optimal level for each group's needs. Cohesive work groups develop internal pressures on their members to conform to group standards, beliefs, and attitudes. Even a "new hire" is socialized to a group's culture very early, and is not likely to remain a free-thinking, rugged individual for long.

Pressures for uniformity serve definite functions. They help a group accomplish its goals and maintain itself. If the group's goals are in line with those of the larger organization, group pressures can help stabilize effective behavior. No formal organization can afford the luxury of completely individualistic and independent thinking and behavior among its employees all of the time. However, group cohesion is a mixed blessing and requires continual attention.

The relationship of group conformity pressures to the development and maintenance of prejudicial attitudes, specialized language development, performance standards, member job knowledge and techniques, time investment and a variety of other work-related behaviors is clear. It is also clear that people, in general, are "controlled" to a significant degree by the task groups to which they belong and feel a part of. To some extent the dysfunctional consequences of such group control are offset by multiple-group memberships. These can provide worthwhile checks and balances highly functional to society and organizations alike, even though they sometimes cause pain for individuals and create organizational conflict.

## IMPLICATIONS FOR MANAGERS

*Conformity pressures within a group have different implications at different stages of the group's life cycle.* For example, during the assembly, organizing and learning stages of a group's life, conformity pressures can lead to premature decisions and inhibit crucial experimenting and problem solving activity. Therefore, high levels of cohesion and conformity pressure probably should be avoided in the early stages. During the jell and closing ranks phases, conformity pressures can be helpful to the group as a whole, by enhancing cooperation, coordination, attendance and energy expenditure. Alternatively, they can act as a *demotivator for new members who find themselves hemmed in by prior decisions, standards, and beliefs established by the original membership.* Even if the group is highly successful and making real progress as a group, the new member who is pressured to conform may instead "turn off," thus planting a seed for later problems when additional new members react similarly, rally around him or her, and form an informal splinter group. *This explains the necessity for active and personal involvement by the manager in orienting and training newcomers.*

Group shared attitudes and norms coupled with conformity pressures are especially pertinent matters during the renewal or rebuilding stage of a group's life cycle. The "old-timers" often become especially defensive during such periods and band together. The manager or any other would-be change agent (consultant or personnel specialist) must do plenty of homework on the group's history before progress can be expected during this stage.

The quest for an optimal level of cohesion in a group, coupled with the development and harnessing of conformity pressures to control its members, is a continuous process. From the time the members are initially assembled to the time the group breaks up or dies (if it ever does), there is a need for a constant juggling act. A group's productivity or task effectiveness depends upon how well it manages this juggling act while matching its resources with task requirements. The mutual accommodation activities among the members, between the members and task requirements, and between the group and its external environment, both reflect and influence the matching process. In brief, group process is an important ingredient of task group effectiveness and encompasses a continuous set of interacting activities.

The factors that impinge upon this continuous set of activities are many and complex. They include motivational factors, member skill and personality factors, external relations with other groups, task and technological factors, leadership factors, group size and structure, financial resources and the larger organization in which the group is embedded. Subsequent chapters will show how these factors operate.

## ENDNOTES

1   Vim, vigor, and enthusiasm in groups was described as "hedonic tone" by psychologist John Hemphill many years ago.

2   The relationship between the two terms "work group morale" and "job satisfaction" should also be clarified. An individual's overall satisfaction with his or her job is the sum of all things about the job which affect the individual positively or negatively. Thus the degree of individual attraction to one's work group is one of many factors (including pay, job duties, etc.) which contribute to making personal

overall job satisfaction high or low.  Job satisfaction is an individual matter and morale is a group matter.

3    Cohesion in a task group is not an unmixed blessing.  Sometimes, for example, groups coalesce around behavioral objectives not consistent with the larger organization's objectives.  See Stogdill, R. M., "Group productivity, drive and cohesiveness," ORGANIZATIONAL BEHAVIOR AND HUMAN PERFORMANCE, 1972, 8, 26-43.

4    A number of individual difference variables have been found to differentiate frequent conformists from nonconformists.  See Krech, D., Crutchfield, R., and Ballachey, E., INDIVIDUAL IN SOCIETY, 1961, New York: McGraw-Hill, 505-529; and McGrath, J. and Altman, I., SMALL GROUP RESEARCH:  A SYNTHESIS AND CRITIQUE OF THE FIELD, 1966, New York: Holt, 24-35.

5    Hackman, R.,  "Group Influences on Individuals," In Dunnette, M. D., (Ed.), HANDBOOK OF INDUSTRIAL AND ORGANIZATIONAL PSYCHOLOGY, Chicago: Rand McNally, 1976.

6    I am indebted to Don Perry, a former student, for this piece of information.

7    Blau, P., THE DYNAMICS OF BUREAUCRACY, 1955, Chicago:  University of Chicago Press, Chapter 10. Also discussed by Strauss, A., NEGOTIATIONS, 1978, San Francisco:  Jossey-Bass, 41-48.

8    Allport, G., THE NATURE OF PREJUDICE,1968, Garden City, N.Y.:  Doubleday Anchor,  292-294 and 38-39.

9    The above discussion differs to some extent from Hackman's perspective on the group's potential impact on member skill and task knowledge.  I consider the potential impact to be greater and more widespread than he does.  See Hackman, J.R., cited earlier, 1512-1513.

10   Krusekopf, C., "Pushing corporate boards to be better," FORTUNE, July 18, 1988, 58-67.

11   See Miller, G. and Rosen, N., "Members' attitudes toward the shop steward," INDUSTRIAL AND LABOR RELATIONS REVIEW, 1957, 10 (4), 516-531; Rose, A., UNION SOLIDARITY, 1952, Minneapolis:  University of Minnesota Press; Purcell, T., THE WORKER SPEAKS HIS MIND ON COMPANY AND UNION, 1953, Cambridge:  Harvard University Press; and Rosen, H. and Rosen, Ruth, THE UNION MEMBER SPEAKS, 1955, Englewood Cliffs, NJ:  Prentice-Hall.

12   Burchard, W., "Role conflicts of military chaplains," AMERICAN SOCIOLOGICAL REVIEW, 1954, 19, 528-535.

13   See the NEW YORK TIMES, March 19, 1972, page 58.

# CHAPTER 5

## THE MATURE WORK GROUP

Thus far I have shown why work groups are significant entities for managerial attention and have illustrated several of the basic processes through which they develop and by which they influence their members. The analysis has emphasized group cohesion as a central factor and has shown its relevance to member control, conformity pressures, overall viability and teamwork. The analysis also has emphasized the dynamics of group formation and the processes of group evolution. Let us now consider some additional factors that relate to these processes in established work groups, i.e., groups that have a substantial history within an organization and that evolved via the processes described earlier.

## THE GROUP'S STRUCTURE

Once a goal is clearly established and accepted by most members, one of its more essential functions is to set a direction for group activities. As a group engages in goal-directed work, a social structure inevitably evolves, stemming from the varied motivations, personalities and abilities of different individuals and their interaction with requirements for task specialization.[1]

**Specialization works** - Groups often find that if they specialize the tasks of their members they are more effective. Usually this specialization is intentionally designed and administered in conjunction with goals to create a structure expected to result in optimal organizational performance. The development of appropriate production, service or technical structures is encouraged to meet the demands of the task. This process is not necessarily completely harmonious, maximally efficient, or completely controlled.[2]

Within these structures, member roles are differentiated according to task requirements and personal preferences, and organized to coordinate efforts toward solving common problems. Each member's role carries with it a set of expectations for behavior and task performance. It also has some level of status built into it. For example, a company president is expected to perform administrative duties, coordinate the activities of other executives, and maintain relations with groups and individuals outside the organization. The president behaves in certain ways which fit the expectations of the people he is dealing with. At a meeting with the board of directors he might show deference to board members, laugh at their jokes, and behave in ways that justify his activities to the board. At a meeting with subordinate managers, however, the president will be the party exercising power and therefore will offer criticism and be the focus of the discussion. Role behavior is not an absolute, but rather is dependent on the context in which the role is assumed.

**Roles are not necessarily clear-cut** - Roles differ in the extent to which they are well defined. The role of a receptionist in the main entrance of a "blue chip" corporation, for example, is well defined. The receptionist's powers, choice of vocabulary, polite treatment of visitors, style, status and condition of clothing are thoroughly prescribed.

The roles of staff employees, such as personnel managers or quality control managers, are another matter. Such roles are characterized by considerable disagreement on expectations among people who deal with their occupants. Consequently, the extent of the personnel manager's power frequently is unclear, making this job difficult to perform effectively. The same is true of first-line supervisory roles.

**Status is a powerful influence** - The status hierarchy within a group affects group cohesion because status is viewed by most of us as a personal reward. *If this reward is too unevenly distributed in a group, interpersonal jealousies and competitive behavior often result which, in turn, damage the group's cohesion and teamwork.* Additionally, a group's status hierarchy also may act as a serious constraint when some technological, administrative, or personnel change is proposed.

People are reluctant to give up their achievement symbols. Job title, location or size of office or desk, whom one reports to, whether or not one punches a time clock, and type of clothes worn are important status symbols throughout the organization from top to bottom. Such matters usually are not discussed openly, however, so one must learn to recognize the symbols and anticipate their reward value, especially when planning to introduce a change. Even in the case of "simple" job rotation, a group member may object to sharing job duties with someone else because of a perceived loss of personal status.

To manage an organization or change it significantly, one must learn what the role and status systems look like. Serious conflict and resistance are likely if the change agent uses a frontal approach instead of working with and around the structure.

**Too much specialization can be a problem** - Finally, the amount of group structure (i.e., role and status differentiation) can influence group cohesion. Too much differentiation among unskilled members working on simple tasks (often routine clerical or manual) can produce competition, petty jealousies, and conflict. This partially explains why unskilled workers often appear to reject status hierarchies. On the other hand, many upwardly mobile members of technical and professional groups demand differentiated roles and status levels as part of their normal reward system. This can foster dysfunctional competition among members thereby adversely influencing group cohesion and teamwork. One must conclude, then, that some tradeoffs between individual motivation and group viability are necessary in some instances.

## HOW THE MEMBERSHIP MIX AFFECTS COHESION

Aside from the role and status hierarchy within a group, the membership mixture is another structural characteristic that can influence group cohesion. Membership mix refers to how similar the members are on such factors as personality types, skills, ethnic origins, socioeconomic backgrounds, sex, or types of specialized training backgrounds represented.

**Similarity makes life easier, but diversity may be needed** - It is easier to develop cohesion in a homogeneous than in a heterogeneous group. This probably is true for two reasons. First, homogeneous group members are more likely to have compatible interests. Second, homogeneous groups develop fewer internal dysfunctional status distinctions resulting in less internal competition. However, lack of diversity can hamper creativity and innovation. Once again, a tradeoff may be necessary.

**Acquiring new members does not always change the mix** - The composition of any given work group varies from time to time as some members are replaced by new ones or as its size is increased or decreased. However, there are various factors in organizations and task groups that operate to maintain the basic member mixture in the long run. First, the task may impose demands that require replacements to be like their predecessors. Second, equity considerations lead groups to maintain reasonably fixed percentages of senior, intermediate and junior level personnel, so that promotions from within will be available and so that the group's "dirty work" (e.g., unpleasant or boring chores) will not forever be concentrated in the same persons' hands.

Once a group has developed a membership mix that seems to "work," the members and their leaders attempt to maintain it, even under pressure for change. This is one reason why "different" kinds of people traditionally have found it difficult to penetrate various occupational groups in organizational settings. Indeed, until recent years group members often were encouraged to recruit their own replacements and other new members. Such a practice is influenced by group-shared attitudes that perpetuate the existing membership mixture - because we tend to recruit people in our own image.

**Too much membership change in a short time span hurts cohesion** - Changes in group composition, if they occur too fast and without proper preparation, can produce social chaos in a viable work group. For example, if a group of long seniority tool and die makers were to find itself being steadily infiltrated by recently trained, young machinists fresh out of a modern trade school, the older, and perhaps partially obsolete members probably would see a need to "fight" or resist in one way or another. They are likely to perceive the newcomers as threats to income and job security. The newcomers might be made to feel unwelcome and probably would band together, themselves, for mutual protection.

The same thing would happen in a payroll or accounting department in the face of an influx of new college graduates in jobs previously filled by high school graduates. Trade unions have the same problem whenever membership characteristics change rapidly (e.g., influx of youthful members having different needs than the older, long seniority members). Management and professional groups, of course, show the identical pattern; so do urban neighborhoods and schools as population characteristics change. Thus, changes in group composition can threaten the previously stable status hierarchy, and create dysfunctional competition and conflict within the group.

## IMPORTANCE OF GROUP'S
## OVERALL STATUS IN ORGANIZATION

**Some groups are more equal than others** - Different units and groups in an organization have different status levels as total groups. The surgical physicians in a hospital and the pilots in a commercial airline are the kingpin groups in comparison with the various support units that back them up. Usually the higher the group's status in the larger organization, the greater its attractiveness to outsiders (nonmembers) and the more cohesive it is internally. There are occasions, however, when low external status can encourage cohesion within a group. For example, a low status group may decide it is being unfairly treated and may band together to fight the rest of the organization for a place in the sun. Some clever leaders might deliberately exploit such an "underdog" perception to enhance motivation.

Groups acquire high status in a variety of ways, including through their past accomplishments, their functional importance to the organization, rigorous membership admission standards, and high financial earnings. Some of these variables can be manipulated by those wishing to change a group's cohesion level. However, it is highly unlikely that status differences among different work groups and units can ever be completely levelled.

## GROUP SIZE, JOB SATISFACTION, AND COHESION

Many studies have compared small work groups (5 to 10 persons) with large work groups (50 or more members) on several variables.[3] The evidence from these studies consistently shows that members of small work groups report significantly higher job satisfaction, on the average, than their counterparts doing similar tasks as members of large work groups. *However, personal job satisfaction does not invariably accompany or contribute to high productivity.*

**Small is beautiful, but** - The more satisfied members of small groups may or may not be more productive than the more dissatisfied members of large groups. Productivity depends on the current state of still other variables that affect production, but which do not have a systematic relationship to work group size. The evidence to date shows that the primary advantages of small groups is in areas other than individual member productivity or output.

The results of research on group size in work organizations match those in a variety of studies carried out in schools and universities.[4] These studies show that smaller classes are more satisfying to both teachers and students than are larger classes. Further similarity is found in the task area because individual student achievement shows no consistently significant and direct relationship to size of class.

**Work group size is not a constant** - Work group size in many organizational settings is not fixed; it varies with seasonal work load requirements (retail department stores), unpredictable market and economic fluctuations (most manufacturing industries), availability of qualified applicants and a host of other factors. In other words, it is more accurate to speak of a group's "typical" size and the range or frequency of its variation. Size research has not taken within-group size variation into account when relating group size to such variables as performance, cohesion, absenteeism and the like.

**Small is practical** - The real key to understanding the influence of size on groups is the variable known as "group cohesion" (or morale). Group size is an important ingredient of this human "glue." In addition to reporting higher than average job satisfaction, members of smaller groups describe their groups as being more cohesive or attractive than do members of larger groups. Small, cohesive groups also are characterized by higher than average cooperation among members, low member turnover and absenteeism, and are attractive to outsiders--that is, nonmembers are more interested in joining small, cohesive groups than large, noncohesive ones. Small, cohesive groups buffer their members against stressful environments.

Finally, where technological conditions permit, and when groups accept the goals of their organization, cohesion or morale is related to group performance levels. One way or another, cohesive groups exercise more influence and discipline over their members than do loosely knit groups.

## WHY SMALL IS BETTER

There are several reasons why group cohesion tends to be greater in small groups than in large ones. First, it is easier to develop a *feeling of "belonging"* to a group which is significantly changed by one's presence or absence. If I "belong to" a five-man maintenance crew, then I know the crew feels my absence when I don't show up. If I "work in" a 50-person assembly group rather than "belong to" a smaller group or crew, then the importance of my being present seems rather small and "nobody will miss me." Indeed, several industrial studies show that absenteeism is related to group size--the larger the group, the higher the absenteeism.[5]

*Recognition* also is more available to members of small work groups; the personal attention of the manager is spread less thin than it is in large groups, and quality performance is more likely to be noticed and rewarded with praise and personal recognition from others. Also, small groups can permit more fulfillment of ego needs by providing more opportunity for the manager to use participative methods. This means that a larger percentage than usual of the group membership can be involved in making decisions which affect them personally. It is easier to get members of small groups to participate and make suggestions than it is to motivate members of large groups in this direction.

Indeed, problem-solving and other meetings of large groups often are plagued by strong, dominating personality types, competition among members and limited opportunity for widespread participation, partly because the time available is usually too short in relation to the number of people in the group. Smaller groups have fewer such difficulties.[6]

Group size is a critical variable in relation to group attraction, cohesion, or morale. Small groups provide more satisfactions for their members than do large groups, which partially explains why small, informal groups develop spontaneously in work organizations. *The large, impersonal units created out of technological, architectural, and financial considerations in work organizations often fail to meet human needs.*

## GROUP PHYSICAL BOUNDARIES AND COHESION

Since small group size fosters group cohesiveness, and that cohesion accompanied by appropriate goals is related to group performance, it is clear that creating small groups within a larger organizational structure can be advantageous. How, then, can organizations foster small group solidarity when technological or financial considerations seem to call for larger work units?

One answer to this problem may be as simple as altering the physical environment of the employees or developing boundaries having psychological significance. Most work organizations experience periodic changes in physical layout. Individuals and small groups are moved to different quarters, functions are redefined leading to mergers or splits, or new offices or work areas are created. All such changes have important implications for the motivation and leadership of groups and individuals either directly or indirectly. The spontaneous development of informal groups is a fact of organizational life. The effective manager attempts to capitalize on the constructive resources of such groups. Changes in physical layout have far-reaching effects on these matters.

**Offices in a skating rink** - The headquarters staff of a corporation I once worked for was located in a former roller skating rink. More than 200 clerical employees worked in a huge central area; they sat at rows and rows of desks. Separate offices were reserved around the periphery of the building, but only for managers. Given what is known from research on group size, job satisfaction and morale, it is safe to assume that many employees in this large, impersonal room were dissatisfied and considered themselves to be insignificant cogs in a large gear box.

One approach to encouraging group development and teamwork in such a setting would be to install waist-high walls. If properly placed, these should help create new feelings of group identity and solidarity among employees within each set of boundaries, or increase the strength of such feelings if they are already present before the installation of the walls. Of course, if the new walls do not correspond with any of the "natural" boundaries previously established, resentment and increased dissatisfaction would result.

**A plan is needed** - It is essential, of course, that such a change be introduced only after the groundwork is laid. The employees (and their neighbors) should be informed so that they will not misinterpret the managerial intent and get the idea that they are somehow being punished, threatened, or inconvenienced. (People can object to being fenced in or out.) They also should be consulted so that the group boundaries can be correctly placed.

**Boundaries can create rivalries** - Increased small group solidarity is likely to bring about improved communication, reduced absenteeism and turnover, fewer grievances and better performance. On the other hand, if the fences promote rivalry and competition between groups, some difficult problems will occur. For example, the more "visible" the groups become because of their more obvious boundaries, the more likely it will be for the members of one group to compare their working conditions with those of neighboring groups. If personnel and supervisory practices are too different from one group to the next, such comparisons can become invidious and disruptive. On balance, however, the positive advantages of cohesive groups will outweigh the disadvantages that may develop in a few improperly managed cohesive groups.

**Keep the communication lines open** - Before such changes are introduced, the manager should carefully answer the question, "What employee perceptions are likely to arise and what implications will this change have on group life in the organization?" Experience shows that almost any managerially imposed change will create attempts among employees to interpret the motives behind the change and assess their personal effects. Walls, like fences, convey very definite meanings to most people. For example, consider what happens when a family in a fenceless neighborhood suddenly erects a fence around its property. New fences in neighborhoods bring different reactions depending upon their physical characteristics. If they are low, decorative fences which children and neighbors can easily step over, that is one thing. If they are high, or have barbed wire at their tops, there will be a much different reaction among neighbors. Similarly, boundaries and space have implications at the work place as well as for geopoliticians and astronauts.

**Beware of unintended boundaries** - Whether management plans it or not, groups also form in relation to natural boundaries at the work place. It is well to examine all unintended boundaries to determine whether they contribute positive, negative, or neutral influences to the organization's efforts.

**There are constraints on experimenting with group size** - Group size is not always easy to control for purposes of influencing group cohesion. Aside from the efforts of occasional "empire builders," work group size in most organizations is fixed by factors outside the control or influence of the group or its manager. Manpower resource availability, technological requirements, number of available desks or machines, raw material supply and inventory control, amount of available floor space, or the structural characteristics of the building are the usual factors determining work group size. Often there is some potential for carving large units into smaller ones, and size also can be controlled when designing task forces and committees.

## GROUP PSYCHOLOGICAL BOUNDARIES AND COHESION

**Symbolic boundaries** - Group boundaries serve psychological purposes and do not necessarily take the form of physical walls.

Psychological group identity sometimes is created and maintained by other visible  symbols such as uniforms, insignias, distinctive clothing, special admissions requirements, and even unique speech or mannerisms.  These symbols or admissions standards serve to differentiate the group from others and to socialize its members to adopt unique behaviors, attitudes, and values.  As pressures for uniformity within the group increase, group solidarity increases. In turn the group functions in a smoother, more integrated way.

**Symbols are functionally important** - The group differentiation process often is joked about and even deplored within organizations, and rightfully so in some extreme cases of group separation leading to hostility and lack of cooperation.  On the other hand, imagine what it would be like to work (or be a patient) in a hospital where every employee wears ordinary street clothing, and no uniforms, caps, and insignias are allowed.  One wouldn't be able to distinguish medical students from doctors, doctors from nurses, or lab technicians from orderlies.  Similar results would occur in other kinds of organizations.  Aside from fostering group identity, cohesion and related behaviors, group boundaries are functional to the organization's tasks and may also have safety implications.

## COMMUNICATION PATTERNS AND COHESION

The typical, often repeated patterns of interaction among group members at work constitutes the group's communication network or communication structure, i.e., who communicates with whom, how and in what sequence.[7]  This communication structure may or may not be the same as the group's role, status and authority structure.  The adoption of one characteristic format or another is influenced by a variety of factors including member characteristics, the manager's style, task demands, customary practice, or the quality of the group's relationship to other groups.

Figure 2 describes two communication system models found in task groups.  They have been given names descriptive of their character.  Network A resembles the pyramidal organizational chart pattern found in most organizations. Each person, designated by an "X" in Network A, interacts with only one or two other persons and the flow of communication is tightly controlled.

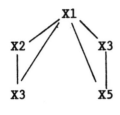
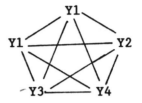

NETWORK A               NETWORK B

PYRAMIDAL            ALL CHANNEL

**Fig. 2.   Two communications nets
frequently used in experiments**

Network B is called the all-channel net. Every group member, designated by a "Y," interacts and communicates with every other member regardless of status difference. Full information is available to every group member.

These communications networks have been found in laboratory studies to differ substantially in their relative impact on the experimental groups where they were imposed. The "all channel" network appears to be the more advantageous on several counts:

- It fosters greater member satisfaction and more group cohesion;

- It promotes sharing of leadership, develops leadership potential, and facilitates leadership replacement;

- It prepares group members to cope with the group's task even when the formal leader is absent;

- It is more effective for dealing with complex problems. Specifically, when doing complex tasks Network B groups reach solutions faster and make fewer errors. These advantages are present even though groups operating an all-channel net may be noisy and appear to an observer as disorganized and repetitive. *However, Network B groups do less well on simple tasks*;

- Members in groups using an all-channel communication net are more thoroughly informed than members in other groups.

On balance, it appears from much experimental laboratory evidence that the all-channel communication network is the optimal communication or interaction pattern to develop in a group performing complex tasks.

**Reasons for task performance differences are less clear** - One group theorist makes a strong logical case that the differences in performance outcomes of the various networks arise as a function of the efficiency with which group members organize themselves and match their potential specialized roles and individual skills with task demands.[8] The all-channel net makes it easier to achieve matching because there is full communication.

## THE PARTICIPATION PRINCIPLE

Questions still exist about performance outcomes of different imposed communications networks.[9] It also is true that network deficiencies do not account for all the communications problems within the larger organizational context. However, there can be little doubt that group cohesion interacts with communications networks in work groups outside the experimental laboratory.

**Communication network effectiveness depends on a combination of several additional factors** - The laboratory-based small group communication net research is closely bound to the larger issues of participation in decision making. Therefore, *despite many of the advantages claimed for all channel or decentralized communications nets, there are contingent conditions affecting their use.* For example, certain kinds of tasks or emergency conditions might preclude the use of the time-consuming all-channel net. Additionally, some group members, including the leader, may not be prepared to accept the responsibilities for thoughtful, informed action implied by the all-channel net. People who are dependent upon others for direction and guidance feel insecure and frightened in situations where many of the traditional or arbitrary symbols of authority are missing. Such persons prefer to receive orders rather than have an authority figure ask them to express their opinion, especially if they are uncertain what opinion the leader holds and cannot assume this as their own.

*An all-channel net therefore gives some people more freedom than they want or can handle. It also may be inappropriate because of low interpersonal trust among the group members.*

**Stage of group development should influence the choice of network** - Communications networks usually vary at different stages of the group's task. Groups often are assembled to perform tasks that require a sequence of activities such as problem definition, generation of alternative solutions, evaluation of alternative solutions and implementation of the preferred solution. The communication network needed among the members may be very different during these various stages of group work. The problem definition stage often requires an "all channel net." The implementation stage, on the other hand, may well require the traditional pyramid.

In other words, the problem solution implementation requirements may, and often do, call for something less than an all channel communication net. It is unlikely that there is one best communication network that should be engineered into all groups at all stages of their development and activity. *The manager's challenge is to encourage appropriate communication net usage for different conditions.*

## UNIQUE VOCABULARY AND COHESION

**Jargon is important** - Unique language, specific to a group, is an often observed phenomenon. Lawyers, medical doctors, electrical engineers, psychologists and all other specialized groups, develop and regularly utilize their own distinctive vocabularies. Some of this vocabulary reflects group status seeking, but it also reflects task demands for precise words carrying unambiguous meaning. A racing sailboat crew, to communicate quickly and effectively, must know the nomenclature for many different parts of the vessel as well as racing "lingo". In football there are "down and out" pass patterns, "prevent" defenses and "tight ends" (not drunk). I have observed more than 300 three-person groups perform a communication experiment requiring the solution of a complex puzzle that utilized dominoes as parts. It is remarkable how much vocabulary development had to occur in these groups before the members could talk intelligently about such simple objects as dominoes.

**Proper choice of words can be crucial** - The speed and extent of specialized vocabulary acquisition in task groups interact with the development of cohesion, performance effectiveness and communications networks. Other things being equal, groups that quickly develop a shared common vocabulary relevant to the task they are performing are more likely than others to succeed. Requests from a surgeon to a nurse such as, "Please hand me that thing over there" rather than, "Please hand me the scalpel" do not facilitate communication and probably will not help develop a lasting interaction pattern between the two parties involved. One reason some groups are staffed initially by experienced "old pros" is to avoid the time consuming vocabulary learning process; experienced people bring the specialized language with them.

**The language required is not necessarily easily learned** - An example of how specialized vocabulary demands interact with group process in a realistic work group setting is found in an account of group development in a mental hospital staff. A nurse on one of the patient wards was encouraged (for purposes of job enrichment and personal development) by other professionals (psychologist and social worker) to "engage in therapeutic contacts with patients." She also was urged to hold group therapy meetings with patients and was offered assistance so that she could learn how to do such activities for which she had no formal training.

According to one experienced observer on this case, the nurse backed away from these assignments: *"Her greatest difficulty was a lack of even minimal psychiatric language, apparently necessary to engage in such tasks."*[10] (Emphasis mine.) The nurse in question realized that participation and job enrichment without appropriate background and training was not a viable strategy.

## PRODUCTIVITY IS LIMITED BY GROUP PROCESS

Up to this point I have said very little about group productivity which is obviously influenced by a combination of the above complex factors. A convenient summary of how these complexities tie together says that how well a group will perform depends upon three factors: task demands, resources, and group process. In combination, task demands and resources determine the theoretical maximum level of productivity that can be achieved. That level is called "potential productivity". Potential productivity can be inferred from a thorough analysis of task demands and available resources. Actual productivity, on the other hand, is equal to potential productivity minus losses due to faulty human processes in the group. According to the author of this summary, group process consists of the:

"...collective actions of the people who have been assigned a task ... by which they evaluate, pool, and assemble their resources; decide who shall do what, when [and where - NR]; assign differential weights to one another's contributions; and extol one another to participate fully in the group's task-oriented activities."[11]

He further suggests that actual productivity will approximate potential productivity when the group's behavioral task sequence matches the [logical] pattern demanded.

This viewpoint assumes that analysis of the task and knowledge of the available resources leads to the specification of the "best" procedure for carrying out the assignment.[12] However, for a variety of reasons, even if the best procedure is correctly identified, it will not necessarily be used by the group. This represents process loss and results in something less than the group's potential performance.

**Group process defined** - The term "group process" has not been defined consistently in the literature. Broadly speaking, it refers to the ways in which group members relate to each other interpersonally in structuring themselves and getting the task performed, the methods they use to communicate with and influence each other, and their decision-making and problem-solving strategies. Thus, mutual influence processes can include the use of persuasion and attempts to "educate" one another, volunteering for or refusing various duties (thereby serving as an example to others), the use of threats and coercion, and appeals to higher level authority (to resolve disagreements). *In brief, group process involves negotiating, a term that has many synonyms: bargaining, wheeling and dealing, compromising, making deals, getting tacit understandings, trading off and even collusion.*[13] Note that the "best" or most logical solution does not always emerge.

## THE GROUP'S INFORMAL CONTRACT

Mature groups in work organizations have a history of informally negotiated agreements regarding such matters as who will do what and when, vacation schedules, overtime schedules, administration of sick leave policy, administration of incentive system rewards, and who will switch to what jobs in the event someone takes ill or resigns. These agreements, which represent realistic accommodations, do not always appear on paper and may not be entirely consistent with organization policies.

The members "keep score" on these agreements and remind each other of imbalances. (Members also will be quick to inform a new manager about these agreements so that he or she will honor them.) The influence techniques used in the negotiating process reflect personality differences, different motives of the members, power imbalances within the group and other matters. Therefore, the totality of group process can't be controlled. Neither maximal matching of members to task requirements nor optimal group structure is likely to occur, at least on complex tasks.

## REASONS FOR PROCESS LOSS

Some of the reasons for process losses are either implicit or explicit in prior sections of this and earlier chapters. For example, too much member concern about status differentials, or an overly competitive reward system can result in a poor match between individual assignments to specific subtasks and can disrupt logical sequencing of work activities. Conformity pressures, group shared attitudes, and prejudices also affect and reflect group process, and help to explain why groups are resistant to change.

Work groups in organizations perform many kinds of tasks. Some require specialization and tightly sequenced operations for success. Others merely require the summation of the members' separate efforts, where all members are doing the same thing. The emerging position among scholars in this field is that the nature of a group's task must be taken into account when assessing other relationships involving such variables as group size, membership composition or reward systems.

The extent of process losses in groups is influenced by a variety of factors, and the nature of the influence is moderated by the character of the task involved. Many of the factors that contribute to process loss are discussed in subsequent chapters of this book.

## IMPLICATIONS FOR MANAGING CHANGE

It is difficult to separate the analysis of group process from group structure. Process and structure develop concurrently as groups evolve and exert mutual influences on each other. This has serious implications for the practicing leader or any change agent wishing to "turn a group around." For example, should one attempt to change the target group's process (characteristic interaction patterns and strategies) or its structure (i.e., role system, size, or membership mix), or both? Advocates of all three positions are represented in the literature.

A work group that evolves out of the developmental processes presented earlier goes through demanding experiences. As the mutual accommodation process unfolds, some members are likely to quit and others may be pressured to leave. Operating procedures and specialized roles emerge through at least a partly competitive process involving status considerations. Disagreements over goals and means to achieve them occur. Dominance battles are won and lost, and ego damage can and does become serious. Moreover, the group must learn how to adapt itself and cope with control systems imposed by the larger organization of which it is a part. This means that the group has to learn how to function both with the help of and in spite of external systems (such as compensation and performance appraisal systems) which often do not match the group's unique needs.

I don't wish to leave the reader with the impression of a hopeless situation. *Dealing with complexity, difficulty, and uncertainty is what managers get paid for.* The challenges involved are what most of them thrive on. However, any outsider when first entering an established task group, whether as a new member or manager, a staff specialist from the personnel department or a consultant, is walking into a network of interconnected variables that will not be quickly understood or easily changed.

The pushing and shoving, arguments and accommodations implied by this and the previous chapter produce stress as a by-product. The next chapter deals with that fact of life.

## ENDNOTES

1    Katz, D. and Kahn, R., THE SOCIAL PSYCHOLOGY OF ORGANIZATIONS, 1978, (2nd Edition), New York: John Wiley & Sons, 211-212.

2    For a classic example, of a non-routine group structuring experience, see Bucher, R. and Schatzman, L., "Negotiating a division of labor among professionals in a state mental hospital," PSYCHIATRY, 1964, 27, 266-277.

3     Krech, D., Crutchfield, R. and Ballachey, E., cited above, 459-462; also see Porter, L., Lawler, E. and Hackman, R., BEHAVIOR IN ORGANIZATIONS, 1975, New York: McGraw-Hill, 250-252.

4     See McKeachie, W. J., "Research on teaching at the college and university level," in Gage, N., (Ed.), HANDBOOK OF RESEARCH ON TEACHING, 1963, Chicago: Rand-McNally, 1118-1172.

5     Porter, L. and Steers, R., "Organizational work and personal factors in employee turnover and absenteeism.," PSYCHOLOGICAL BULLETIN, 1973, 80, 151-176.

6     Hoffman, R., "Group problem solving," In Berkowitz, L., (Ed.), GROUP PRO-CESSES, 1978, New York: Academic Press, 75.

7     This discussion is based primarily on Shaw, M. E., "Communications Networks," and "Communications Networks Fourteen Years Later," in Berkowitz, L., (Ed.), GROUP PROCESSES, cited above, 313-361.

8     Steiner, I., GROUP PROCESS AND PRODUCTIVITY, 1972, New York: Academic Press, 54.

9     Porter, L. and Roberts, Karlene, "Communication in organizations," In Dunnette, M.D., (Ed), cited earlier, 1579.

10    Strauss, A., NEGOTIATIONS, 1978, San Francisco: Jossey-Bass, 113.

11    Steiner, I., cited above, 6-9. See, also, Shiflett, S., "Toward a general model of small group productivity," PSYCHOLOGICAL BULLETIN, 1979, 67-79.

12    Steiner's view that there is some one "best way" is reminiscent of a similar view often found among industrial methods engineers. Many people dispute such a view when espoused by engineers; I personally suspect that for some or many combinations of task demands and resources there are several preferred ways, all about equal and all better than a number of other ways. This does not detract, however, from the overall logic of Steiner's argument.

13    Strauss, A., cited earlier, page 1.

SOME ADDITIONAL LITERATURE FOR THE INTERESTED READER:

-     Yetton, P. and Bottger, P., "The relationships among group size, member ability, social decision schemes, and performance," ORGANIZATIONAL BEHAVIOR AND HUMAN PERFORMANCE, 1983, 33, 350-359. (technical)

-     Snyder, R. and Morris, J., "Organizational communications and performance," JOUR-NAL OF APPLIED PSYCHOLOGY, 1984, 69, 461-465. (technical)

-     Gist, Marilyn, Locke, E. and Taylor, M. Susan, "Organizational behavior: group structure, process, and effectiveness," JOURNAL OF MANAGEMENT, 1987, vol 13, 237-257.

# CHAPTER 6

## STRESS, STRAIN AND CONFLICT:
## BY-PRODUCTS OF GROUP PROCESS

When people are brought together to work in a group they bring with them different agendas, moods, personalities, and cultural backgrounds. It is inevitable that during the continuous interplay among them - given the numerous unpredictable changes that occur in work settings - friction, rivalry, and outright competition will occur as individuals strive for dominance, security, and recognition.

Friction between individuals and groups, and their attendant frustrations or stresses, have both good and bad consequences. The good news is that extra effort, problem-solving, and innovation can result. The bad news is that group process can be disrupted, extra demands on managers can occur, and the effects of otherwise useful motivational strategies may be blunted.

Employees' frustrations are reflected in their attitudes. When frustration is sufficiently serious, a variety of disruptive behavioral results occur. Some people become hostile, thereby disturbing the peace or even "sabotaging" work processes. Others become discouraged, leading to reduced motivation and teamwork, lower standards of performance, absenteeism, and general lack of enthusiasm. Still others develop stress related health problems, alcoholism for example, that bear on the cost of doing business. *There is no question that these human costs are closely tied to organizational effectiveness. Frustration reactions can affect anything from quantity and quality of work to discourteous behavior toward customers.*

## SOURCES OF EMPLOYEE FRUSTRATION

Figure 3 organizes employee frustration sources in three clusters:

A. stress inducing obstacles encountered in the direct performance of one's job;

B. obstacles encountered while balancing the often conflicting demands of one's role at work and the demands of daily living; and

C. obstacles encountered when dealing with the employer's system of rules, policies and their administration.

## A. OBSTACLES ENCOUNTERED WHILE DOING ONE'S JOB

inadequate equipment

inadequate or too much skill

uncooperative or otherwise inadequate co-workers

ineffective or inappropriate supervision

faulty group decision making process

inappropriate or lack of task goals

inadequate task procedures

ambiguous job duties

frequent task reassignments

actions by competing or rival individuals or groups

## B. OBSTACLES TO MAINTAINING A DESIRED BALANCE BETWEEN WORK ROLE AND REQUIREMENTS OF DAILY LIVING

work schedule/location does not match schedule needed in private life

income inadequate--leads to anxiety, moonlighting, need for spouse or children to take job

employer affords inadequate growth opportunities via promotion, training, and tuition support policy

current job security does not match needs imposed by personal responsibilities

job duties conflict with health needs

occupational status does not match desired social status in family/community

transportation difficulties

## C. OBSTACLES WHEN DEALING WITH WORK ORGANIZATION'S SYSTEM OF RULES, POLICIES AND THEIR ADMINISTRATION

unavailability of important functionaries or clerks when needed

officiousness and prejudices of functionaries and clerks

rigidity of policy interpretation and administration

unreasonable rules, e.g., hair length, clothing, parking regulations, snacks at desk

incompetent/uncooperative or rigid personnel in support departments providing services to others

sudden and arbitrary changes in personnel policy

failure to receive an expected promotion

political maneuvering by policy makers

Fig. 3. Sources of employee stress: some examples in three categories

**All cylinders of the motivation engine are needed** - Full energy mobilization for task accomplishment cannot be achieved if the total frustration level produced by the above, in combination, is allowed to get out of hand. All three sources of frustration contribute to process loss in work groups, and process loss as explained in Chapter 5 leads to productivity loss.

Further, I believe that Category B, maintaining a desired balance between the demands of one's work role and the requirements of daily living, has the most significant impact on available task-related energy. It also has the most critical impact on absenteeism and turnover.

**Job vs. outside pressures is the key issue** - Most working people, in my experience, are primarily attentive to the kinds of obstacles listed and implied under Category B, adapting one's work role to the requirements of daily living. If they can't create an acceptable fit with one employer (or job), they are likely to seek another, if possible. Most manage to work out a compromise which enables them to meet their basic obligations, but there is frequent if not continual friction involved which leads to energy diffusion at work, irritation, and, when provoked, anger and aggression.

For example, a key member of a task group or task force who is chronically late for morning meetings because of transport difficulties can cause problems for the entire group. Another example is suggested by the interpersonal squabbling that broke out among several members of the New York Mets baseball team during the summer of 1987. The Mets were several games behind the division leader, at the time, and were struggling to regain their former championship form. One key player was publicly criticized by some teammates for missing too many games due to minor illness and possibly other reasons. He, in turn, threatened them with physical retaliation for their public criticism. The reported behavior pattern strongly suggested that this player was experiencing serious difficulties in dealing with life stresses beyond his occupation. His teammates, on the other hand, were angry because they believed he was letting them down.

**Compromise is typical** - Most people who work out a reasonable accommodation between their work role and requirements for daily living accept or adapt to task-related obstacles. They resign themselves to undemanding jobs, inadequate supervision or inadequate procedures and perform at an acceptable level. This accommodation often but not necessarily includes a fair amount of grumbling. Some will also engage in problem-solving behavior to deal with the sources of these frustrations, if possible. However, not everyone has viable alternatives and some become "problem" employees. If group progress or survival depends on such people, and if it is necessary to excite them, mobilize maximal energy, and sustain it, then the organization must attend to the obstacles involved in all three categories.

**Bureaucracy and poor internal service alienate employees just as they irritate consumers** - Yes, even Category C, obstacles employees encounter when dealing with their employer's system of rules, policies and administration, contributes to the overall level of irritation and friction. Bureaucratic procedures and their administrative handmaidens often cause irritation and thereby induce retaliatory action. The time and energy spent "beating the system" or getting even is not optimally spent.

**Available energy is limited and unevenly distributed** - It seems to be a fact of organizational life that most employers focus their motivational resources on the task--Category A. They assume that employees will work out their own accommodations with the requirements of daily living. *Many managers, especially at executive levels, further seem to assume that these accommodations are made with equal energy sacrifices by all employees.* Indeed, some behavioral scientists advocating job enrichment strategies and participative management plans (which often require large increases in employee energy expenditure) seem to be making the same assumption. *The fact is, some people have much more available energy potential for their jobs than others, just as some people have greater ability than others.* Many employees lack the resources to do much more than compromise between competing energy demands.

## CONSEQUENCES OF STRESS

Stress-related tension usually is accompanied by increased concentration and energy expenditure. Frustration (blockage or threatened blockage) of goal-directed behavior produces additional tension. For example, if you discover that a vital part is missing from a do-it-yourself kit so you can't finish your child's birthday bike, or that your airline flight home on a Friday evening is cancelled, your tension is likely to increase.

An escalated tension level (which some writers equate with "stress") produces psychological and physiological by-products. Physiological effects can include heart beat, pulse rate, blood pressure, perspiration, and blood chemistry changes, among others. Psychological effects are likely to include arousal of certain emotions and attitudes, e.g., anger, distrust, desire for revenge, or disappointment. Such emotions and attitudes, of course, can cloud our judgment, among other things.

**Pressure affects performance** - Some organizational managements, in the belief that "pressure keeps employees on their toes," put great pressure on them to get the work out. (Pressure in this sense refers to the motivational stress or tensions created by production schedules, deadlines, accuracy demands, competitor's actions, machine requirements for fast work or managerial threats (such as, "If you don't make your deadline, you are in big trouble").

The good news is that pressure in the right amount keeps employees on their toes. Task-relevant frustration can increase the challenge involved and enhance energy mobilization. In the right amount, it can also produce problem solving behavior and innovation, which often are necessary group process ingredients.

The bad news is that if the pressure is too great or too continuous, some employees will seek ways to avoid it. Employees frustrated by too much pressure from the organization very often try to beat the system.

For example, some managers take the position that their subordinates should never make any mistakes. They place their employees under great pressure to avoid errors. Some individuals under such extreme accuracy pressure may hide errors from their supervisor, or may learn the proper procedures but not use them out of spite. Under extreme circumstances some people may temporarily lose the ability to make decisions.

Hiding errors or stubbornly refusing to use proper procedures while under pressure are some of the things that employees do to "get even with" authoritarian supervisors on occasion. They represent aggressive reactions to frustration. Thus heavy pressure on employees may keep some of them on their toes, but it can also create serious problems.

*Look for the optimum balance*: Rather than choosing between high and low pressure, it is best to find that optimal pressure point where particular individuals or units work most efficiently. This point varies from one person or group to the next. Figure 4 illustrates this.[1] You can see that where pressure is low, performance also is low. As pressure is increased through a moderate range (which might be considered as challenging), performance improves markedly. However, a point of diminishing returns eventually is reached beyond which performance may suffer, sometimes disastrously, if pressure is increased too much. The relationship in the graph between motivation (energy arousal) on the one hand and performance on the other is hypothetical.

The actual location of the critical point on the graph varies from one person to the next, and there are no handy ways to measure this. You may wish to keep this point in mind when reading about "goal setting" in a later chapter. (The curve in Figure 4 often is referred to as the "inverted U" relationship, a term encountered again later in this book.)

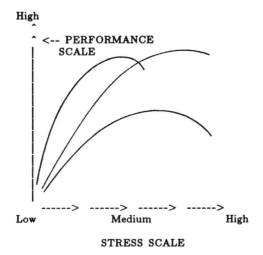

High

<-- PERFORMANCE
SCALE

------>  ------>  ------>  ------>
Low          Medium                High

STRESS SCALE

Fig. 4: Stress and performance - the inverted "U" relationship for three hypothetical persons

**Pressure affects perception** - Let us now consider another relationship--when people are placed under high pressure accompanied by high tension, what happens to their ability to perceive differences among other people and objects? Do they become more or less discriminating, or remain unaffected? It is essential for all of us to make accurate and efficient perceptual discriminations among people, objects, plans of action or alternative diagnoses of trouble throughout our lives. *In many instances such perceptual ability is an important aspect of task performance.*

The basic relationship here is very similar to the one discussed above in relation to performance. As we increase the amount of pressure that we place on a person from zero to some moderate amount, performance and discriminating ability increases.

*But there is a point of diminishing returns.* When we increase tension beyond some hypothetical "moderate" level and approach the "high" level, however, the rate of increase in discriminating behavior slows down and eventually deteriorates. This happens because, when people are under sufficiently high tension, they either are able to observe fewer cues or stimuli in their environment, or they develop internal neural interference with the mental processes involved in interpreting the stimuli.[2] Presumably such interference or perceptual narrowing occurs because of the tension effects on the nervous system.

**Pressure can disrupt group process** - When we are stressed sufficiently, our ability to judge other people's character and abilities also may suffer. This can facilitate scapegoating and contribute to interpersonal and group conflict because in such circumstances many of us have a tendency to focus only on the negative characteristics of our "antagonists." Such narrow thinking will disturb the negotiating process by which group members develop their structure, work assignments, and general ground rules. Pressure is a motivational prescription whose dosage must be carefully controlled. Too much of this medicine can create unintended side effects.

**Pressure can contribute to disease** - In addition to task performance, perceptual, and behavior problems, tension or stress created by pressure can help produce a number of health problems. Evidence provided both by experimental research workers and clinical doctors indicates that a large number of health problems can be triggered or contributed to by psychological problems at the work place.[3] Thus high blood pressure, menstrual problems, obesity, hay fever, arthritis, skin rashes, asthma, heart disease, diabetes, and even some forms of tuberculosis may be affected by stress at work.

Apparently this is true because all of these physiological reactions are sensitive to fluctuations in mental processes. Avoiding such consequences of stress is not merely a question of "will power" and "standing up to your troubles." Frustration induced stress has physiological as well as mental aspects, as indicated earlier in this chapter. Prolonged or overly frequent frustration evidently can produce tissue fatigue in the weakest system of the body.[4]

Thus there appears to be a subtle interaction between resistance to disease and social-psychological aspects of one's environment. Clinical evidence also suggests that extreme or overly long job insecurity, blocked promotion opportunities, overly frequent task interruptions, overdoses of autocratic management, and task demands in excess of personal skills all can contribute to an individual's susceptibility to disease.[5]

This does not mean that such factors cause heart attacks, diabetes, or high blood pressure. It merely means that these job pressures lower resistance and make it easier for diseases to gain a foothold. It seems possible, given the sketchy evidence available, that membership in a cohesive work group can go a long way toward alleviating the effects of the above pressures.[6] A strongly cohesive family can also serve this purpose.

## STRESS ANALYSIS APPLIES TO GROUPS, TOO

So far we have focused on how frustration factors operate at the individual level of analysis. However, the central thrust of this book is the task group. The individual analysis can be extended to help explain energy mobilization and channeling in such social units.

**Groups react to stress like individuals do** - Research data support this argument. One study, for example, suggests that under extreme survival conditions in World War II, some U. S. Air Force bomber crews that survived crash landings subsequently panicked, suffered internal communication breakdowns, and acted as competitive individuals - each member out for himself; other bomber crews under similar conditions, but apparently more cohesive, held together and problem-solved collectively. Survival rates were higher in the latter cases.[7]

A research program on human behavior during natural disasters (such as earthquakes, storms and floods), on the other hand, showed considerable teamwork in almost all cases, perhaps because the circumstances were less stressful than an airplane crash landing in wartime.[8] Other studies of groups under stress shows an increased need for authoritarian leadership,[9] internal scapegoating behavior,[10] leadership replacement,[11] increased authoritarian behavior by leaders,[12] and greater effectiveness of authoritarian rather than more participative leaders.[13]

In still other groups stress was accompanied by negative stereotyping, accidents and psychosomatic disease.[14] However, some groups become more cohesive under stress while others become less so, probably because of the "inverted U" effect.[15] Finally, *there also is evidence of an inverted-U relationship between stress and group performance; total group performance increases with stress until stress becomes too high.*[16]

## FACTORS INFLUENCING REACTIONS TO STRESS

While stress research on groups is not nearly as common as stress research on individuals, two themes common to both sets of literature do suggest themselves. First, the effects of stress on groups and individuals depend on a number of factors common to both such as the duration, frequency or nature of the block (or threat), whether the source of the frustration is external to the group (or individual) or internal, and the condition of the group or individual at the time. Second, some groups, as is the case with individuals, cope with frustration better than others. *Well integrated personalities are more likely to problem-solve under stress; well-integrated groups (having sound group process and adaptable structures) are likely to do the same.*

## COMPETITION AND CONFLICT

Frustration and stress produced by the factors discussed thus far are compounded by competition and conflict. Both can have either positive or negative impact on group process.

**Competition and conflict can induce stress symptoms** - The behavior of groups in conflict or competition with other groups follows a general pattern similar to the one observable among frustrated and/or competing individuals.[17] A group whose goal-directed activities are perceived to be interfered with by the goal-seeking activities of another group may engage in collective problem-solving behavior, become aggressive in varying degrees, display immature behavior, or give up. It also can become "sick" or lose its efficiency, much the way some individuals do under excessive stress.

**The existence of frustration among individuals within groups can affect the relations between groups** - For example, widespread economic depression and its attendant frustration often lead to scapegoating. In the larger society this historically has been accompanied by deterioration of relations among racial, ethnic and religious groups.[18] A similar phenomenon occurs in work organizations. If employees become too frustrated by ineffective or arbitrary supervisors, stressful working conditions, or by external, societal stresses, they may very well engage in hostile collective action against an "out group"--management, or ethnic and religious minority group members at work. A rival work unit in the organization also may become a target. Strikes, rumor mongering, scapegoating, and other hostile actions become the order of the day.[19] The same type of social process also can occur within and between labor unions. In such cases the union leadership becomes the "out group," or else jurisdictional battles occur between rival unions.

**An example of escalated conflict** - The Charing Cross Hospital strike, reported by the Associated Press from London, England on November 28, 1979 in the ITHACA JOURNAL, is an interesting case in point. A maintenance man refused to install an air filter in an operating room, claiming that it was "not his job" to carry the lightweight filter from the Supply Room to the Operating Room. Management fired him, thereby setting off a "wildcat" strike by all of the maintenance workers (not authorized by their union). Their union officers could not control them.

Bitterness and violence subsequently erupted between the health care staff and maintenance men on the picket line. The hospital's cancer patients, three hours before the fuel supplies were to expire, wrapped themselves in blankets and went into the streets to plead with the maintenance men to allow a fuel truck to cross their picket line. Thus, from one man's refusal to carry out an assignment emerged a chain of most unfortunate events.

## CONSTRUCTIVE VS. DESTRUCTIVE CONFLICT

Most behavioral scientists believe that rational problem-solving is superior to the use of naked power and emotionally charged hostile behavior. Some of them accept the proposition that while extreme forms of aggression, particularly at the work place, generally have unfortunate consequences both for the individuals involved and the organization, there are occasional circumstances where aggressive outbursts are useful. Let me define some terms:

A destructive conflict is a condition or state of an interpersonal or intergroup relationship which can't be severed easily. It is characterized by a sustained, interrelated pattern of mutually or unilaterally damaging beliefs, attitudes and behaviors such as chronic and persistent:

- Hostility, antagonism, punitiveness, dominance striving and threat

- Perceptual distortion, stereotyping and scapegoating

- Trickery, feelings of betrayal, and revenge seeking

- Institutionalized practices, such as publicizing performance data, that keep the conflict from dying

- Mutual disrespect and denigration

- Inconvenience, discomfort, or damage to bystanders

A <u>constructive</u> conflict is characterized by a sustained and interrelated pattern of:

- Disagreement over goals, priorities and methods

- Sharpening of issues

- Argumentation and insistence on considering alternatives

- Mutual respect among the parties, but probes for weakness

- Mutual efforts to insure there is no permanent winner

In the case of constructive conflict one or both parties operate from an assumption that mutual benefits will arise from such a relationship, and they cooperate with each other between arguments. In the case of destructive conflict, on the other hand, such attitudes and behaviors are both unlikely and difficult to cultivate.

## SPONTANEOUS VERSUS PLANNED
## COMPETITION BETWEEN GROUPS

Competition is another process by which a relationship among individuals, work groups, departments, divisions or nations may be defined. It can be either spontaneous and natural or deliberately planned and encouraged.

Some spontaneous or "natural" rivalry is normal and to be expected in all organizations. Whenever group boundaries are observable, the members of separate groups tend to identify themselves with their groups and make comparisons between "their" group and "other" groups. They compare working conditions, effort requirements, political "influence" within the organization, administrative policies, leaders, performance standards, and rewards. They also try to achieve and maintain appropriate "balance" on such matters. Usually such activity merely reflects mild rivalry--there are no clear-cut "winners" and "losers."

**For example** - Two craft groups (machinists and plumbers) may vie with each other within a maintenance department for new equipment or other resources. Or, a welding group and a neighboring assembly group may "compete" over floor space needs. Such competition generally is at a low emotional level, and both sides take their share of wins and losses in the long haul.

If the group members get the idea that there will be permanent winners and losers, or that their status in the larger organization is at stake, there will be a direct increase in the level of emotional activity and a proportionate decrease in the level of logical thinking. Economic retrenchment aggravates this process and can convert mild rivalry into a destructive conflict.

**Competition can get out of hand** - When competition is deliberately planned and encouraged, it normally occurs within the context of a system of rules, rewards, and penalties. Despite controls, however, normally such competition is more heated than the mild departmental rivalries because there are clear-cut winners and losers, and because the stakes tend to be higher, e.g., budget allocations, manpower allocations, task difficulty issues, such as which group will get which product to market or which client sector to deal with, and others.

Analogous issues arise in all work organizations. By definition, "pure" win-lose competition means that some groups win at the expense of others. The losers, therefore, find (or perceive) their behavior pathways to important goals blocked, and even the winners, during the course of the contest, find numerous blocks and experience stress to some degree. In the long run such a situation often becomes cyclical and self-defeating for all parties concerned.

## THE INTERGROUP
## CONFLICT ESCALATION PROCESS [20]

Substantial research evidence and observation of many case studies show that the following phenomena occur more or less sequentially under conditions of <u>prolonged</u> win-lose competition between groups as the process gradually escalates:

- Increased group cohesiveness, at least initially; each competing group becomes more attractive to its members who draw together, assuming they have common objectives, which helps the group in its problem-solving stage. Beyond the group's tolerance level (critical point--see Fig. 4) for competitive stress, however, the problem-solving trend is likely to reverse itself;

- Increased spirit; more interest in the group's activities and willingness to help; increase in the number of members who initiate leadership acts, i.e., members encourage each other toward group goals;

- Strengthening of the existing power structure;  the leader of the group usually gets increased support from followers as a result of battle between the group and outsiders, at least in the short run;

- Increased conformity trend; those individual members who disagree with the majority increasingly find themselves facing social isolation or outright rejection or expulsion as the competition heats up;

- Reduced objectivity in evaluating the competing group's efforts and capabilities; this is the familiar "over-confidence" phenomenon which affects many groups in competition--the "other side" is considered weak and inferior only because it is the other side, not because of objective evidence which might, in fact, show the reverse is true;

- Increased use of inflammatory rhetoric and propaganda directed at the "enemy," but published for the rank-and-file members in order to increase their cohesion and will to fight.  However, this frequently increases the enemy's will to fight also because such propaganda, if publicized, either frightens or angers them.

- Increased stereotyping; that is, members of the opposing group all are perceived to be "bad" simply because they are members of the enemy group.  This reflects reduced perceptual discrimination which, as pointed out earlier, occurs under high stress and hampers problem solving;

- Increased distortion of the issues; common ground in counter-proposals made by management and labor, for example, is likely to be ignored as each side exaggerates the differences instead.  It also has been found that group members' knowledge (as measured by tests) of their own group's position is greater, under competitive conditions, than is their knowledge of the opposing group's position, even after information on both positions has been made available and publicized;

- Loss of objectivity among group leaders and spokesmen because of the pressures they experience toward being "loyal" to their group; once the group (or a nation) commits itself to a competitive stance or battle, the leader's hands are tied, by and large, especially if faced by the prospect of defeat; any attempt by the leader at cooperative problem solving or compromise with the "enemy" is likely to be viewed by members as a "sellout;" [21] and

- Inability to accept neutral, third-party judgment as valid, especially if it is not in favor of one's own group.

**Impact on group process is profound** - It may reasonably be inferred from the conflict escalation sequence described above that group process in task groups can be strongly affected by the stresses arising from external group relations. *The fundamentals of who is to do what, when, how and where within a task group can be profoundly influenced by the presence or absence of external conflict and competition.* In Little League sports, for example, poor players sometimes are encouraged by their teammates to stay home on "big game" days.

**Politics are part of the game** - It also is possible that process decisions will enhance the prospects for external conflict or competition depending on whose views and preferences prevail inside the group. A faction that has lost an internal group process battle, for example, may instigate a battle with an external rival group in order to embarrass its own group's leadership, weaken the leader's position and possibly get another chance for itself. Such "political" maneuvering is common in organizational life and needs to be taken into account when trying to develop groups for task performance.

**Group reactions to conflict aren't always predictable** - The typical conflict escalation model just described affects different groups in different ways. Highly cohesive groups at the start of the escalation process behave differently than groups lacking cohesion. Additionally, if a group lacks cohesion initially, the onset of battle or competition will not necessarily pull it together. Sometimes it will, and sometimes not. The time-honored practice by political leaders to go to war against a traditional enemy will not always serve to bind the followers together.[22,23] If cohesion does increase in such a group, it is likely to give way to internal bickering and finger pointing fairly quickly in the face of losing.

## STRESS AND GROUP DEVELOPMENT:
## THE PRACTICAL SIDE

The above analysis of stress, frustration, competition, and conflict has several practical implications for the development, performance, maintenance and renewal of groups. First, the development stage (Periods 1-3 in Figure 1) is likely to be characterized by task-related frustration as people work out their role-relationships and learn their jobs. Managers should be especially attentive to their employees' outside requirements of daily living and the policy-rules-administration obstacles during this period so that task concentration can occur.

Second, a group undergoing renewal may experience even greater stress than one in its initial developmental phase, because newcomers are likely to be perceived by old-timers as threats. There will be the usual sources of frustration plus conflict over ideas, procedures and other matters, all influenced by strong needs. This is a period during which personnel support services may be especially needed.

Third, nothing remains the same. Key group members get sick, members of their families get sick, someone falls in love, another lands a part-time extra job, someone else enrolls in night school, and so on. Complications may arise because of budget cuts, a new manager, or a change in demand for the group's product or service. All of this calls for continual monitoring because it will affect the supply of potential human energy available to the work group. *If the available energy becomes too unevenly distributed among group members, serious frustration can occur.* Indeed, an entire group effort can fail. Sometimes this can be taken care of by appropriate reward systems--pay being based upon contribution. Thus, some members may be willing and able to take up the slack for others. Sometimes individual members may have to be replaced. This is what energy mobilization on a continual basis is all about.

Fourth, an overload of frustration among group members, whatever the sources may be, increases the likelihood of irritation, prejudicial attitudes, scapegoating and conflict--both within the group and between the group and other groups. The likelihood of these disruptive outcomes is increased by the presence of intergroup competition. The behaviors involved are not goal directed; they represent a diffusion of energy that would otherwise be potentially available for task accomplishment.

**The manager as buffer** - Frustration and stress are especially pertinent matters for the group's manager. Group members expect their manager to serve as <u>their</u> <u>buffer</u> against sources of frustration, and to help them minimize stress within the group. The manager who fails to perform this critical aspect of team maintenance usually will lose the group's confidence and support. Senior managers frequently are the major problem in not understanding that the stresses they create from above cause deteriorating team relations further down the structure.

Task groups may be viewed as living systems that both influence and are influenced by their environments. Previous chapters explained something about their inner workings which produce internal processes and mechanisms that help them cope. To a considerable extent, the group's structure (e.g., role-status system, membership mix, communications system) arises to help the group adapt, and to cope with frustration-induced stresses in the group's environment. The group, then, serves as a buffer for its members; at the same time its structure and internal processes may create internal sources of tension. Out of this complex maze emerges energy, various channels for its expenditure, and obstacles to its effective use.

Managing such a process is an ambitious undertaking . Let us turn to several motivational strategies, including planned competition, used to facilitate the task.

## ENDNOTES

1   This figure is similar to the one proposed by most stress theorists. For more technical discussions see Selye, H., STRESS OF LIFE, 1956, New York: McGraw-Hill, and McGrath, J. E., "Stress and behavior in organizations," In Dunnette, M. D., (Ed.), HANDBOOK OF INDUSTRIAL AND ORGANIZATIONAL PSYCHOLOGY, 1976, Chicago: Rand McNally.

2   Easterbrook, J. A., "The effect of motivation on cue utilization and the organization of behavior," PSYCHOLOGICAL REVIEW, 1959, 66, 183-201.

3   Brown, J. A. C., THE SOCIAL PSYCHOLOGY OF INDUSTRY, 1962, Baltimore: Penguin, Chapter 9; Sales, S., "Organizational role as a risk factor in coronary disease," ADMINISTRATIVE SCIENCE QUARTERLY, 1969, 14 (3), 325-336; House, J. S., "Occupational stress and physical health," In O'Toole, J., (Ed.), WORK AND THE QUALITY OF LIFE, 1974, Cambridge, Mass: MIT Press.

4   Not all writers agree in their usage of such terms as stress, frustration, anxiety and tension. See Costello, T. W. and Zalkind, S. S., (Eds.), PSYCHOLOGY IN ADMINISTRATION, 1963, Englewood Cliffs, N.J.: Prentice Hall, 125-129 for a discussion of this matter; see also Cooper, C. L. and Payne, R., (Eds.), STRESS OF WORK, 1978, New York: Wiley.

5   Brown, J. A. C., THE SOCIAL PSYCHOLOGY OF INDUSTRY, 1962, Baltimore: Penguin, p. 251, Halliday, J., PSYCHOSOCIAL MEDICINE, 1948, New York: Norton. Chapter 10. See also, Locke, E. In Dunnette, M. D., (Ed.), cited above; and, "A compendium of articles on stress," PSYCHOLOGY TODAY, 1969, 3 (4), 24-38+.

6   Friedman, S. and Glasgow, L., "Psychological factors and resistance to infectious disease," PEDIATRICS CLINICS OF AMERICA, 1966, 13 (2), 315-335. See, also, Cobb, S., "Social support as a moderator of life stress," PSYCHOSOMATIC MEDICINE, 1976, 38, 300-314.

7   Torrance, E. P., "The behavior of small groups under the stress conditions of survival," AMERICAN SOCIOLOGICAL REVIEW, 1954, 19, 751-755.

8   Quarantelli, E. and Dynes, R., "When disaster strikes," PSYCHOLOGY TODAY, 1972, 5 (9), 66-70

9   Mulder, M. and Stemerding, A., "Threat, attraction to group, and need for strong leadership," HUMAN RELATIONS, 1963, 16, 317-334.

10  French, J., "The disruption and cohesion of groups," J. OF ABNORMAL AND SOCIAL PSYCHOLOGY, 1941, 36, 361-377.

11  Hamblin, R., "Group integration during a crisis," HUMAN RELATIONS, 1958, 11 (1), 67-76.

12  Fodor, E. M., "Group stress, authoritarian style of control and use of power," J. APPLIED PSYCHOLOGY, 1976, 61 (3), 313-318.

13  Rosenbaum, L. and Rosenbaum, W., "Morale and productivity consequences of group leadership, stress and type of task," J. APPLIED PSYCHOLOGY, 1971, 55 (4), 343-348.

14  Paterson, T. T., MORALE IN WAR AND WORK: AN EXPERIMENT IN THE MANAGEMENT OF MEN, 1955, London: M. Parrish.

15  Stein, A. A., "Conflict and cohesion: a review of the literature.," J. CONFLICT RESOLUTION, 1976, 20 (1), 143-172.

16  Pepinsky, Pauline, Pepinsky, H. B. and Pavlik, W. B., "The effects of task complexity and time pressure upon team productivity," J. APPLIED PSYCHOLOGY, 1960, 44 (1), 34-38.

17  I arrived at this generalization while reading and comparing numerous historical accounts of strikes, race riots, and prison rebellions in the United States, and various lengthy political struggles in Northern Ireland, the Middle East, Latin America and Asia. An especially turbulent period of U.S. history is reviewed in this context by several publications. See, for example, Graham, H. C. and Gurr, T. R. (Eds.), VIOLENCE IN AMERICA: HISTORICAL AND COMPARATIVE PERSPECTIVES, Staff Report to the National Commission on the Causes and Prevention of Violence, 1969, Vol. 2, Washington, D. C.: Government Printing Office.

18  Allport, G. W., THE NATURE OF PREJUDICE, 1954, Cambridge: Addison-Wesley, is still pertinent today.

19  Various writers have listed the following forms of aggression or hostility by employees: Damaging equipment; malicious gossip; stealing employer's merchandise and tools; excessive criticism of management; attacking physically or shooting one's

supervisor; militant political attitudes; planned absenteeism; strikes; slowdowns; overly literal interpretation of orders and instructions; and sabotaging the work of competing groups. It is readily apparent that people at the work place have a range of learned hostile behaviors from which to choose. See Brown, J. A. C., cited earlier, and Stagner, R., THE PSYCHOLOGY OF INDUSTRIAL CONFLICT, 1956, New York: Wiley, Chapter 6.

20    The following analysis is freely adapted with my own elaboration from Blake, R., Mouton, Jane and Shepard, H., MANAGING INTERGROUP CONFLICT IN INDUSTRY, 1964, Houston: Gulf, Chapter 2, and is supported by a considerable body of literature on social conflict. The chapter as a whole has benefited materially from the prolific writings of Morton Deutsch, and from the many conflict case analyses prepared over the years by my students.

21    Realistic examples of how leaders' options are limited by their followers may be found in Killian, L., "Leadership in desegregation," in Sherif, M., (Ed.), INTERGROUP RELATIONS AND LEADERSHIP; APPROACHES AND RESEARCH IN INDUSTRIAL, ETHNIC, CULTURAL AND POLITICAL AREAS, 1962, New York: Wiley and in Wicker, T., A TIME TO DIE, an eyewitness's account of what went on behind the scenes during the Attica Prison negotiations.

22    The effects of external conflict on internal cohesion are discussed in an extensive, multi-disciplinary literature review by Stein, A., "Conflict and cohesion," JOURNAL OF CONFLICT RESOLUTION, 1976, 20, (1), 143-172. See also Janis, I., "Group think," PSYCHOLOGY TODAY, 1971, 5, (6), 43 and Hall, J., "Decisions, decisions, decisions," PSYCHOLOGY TODAY, 1971, 5, (6), 51+.

23    The reader might find it useful to apply the above escalation analysis to internal tensions within the USA during the War in Viet Nam, to France and its painful experiences in withdrawing from Algeria, or to the Attica Prison takeover and the Kent State University student-National Guard tragedy during the 1960s.

SOME ADDITIONAL LITERATURE FOR THE INTERESTED READER

-    Baker, D., "The study of stress at work," ANNUAL REVIEW OF PUBLIC HEALTH, 1985, 6, 367-381.

-    Sharit, J. and Salvendy, G., "Occupational stress: review and appraisal," HUMAN FACTORS, 1982, 24(2), 129-162.

-    Schuler, R. and Jackson, Susan, "Managing stress through PHRM practices: an uncertainty interpretation," RESEARCH IN PERSONNEL AND HUMAN RESOURCES MANAGEMENT, 1986, 4, 183-224.

-    Hall, K. and Savery, L., "Stress management," MANAGEMENT DECISIONS, 1987, 25 (6), 29-35.

# CHAPTER 7

# MOTIVATION IN TASK GROUPS

The organizational purpose of motivational systems is to find ethical ways of getting groups and their members to do what needs to be done under a variety of conditions. In group process terms, this means managers must try to motivate group members to match themselves with the tasks for which they are best suited, encourage the most advantageous sequence of work activities, and provide rewards for continued, effective performance in this advantageous structure. In addition, the manager needs to apply motivational techniques to develop and maintain group cohesion, morale, and teamwork; most group members expect it.

**Group process re-shapes the employer's reward system** - Whatever system is used to motivate energy mobilization for task performance, it will interact with group processes as described in the previous chapter. As members relate to each other interpersonally while structuring their group, and communicate with and influence each other, they bring into play their personal beliefs, attitudes, prejudices and value systems. Therefore, rewards and punishments and administrative matters involved in the larger organization's motivational system are *interpreted, debated, accepted, rejected or compromised as the group irons out its internal disagreements and develops group shared attitudes and norms.* The dynamic process of group conformity development, while subtle and often difficult to observe, modifies or influences the linkage between the employer's motivational strategies and individual attitudes and behavior. Energy mobilization in task groups reflects both individual and on-going social processes.

**Theories have practical impact** - The employer's motivational system and related administrative policies can be no better than the implicit theories and beliefs on which they are based. Therefore it is appropriate for managers to develop an understanding of motivational factors so they can do their best to match incentives with teamwork behavior. This chapter deals with strategies for motivating teams - goal setting, providing knowledge of results, managing for success, and the use of competition.

## GOAL SETTING AND KNOWLEDGE
## OF RESULTS AS MOTIVATIONAL PROCESSES

**A hypothetical case** - Goal setting is a process by which objectives are established so that human effort will be channeled in appropriate directions and on an appropriate time schedule. However, the processes of goal setting and feedback that provides knowledge of results (i.e., progress toward the goals) are so closely related and mutually dependent that they are discussed jointly, below. Both of these processes must be utilized in appropriate ways if reward systems are to operate with maximal effectiveness.

Let's begin with an example from outside the work world. Assume we have experimental control over two well coordinated athletes who have been taught how to hit a tennis ball but have never seen the game of tennis played. While capable of hitting various kinds of shots, *they do not know how to keep score.* Their manager (you) agrees to pay the athletes a solid weekly salary in return for which they are to "play tennis" (hit balls back and forth to each other) from 9 a.m. to 5 p.m. each day. There are lunch and two official rest breaks each day. The manager is present at all times to make sure the players keep busy, *but for the first two or three days, sets no goals, does not keep score and provides no feedback on progress.* That is, the players simply have to do whatever it means to them to "play tennis". The following are some behaviors likely to occur during the first two or three days of the week:

- The players at first practice various shots and "warm up"; balls are played on first, second or even third bounce;

- At some point they get bored and pressure you (the "manager") for further rules or structure and objectives; none are provided. Instead, the players are told, "Just keep busy and do your job;"

- The players subsequently invent their own objectives. They decide jointly to do a number of things. For example,they may count how many strokes they can accumulate jointly prior to either player missing a shot, and attempt to maximize this number. They may or may not insist on playing first bounce only; or they may practice certain shots such that each takes turns, with the other's cooperation, at hitting lobs, overheads, backhands or whatever.

- Eventually the players will invent some kind of game which will structure their activity, give it meaning and help the passage of time. *While "playing tennis", however, they are striving to achieve only their own goals, or some combination of theirs and what they think are yours.* A lot of their energy is wasted partly because their own improvised feedback system is not optimally effective.

At the beginning of the fourth day, you explain that you expect the players to earn points, and that one point is earned by a player when he hits a shot that the other fails to return, in bounds, prior to a second bounce. You further explain that you will keep score and will announce each player's score at 20 minute intervals throughout the day.

**Feedback has many implications** - You may speculate as to the motivational and performance impact of this new feedback system. The players probably now will make a game out of the activity-- who can compile the most points, all day, per 30 minute time period, before lunch, and so on.

The point feedback (how many points each player has accumulated) at 20 minute intervals serves as a cue to most athletes, who do tend to be competitive creatures, suggesting that they should be trying to outdo each other. In other words, *the feedback is much more than a mere verbal announcement on numbers of points per player at 20 minute intervals.* Rather, it is a complex stimulus which is interpreted by the players and influences not only energy mobilization, but also channels the energy in some direction or other, and has implications for the maintenance of energy expenditure in relation to time schedules. The feedback could be at 10 minute, 60 minute, half-day or daily intervals. Moreover, the feedback stimuli alone should provide enough information to enable the players to structure their task, make plans, compete with each other, and pace themselves so they'll have enough strength left at the end of the day to walk home.

**Feedback isn't the whole story** - The feedback also permits and encourages the players to establish goals, *although it does not guarantee that they will do so.* If the feedback were to be combined with an intentional goal-setting activity, then the likelihood of player goal-setting would be further increased. At least they would be further sensitized as to priorities involved. And, if rewards were to be provided, such as praise for well-played points, extra rest breaks, soft drinks, money, prizes or tickets to interesting cultural or athletic performances, the reader can judge the likely results.

The above hypothetical "experiment" illustrates the complex interplay of job duties, time, supervision, goal setting, knowledge of results, attitudes, personal background, perception, interpersonal influence, energy mobilization and performance. Is it any wonder that "routine" applications of Management by Objectives (MBO) systems in industry do not work very well? Much is required beyond writing down a few goals and a timetable. Let us now turn our attention to some serious organizational and experimental literature on this complex matter.

**Some examples from industry** - A few years ago Emery Air Freight, Inc. embarked on a strategy built upon B. F. Skinner's theory that behavior can be affected by positive rewards. They maintain that their experiment saved the company an estimated $2 million over a three year period.[1]

This experiment was initiated when the company discovered that employees in the customer services division were not responding to customer queries within the expected company norm of 90 minutes. In fact, the employees thought they were doing so, but actually were meeting this objective only 30% of the time. Therefore, an individual record keeping form was provided for each employee so that he or she personally could keep track of actual performance. Previously there was no feedback or record keeping mechanism. According to the account, performance improvement was buttressed by "praise and recognition" from supervisors.

Performance in the test office reportedly jumped from 30% of standard to 95% in a single day, was matched by similar spectacular results when the system was installed in the remaining offices of the division, and persisted after three years. One office staff reportedly set even higher standards by saying that they would not only respond to all customer queries in 90 minutes or less, but that they also would provide all the requested information in that time period.

The same strategy subsequently was applied to the Shipping Department, to encourage the cost-saving use of oversize containers for packing many smaller packages into one shipment. After an individual worker checklist was introduced, which the workers filled out themselves, coupled with supervisory praise and recognition, remarkable results again materialized. Container use reportedly jumped, nationwide, from a prior level of 45% to a new level of 95%, and in more than 70% of the offices the increase occurred in a single day. Moreover, as in the case of the Customer Services Division, these increases also persisted for a long time (nearly two years), *except in a few locations where the system was "temporarily interrupted" because of managerial replacements.* In these cases, performance regressed to its pre-experimental level but came right up again when the new manager reinstituted the system. While the PSYCHOLOGY TODAY article doesn't deal with this point, the reader is encouraged to remember the slumps that developed in Emery shipping offices when managerial replacements occurred. These slumps sound very much like one that occurred in another goal-setting experiment discussed below. That study found that goal setting was correlated with high performance only when accompanied by close supervision.[2]

**So, what's new?** - The above account of a modern action research experiment corroborates the classic "knowledge of results" study reported in 1932 by Walter V. Bingham, the grandfather of American industrial psychology. (His book, by the way, is entitled PSYCHOLOGY TODAY!) He arranged for simple feedback gauges to be installed on each worker's boiler in an electricity generating plant. Remarkable performance increases were observed. "For the first time," according to Bingham, "the men really knew when they were being successful in their work. A new spirit spread among them. A fresh pride replaced the old indifference. Graphic daily and weekly records for each boiler were posted. Rivalry sprang up, (and) competition between the three eight-hour shifts. Moreover, each man could compare his own performance today with his last week's record, and try to improve it."[3] These are precisely the kinds of findings one would expect in the case of our hypothetical tennis players. They also closely match the Emery Air Freight findings of more recent vintage.

Both the Bingham and the Emery Air Freight, Inc., accounts rest upon experiments conducted without benefit of control groups and other desirable scientific attributes. Nonetheless, they corroborate other, more scientifically acceptable and recently reviewed studies in which knowledge of results or performance feedback was provided to people who previously had none or had to invent their own, as was the case with our fictitious tennis players, above.[4]

**Group feedback also is needed** - The presence of a group imposes extra considerations when weighing motivational methods. Special emphasis is due a conclusion drawn by one of the country's foremost authorities on group dynamics. After reviewing a large number of group studies, he makes clear the need for providing performance feedback (knowledge of results) *on the score of the group as a whole*, as well as feedback to individual members.[5] Unfortunately, the need for a total group "score" typically is not recognized by performance appraisal systems used in the world of work.

**Laboratory and other research** - Goal setting, as distinguished from knowledge of results, has been studied extensively in laboratories under carefully controlled conditions. In addition, a large number of published and unpublished studies on goal setting have been conducted in recent years. Most of these were conducted in work organizations and represent a variety of occupational groups--- vending machine servicemen, female telephone operators, production workers, managers, salesmen, truck drivers, logging crews and United Fund Campaign teams. Here are some major findings from all of this work, as I interpret the results:

- Specific goals are more effective motivators than general goals, or no goals at all;

- Competition sometimes arises as a spontaneous by-product of goal-setting applications in work settings, and complicates the interpretation of results;

- The continued presence of a supervisor or manager, for several possible reasons, seems to be a requisite condition, in some circumstances, to ensure positive effects of goal-setting; and

- Difficult goals inspire greater performance than do easy goals, provided that the goals are accepted.

**The research results are consistent** - The accumulated evidence both from realistic employment settings and the experimental laboratory supports the use of knowledge of results and goal setting as motivational tools. It is also apparent, however, that there are complexities involved that can modify the effectiveness of either. Best results are more likely when both techniques are used in concert, and when combined with an appropriate reward system. Controlled competition also may help. These conditions may further require, or at least would be buttressed by, *the effective presence of appropriate leadership or supervision.*

**Feedback alone is not enough** - Performance feedback on a regular basis will not automatically motivate people to do better. Some may find the feedback threatening or at least annoying, others may not mind it but will pay only partial attention to it, and some may set inappropriate future goals based on the feedback. The feedback will be interpreted differently by different people, and where groups are involved, shared attitudes and norms will develop autonomously *unless further structure, interpretation, and encouragement are provided by the manager.*[6] Therefore, one may also conclude that incentives are not an effective substitute for leadership.

## A USEFUL MODEL FOR UNDERSTANDING GOAL SETTING

It is clear that managers can influence employee and group behavior through appropriate use of goal setting and knowledge of results. One school of thought (and there are several[7]) in the field of organizational psychology says that motivated behavior is a function of several factors, only one of which is captured by the terms "hard" or "easy" goals. Let's begin by identifying and formalizing the kinds of factors that are likely to influence a group member's thinking when considering goals and the available behavior pathways to achieve them.[8]

The first factor I'll consider here is Net Profit. This factor might be roughly represented as: Net Profit = (Perceived Value of Reward) - (Perceived Cost of Reward). To calculate the Cost of Reward, a person estimates at least three things:

- What one has to invest in the way of energy, time, and other resources while trying for the reward;

- The total of the sure profits from other rewards that can be obtained if resources are not committed to this particular goal activity; and

- Any negative aspect of the reward which has to be accepted along with the positive (e.g., a bonus may put one into a different tax bracket; a promotion can have undesirable as well as desirable consequences).

**There are different types of rewards** - When "estimating" Net Profit one considers the value of more than one kind of reward. For example, suppose an executive says to a life insurance salesman: "Mortimer, if you will increase your dollar volume by 25 percent in your present territory during the next six months, I'll promote you to district manager." Mortimer will consider, among other things, the potential value of the promotion to district manager and what that title would do for his salary, status, future with the organization, and bargaining position with other employers. He also may consider the challenge involved in pursuing the 25 percent improvement. In other words, the intrinsic nature of a behavior pathway may be rewarding in and of itself, regardless of the promise of future extrinsic rewards. Indeed, at least one well-known psychologist believes that the intrinsic rewards derived from task performance are the most significant motivators in the world of work.[9]  There is good reason to question the extent of his emphasis, but such rewards can't be overlooked.

**Net profit is not the only issue** - In normal circumstances a person does not automatically decide to try whenever his calculations show there will be a profit in succeeding. Most people want to know what will be lost if they try and fail, as well as the potential net gain from trying and succeeding. First of all, the person who tries and fails loses the Cost of Trying, the investment of energy and resources plus the loss of other sure profits from the activities passed by. Secondly, in some cases, there is actually a penalty for having tried and failed, which may be either material or psychological, as in weakened self-confidence and new awareness of a person's limitations on the part of others who watched him try and fail. We can represent the person's calculation of risk as: Cost of Failing = (Cost of Trying) + (Penalty for Failing).

**Estimated chance of succeeding also is important** - In the case of financial incentive systems, for example, a salesperson may ask, "How likely is it that I have enough potential ability to make up the difference between my present performance and the level required for the reward?" This "Perceived Probability of Success" is an estimate reached after one compares the things in his or her favor against the potential obstacles which could produce defeat.

Finally, since all the factors considered so far are only the person's subjective calculations rather than certainties, the decision will also be affected by "Confidence in Calculations." Many things can affect this factor. Two that are especially important are:

> Clarity of behavior-incentive link. The linkage between the expected behavior and the incentive will be unclear if management's communications about it are confusing, if management fails to reward enough instances of the behavior, or if management allows a long time lag between the occurrence of the behavior and administration of the reward. Whenever the linkage is unclear, a person's confidence that he has correctly calculated the Probability of Success will be low; and

> Knowledge about the reward. If the reward is a new or not previously experienced one, a person may wonder if he knows about all the positive and negative aspects of the reward. Such a person will be especially uncertain if opinion is divided among other trusted people. In such cases, confidence in calculated Net Profit and Cost of Failing will be low. Confidence in Calculations also will be affected, in all likelihood, by individual differences in personality characteristics.

**Emotions influence the decision making** - While the above discussion suggests a great deal of objectively accurate and deliberate human calculation, such is not necessarily the case. Subjective emotional factors (some that may even seem irrational to the objective observer) affect the entire process. The presence of strong tension-related needs, fear, severe insecurity or anger will strongly affect the individual's perception of the behavior-reward link. Thus a technologically obsolete worker threatened by a permanent layoff may refuse a chance at a retraining program because he did poorly in school as a boy. Or, he may reject this golden opportunity because his fellow work group members influence him with their negative attitudes. A task group's conformity inducing tendencies relate directly to the incentive "calculations" made by individuals. Figure 5 illustrates how it all happens... (Have another cup of coffee before examining it.)

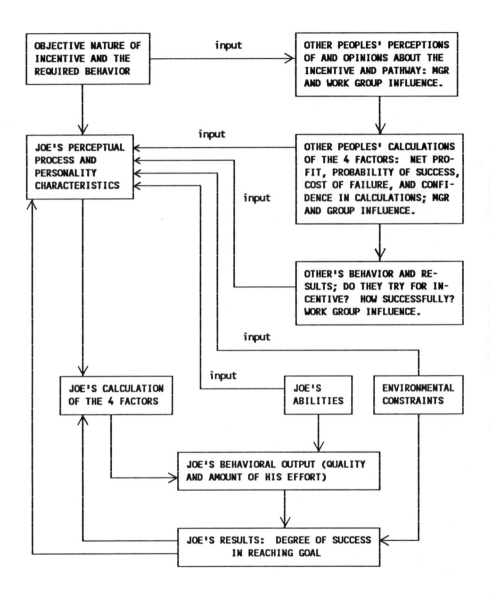

Fig. 5.   The social process of motivation, decision making and per-
          formance at work (adapted with modifications from Rosen, N.
          SUPERVISION: A BEHAVIORAL VIEW, Columbus, Ohio:
          Grid, Inc., 1973)

## HARD TO ACHIEVE GOALS

Many managers like a demanding approach to motivation. They set exceptionally difficult goals for their subordinates in an apparent attempt to build their organizations on the shoulders of an exclusive group of people having unusually high achievement needs and who respond enthusiastically to difficult challenges with limited chance of an extrinsic reward. The strategy is presumably designed to discourage all but the "most able and motivated" from joining or remaining in the group. However, there is no necessary relationship between the type of risk-taking behavior being sought on the one hand and talent or ability on the other.

**Valuable employees may leave** - The high pressure environment that such an approach to motivation creates encourages stress, turnover and turmoil, but it is not true that only poor quality employees will be turned off and quit. Talented people also are likely to leave for opportunities where they can have a better chance at important extrinsic rewards. Moreover, some poor quality people may remain because they have a realistically low level of aspiration, knowing that they will not accomplish more than the minimum for whatever job they take. The basic strategy, while perhaps applicable in special cases, in general is questionable.

**Managers' values complicate the issue** - Some managers believe that "hard-to-get" rewards are seen as more valuable than "easy" rewards. This interpretation appeals to common sense, but it is probably true only when certain needs are present. For example, a promotion that is a sure thing and a promotion for which there is only a 20% chance both have the same potential for satisfying many needs. But the harder-to-get promotion, if received, can also act as a symbol of achievement or an indication of high status. Since achievement and status needs are not active in everyone, and since there are many other needs which might conflict, it is not always true that hard-to-get rewards are perceived as valuable. A promotion may be hard to get, but it actually may be seen as something to avoid by a person with low status and achievement needs and high social and safety needs.

**Hard-to-get rewards are not always seen as valuable** -The belief among many managers that they are so perceived by rank-and-file employees probably follows from the fact that managerial occupations attract a disproportionate share of self-confident people characterized by high achievement needs. In short, *many managers project their own need structures and personalities onto others who often are different.* To the extent they build their organizations' reward systems on such premises (and then find that the rank and file does not respond), their organizations suffer.

## SUCCESS AS A MOTIVATOR

It has long been recognized that nothing succeeds as well as a dose of success when it comes to motivating people, both individually and in groups, when there is a desire to do well. Thus, the wise coach, when teaching someone to play a difficult game (such as chess or ping-pong), will hold back or "throw" a game, or give the inexperienced player a handicap (golf, bowling) so that the learner can feel the accomplishment of scoring or winning, and therefore develop confidence. Athletic team managers often accomplish this by arranging a game schedule that includes some easy opposition early in the season, just as prize-fighter managers do when developing a new, inexperienced contender.

**Success frequently inspires self-confidence** - Increased self-confidence changes the calculations people make regarding their probabilities of future success--and may result in the individual re-evaluating the value of a reward or activity. It's not much fun playing a game that you know you have no chance of winning--one at least likes to come close. In short, increased self-confidence releases energy. When interviewed after winning the Professional Indoor Tennis Championship final match in 1977, Bjorn Borg said that he wasn't fully confident until after he beat Jimmy Conners in the first set. That early victory, he explained to reporters, gave him the confidence he needed to win two more.

**Groups also react to success** - Just as success can enhance self-confidence and release energy potential for individuals, it also can help develop cohesion and camaraderie in groups. An example of this was reported on the basis of undersea marine research teams.[10] Each successful undersea mission, according to the account, led to increased group cohesion.

Extensive experimental laboratory support for this phenomenon also exists. One author, on the basis of realistic laboratory studies, states that, "After repeated success, members perceive that the future promises a greater likelihood of success at that difficulty level, raise their anticipated level of aspiration, develop feelings of success and pride in the group, assign a favorable evaluation to their group's performance, attribute greater value to future success, develop a disposition to seek further successes, perceive their group to be an attractive one, and become committed to the process of setting future goals."[11]

In connection with these experimentally based conclusions, the reader once again is referred to Figure 1 in Chapter 2; *the above research conclusions describe a viable, developing group that is likely to become a "winner" by anyone's standards.*

**Failure also affects groups** - The same author's review of extensive research on repeated failure by groups is summarized as follows: "After repeated failure members are less inclined to be concerned about the probabilities of future failure or success; instead, they seek means that will help them to avoid the unfavorable consequences of failure. They tend to: lower their group's goal...., give an unapproving evaluation to their group's performance, see the activity as less important, believe success on the task is less desirable, are less attracted to their own group.... (and) would gladly abandon altogether the practice of setting aspiration levels."[12] Imagine the Baltimore Orioles baseball team's collective self-confidence during their 21-game losing streak at the beginning of their 1988 season.

**Face-saving** - Members in failing groups appear to have a strong preference for unreasonably difficult tasks which makes them vulnerable to subsequent failure. Preference for unreasonably difficult tasks is a "face saving" mechanism which reduces the onus of future failure--the psychological penalties for failing difficult tasks are less than those for easy tasks. It is clear, then, that groups suffer from failure experiences in ways that parallel individual failure cases. Success and failure strongly influence group motivation and process.

The interplay of morale and performance, when a relationship does exist,[13] is dynamic, subtle, and can be influenced. It is likely to be strongest in those technological circumstances where there are clearly observable performance standards against which groups can compare themselves over time. As we will see in the next chapter, such performance standards are not always readily available to a group. However, this is a deficiency that can be corrected.

## CONVERTING FAILURE INTO SUCCESS

**Tactics** - While success is the goal, every organization has its share of employees (and groups) considered to be chronic losers. Even private corporations rarely fire such people; they usually try to do something with them. Such cases are brought in here because the problem is best seen in a motivational context. A chronic failure (both individuals and groups) becomes a self-confidence problem because he (or she) usually is a failure in his own eyes as well as in the opinion of others.

Here is a speculative list of possible salvage tactics:

- Reduce "audience effect" which builds tension and causes loss of face, either by removing the audience or by moving the person or group to a new location;

- Modify the schedule - reduce amount of effort required (re-set goals, at an achievable level);

- Modify the job definition, making it less difficult;

- Transfer the individual to a different job but at same pay level;

- Arrange temporary demotion - same type of job but at an easier station;

- Bring extra resources to bear - such as an understanding coach or trainer - or a re-engineered procedure that will help the employee or group;

- Provide extra persuasion and support, from the boss and/or colleagues; and

- Protect the employee from non-job sources of frustration so that overall tension level can be reduced.

Effective use of the above tactics can be hampered by the presence of co-workers who may resent the "special attention" that the chronic failure case is receiving. Thus, *whatever strategy is used to assist either an individual or group that is in difficulty must deal with spectators and make them part of the solution.*[14]

**Homogeneous grouping** - An additional managerial tactic for dealing with failure cases is exemplified by one firm's practice of transferring "failure" cases to the timekeeping department. Here such employees were not required to interact with others, and the task was mentally undemanding. This practice was deemed far more humane than outright dismissal by the company, known for its paternalism. Over the years, however, this became a 40 to 50 person department staffed largely by marginal people. In other words, the policy created an accidentally homogeneous group of limited capacity. There was no major problem for years, however, until the organization decided to computerize its records. The management found at that time that relatively few of the timekeepers were retrainable, most were made obsolete by the change, and there were no other places in the company to hide them. There are few viable solutions, but homogeneous grouping of failure cases is not necessarily the answer, in either work organizations or schools.

**Training** - When people fail, they tend to lose self-confidence and hope, particularly if they fail frequently or badly. If they see few or no satisfactory behavior pathway alternatives to their goals, many are likely to develop what is called the "withdrawal syndrome." Such has been the case for many under-educated members of our society who are chronically unemployed or under-employed.

In the 1970s massive, governmental financed training and retraining programs were conducted to help salvage some of these casualties of the economic war in American industry. They did not solve the problem, but some of the programs may have helped. After reviewing the research literature on such programs for the period 1968-1976, one author concluded, "...the studies do show that the hard-core unemployed can be trained to become productive, self-respecting members of society. The literature (further) seems to indicate that *the most successful programs (treat) the individual as a whole person, and attempt to give him a great deal of emotional and material support...*"[15] (Emphasis mine.) The same can be applied validly to groups in trouble--a comprehensive support strategy is required. (See discussion of frustration in Chapter 6.)

## THE PROS AND CONS OF COMPETITION
## AS A MOTIVATIONAL STRATEGY

Competition is a major factor in our lives from the earliest days of our sibling rivalries at home through contests in the school room, athletics, and finally through most of our careers. Many employers try to capitalize on competitive tendencies and rivalries to generate increased motivation within and between various classes of employees, and among individuals. The common belief is that competitive strategies lead to greater effort, more work being done, enhanced group cohesion, and higher quality work. While it is true that such outcomes may result from competition, the reverse also may be true, as well as other unintended consequences. Therefore, the deliberate use of competitive strategies to enhance work motivation and team building requires planning and control.

Competition is a complex, interpersonal or inter-group process which arouses, directs and sustains energy expenditure of the parties engaged in a relationship. The competitive process can arouse varying degrees of emotional involvement ranging from mild to intense. Competitive strategies can be divided into three categories, each of which induces different amounts of stress or tension.

**Competition for fun** - Low levels of stress are associated with mild competitive strategies such as safety, sales, or attendance record contests. These are in the same general category as spelling bees and similar tactics used in schoolrooms by teachers trying to liven up an otherwise dull activity. The Philadelphia Flyers professional hockey team has used such tactics to achieve physical conditioning and weight control among their players. Shunning the traditional drudgery of routine exercises and wind-sprints, the Flyers were divided up into four squads which competed, on off days, at soccer, football, softball, speed skating and other games. Cumulative records were kept; each squad received a point for every contest it won. Coach Pat Quinn explained, "It gives the guys an opportunity to laugh at themselves. ...if there's no chance for humiliating each other a little bit, this [long hockey season] gets to be an awful job to come to every day."[16]

**Competition for development** - Competitive strategies in this category are somewhat more stressful, but not in the extreme. Playing the game is the important thing, not winning. An example may be found at a tennis court where some individuals, wishing to improve their own game, seek to play with others who are better players than themselves. Such players don't expect to win, but they expect a better than usual challenge and will try harder than usual so they won't waste the better player's time. In the process, they expect to polish up their strokes or get better than usual exercise.

**Competition for high stakes** - This usually involves competitive strategies that produce high stress. The outcomes can be either constructive or destructive and the risk of unanticipated dysfunctional outcomes is high. These were described in Chapter 6. Our immediate concern at this time is with milder forms of competition for purposes of enhancing task performance.

**Managing competition** - If mildly stressful competitive strategies are to be used effectively for motivating individuals and groups, they must be based on the same motivational principles we have discussed before. The value of the rewards involved (prizes plus the fun or challenge of competing) must exceed the costs by an appropriate amount. And, the perceived probability of success must be reasonable, say in the .40 to .60 range. Also, the costs of failure must be kept low. Moreover, goals must be set, feedback on performance has to be available, and the participants must know how to play and what the rules and constraints are. One also must experiment to determine how often a "contest" should be held and for how long. The competitive strategy, if overdone, can lose its potential effectiveness.

**The negative side always lurks** - Competitive strategies, even of the mild variety, also can backfire if the wrong individuals are involved. Consider the extreme behavior of some parents publicly berating their child players during Little League athletic contests, for example, or other people you have known to become ugly at some point during a game of MONOPOLY. There are some individuals who simply can't control themselves under competitive conditions--they become hostile and destructive.

Many of the unwanted effects of competition are related to the employee's perceived probability of winning. A person faced with what appears to be unequal competition, may simply maintain the status quo and pray for a miracle, or reduce his or her effort (to cut losses), or try to "equalize" the competition through subtle interference with competitors.

A person faced with what appears to be unequal competition also may try to gain advantage by building shortcuts into task procedures. This can be done to save time and sneak by inspection, even though the work done is inferior. In a factory I once worked for which produced one-wheel trailers pulled by autos for baggage such as camping gear and other light loads, two young, bored workers invented their own game to liven up the job. They bet beers on which man could assemble the most wheels per hour for such trailers. One of them, to gain a competitive advantage which nobody knew about until much later, left the cotter pin out of an occasional wheel. The cotter pin held the assembly together, and its presence or absence was not observable to inspectors because the hub cap covered its location. This undesirable by-product of competition came to light when several wrecked trailers were returned to the factory by the parent company for analysis and repair.

In competitive situations, job-related information sometimes is deliberately withheld, or is communicated inaccurately or deceptively. This may be in the individual competitor's interest, but it may not be good for the overall organization.

Individual competition among its members may not be the most desirable motivation system for some work groups because the total group output may end up lower than if the members see themselves as a cooperative unit, dependent on each other for achieving rewards. This is particularly true of groups whose ability range includes a few obviously superior members. It's also true of work groups working on complex tasks where open communication is vital to overall efficiency.

**Choosing up sides** - As in the case for individual competition within a group, competition between groups also has its pros and cons. Before introducing competitive motivational techniques, the task and group situation should be evaluated carefully. The manager might ask, "What are the conditions under which the negative effects may not be worth the benefits?" Answering this question requires a listing of the major possible effects:

- Increased interest may develop in an otherwise dull, routine task situation;

- Increased small group cohesiveness under the competitive situation may give individuals a greater sense of the importance of their own efforts, and lessen tendencies to "let George do it;"

- Competitors may develop shared negative attitudes toward each other, tending to underestimate contributions and becoming suspicious of motives;

- The frequency and constructiveness of interpersonal communication may be disrupted;

- Risk taking, or willingness to by-pass successful precedent in order to test promising innovations, may be depressed;

- Competitors may "shave" the rules or invent short-cuts that may or may not be organizationally acceptable; and

- Unless the winners are clearly superior, the losers may suspect the incentive administrator of favoritism or incompetence.

There is a tendency for competitors to strive for permanent dominance. Regulatory attention therefore must be given to competing individuals, groups and departments within organizations so that mild rivalry will not escalate into open warfare.

**Competition as a motivational strategy is not always a good idea** - Finally, the nature of the task involved is a crucial factor in deciding whether or not a competitive motivational system should be employed. All questions on this matter are not yet answered, but evidence to date suggests that complex problem solving and learning activities are likely to be more productive under collaborative rather than competitive circumstances.

## APPLICATION TO THE TEAM BUILDING PROCESS

It is clear that there is more than one way to motivate people and groups to perform tasks and achieve goals in work organizations. There are several ways to build interest and challenge into a work situation and to reduce the burdensome effects of routine and boredom. *A comprehensive and integrated reward system is needed, which must be monitored continuously and altered frequently to meet changing circumstances.*

**The four-factor model applies** - Now, how can we relate the above arsenal of motivational artillery to the four cycles of group evolution?[17] Let me begin with the process of group development during which an initial collection of members assembles, is named and explores the nature of their mission, goal(s), and tasks. First, potential members must be attracted to the group by some means.

This suggests that recruiting efforts must be designed so they will appeal to real needs and arouse interest in this group. During the early organizational efforts of the group, all elements of the four-factor model come into play for each new member -- "What will I get out of this activity? What will I have to pass up in order to do this? What will my own job require? What performance standards will be set? How often must I be here? Do I have the time? The inclination? Are the other members interesting? Dependable? Is the objective worthwhile? How likely am I to get by, or to excel? What are my penalties for failing?" The new group member's answers to such questions will be influenced by the group's other members and the ways in which they interact. Subtle pressures for uniformity begin early.

Some individuals will come up with a favorable balance in answering these questions while others will not. So, even during the early developmental stage, some members drop out entirely or decide to stay but play a passive role. Those who find a favorable balance in their answers have been successfully aroused -- the first stage of the motivational process in the direction of cooperative behavior.

**Goal setting, feedback, and rewards become increasingly important** - The next step is to transform their potential energy into expended energy. If there are not too many disinterested individuals acting as wet blankets (and it is probably wise to screen these out before it is too late), the enthusiasm of the interested members should be enough to get them started in task and organizing activities. It is useful to relate this process to management training programs. Some courses include both voluntary members who want to be included, and involuntary members who are required to be in them. Some of the involuntary members can be reached motivationally while others may become outright disruptive. If the system adopted for the majority is inadequate to motivate the disruptive minority, other control measures must be brought to bear. From that point on, the degree of challenge and intrinsic reward in the task, the establishment of meaningful and challenging goals, feedback on goal attainment, and the appropriate use of extrinsic rewards, all become important so that energy will continue to be expended, in constructive directions and on a timely basis. *The group's manager is often the key to making these factors come together properly.*

While considerable goal setting research evidence suggests that difficult goals work better than easy goals as motivators, it is premature to draw a fixed conclusion about goal difficulty. Groups that are just starting out require a different level of goal difficulty than mature groups with established accomplishments. Thus, gradual escalation of goal difficulty is a strategy that bears consideration. Moreover, there is the more fundamental question as to the source of group goals. That is, who should set them--the management or the group itself? Some combination of the two is probably best. Gradual escalation of goal difficulty, for example, is likely to breed resentment unless the group members agree to it.

Knowledge of results should be provided on a reasonably frequent basis so that groups can assess their progress toward goals. However, the feedback should not be so frequent as to irritate the members or make them nervous. This entire process requires that creative task analysis be conducted so that significant progress data can be utilized. Baseline data will be necessary so that groups can compare themselves with other groups as well as with their own performance on prior, comparable occasions.

**Additional matters for the manager to bear in mind** - All of the above are matters over which many individual managers have considerable potential influence. As the group evolves, several additional matters also are likely to require special attention from the manager:

- Adjustments will be required to deal with the individual members whose motivational level and contributions to group activity may change either up or down;

- Effort and methods will be required for incorporating newcomers to the group--the group's goals must become the newcomer's goals too; and

- New group goals will need to be developed as time wears on in many instances.

**Cyclical variations occur for individuals and groups** - The motivation of people and groups at work is much easier talked about than accomplished. We know more about the processes involved than we have been able to implement in most organizational settings. There are difficult, unresolved problems. One of the major ones is what to do about group members who start out well as highly motivated performers, establish themselves, and subsequently relax and go downhill for any of the following reasons;

- Sickness;

- Changed personal circumstances, such as marriage, becoming the parent of twins, or the acquisition of a new and fascinating hobby which drains off energy outside the work place;

- The pursuit by a member of "extra-curricular' activities of value to the larger employing organization but not of immediate benefit to the work group; and

- Close proximity to retirement age.

Group members react differently to their colleagues depending on which of the above reasons apply. A group member who suffers a heart attack may be "carried" by the group for a considerable period of time. One who acquires twins may also be carried by the group until he or she makes the necessary adjustments. In the third case, however, group members may become resentful that one of their colleagues is increasingly engaged in extra-curricular organizational activities such as task forces, administrative work, special missions for a senior manager, and the like which interfere with the group's ability to get its job done. The fourth situation, imminent retirement, causes many problems for task groups if they do not see where the replacements are coming from.

Cyclical variations in energy required by the task will be identified as experience accumulates. Retail stores, for example, have to deal with holiday rush periods, as do commercial transporters. College professors know about the student "let down" between Thanksgiving and Christmas vacations. Both the reward system and task need to be engineered to cope with such matters.

Ultimately, a viable performing group, depending on its function in the organization, may require extensive renewal because too many members change their calculation of the four factors in the model (usually the Net Profit calculation).

A group that loses its edge and starts going downhill probably will require a return to group development strategies to attract new members or shape new expectations and attitudes. *Motivational shaping processes occur in cycles, frequently change, and must be adaptive to changing conditions. And, as is the case for individuals who in most instances require different approaches to motivation at different stages of their personality development in life, task groups, as they evolve and develop through their life cycles require appropriate changes in their motivational systems.*

**Group membership mix emerges again** - The problem of motivating individuals and work groups is further complicated by heterogeneous staffing patterns. An appropriate reward system for the sales division, for example, might not fit a research and development division; what works for young hamburger cooks at McDonalds' may not be appropriate for financial analysts on Wall Street. Task and personal background characteristics are different.

**In conclusion** - Perhaps the best we can expect from psychologists are a few guiding principles and concepts that practitioners will have to adapt to the specific needs of their organizations on a trial and error basis. Several such principles include:

- Goals are motivators; in their absence people will set their own and probably will waste a lot of effort;

- Knowledge of results on an appropriate informational feedback schedule arouses interest and focuses people on goals and the means available by which they may be reached;

- Success breeds more success, to a point; and

- Mild, properly managed competition applied as a motivational technique in appropriate groups can be fruitful.

Finally, a combination of all of these principles has great potential for stimulating challenge at the work place, and for building and re-vitalizing task groups. Application of these principles, however, requires appropriately designed administrative mechanisms to incorporate what is known about psychological reinforcement, goal setting, and knowledge of results. The next chapter examines such administrative mechanisms.

# ENDNOTES

1    See PSYCHOLOGY TODAY, April 1962, 68-69, where a digest of a longer article appears. The digest is based on a December 18, 1971 article in BUSINESS WEEK, copyright by McGraw-Hill.

2    Ronan, W., Latham, G. and Kinne, S., "The effects of goal setting and supervision on worker behavior in an industrial situation, "JOURNAL OF APPLIED PSYCHOLOGY, 1973, 58, 302-307.

3    This account is taken from a secondary source, Viteles, M., MOTIVATION AND MORALE IN INDUSTRY, 1953, New York: W.W. Norton and Co., 144-145. According to Viteles, the original source is a book by Bingham, W. V., PSYCHOLOGY TODAY, 1932, Chicago; U. of Chicago Press, 262-263.

4    Latham, G. and Yukl, G., "A review of research on the application of goal setting in organizations," ACADEMY OF MANAGEMENT JOURNAL, 1975, 18 (4), 824-45.

5    Zander, A., MOTIVES AND GOALS IN GROUPS, 1971, New York: Academic Press, 202-203.

6    Aside from Latham and Yukl, above, see Nadler, D. A., "The effects of feedback on task group behavior; A review of the experimental research," ORGANIZATIONAL BEHAVIOR AND HUMAN PERFORMANCE, 1979, 23, 309-338, and Locke, E. A., "Toward a theory of task motivation and incentives," JOURNAL OF ORGANIZATIONAL BEHAVIOR AND HUMAN PERFORMANCE, 1968, 3, 157-189.

7    See Pinder, C., WORK MOTIVATION: THEORY, ISSUES, AND APPLICATIONS, 1984, Glenview, ILL.; Scott, Foresman and Company for a wide ranging, readable review of many theoretical perspectives about motivation at work. My approach in this book cuts across several of them but doesn't pretend to encompass the whole field.

8    The model which follows is derived from something known as VIE theory. See Miner, J. and Dachler, P., "Personnel attitudes and motivation,: ANNUAL REVIEW OF PSYCHOLOGY, 1973, 24, 384; Locke, E., "Personnel attitudes and motivation,: ANNUAL REVIEW OF PSYCHOLOGY, 1975, 26, 457-480; and Pinder, C., cited above, for important criticisms of the substance and research underlying this model.

9    Herzberg, F., WORK AND THE NATURE OF MAN, 1966, Cleveland: World Publishing Company.

10   Radloff, R. and Helemreich, R., "Stress under the sea," PSYCHOLOGY TODAY, 1969, September.

11   Zander, A., cited above, 202-203.

12   Zander, A., cited above, 200.

13    The group cohesion-performance relationship studies have not produced consistent results over the years. A probable reason is the lack of control for time lags and trends. One longitudinal study controlling for time shows clear support for the above argument. See Rosen, N. A., LEADERSHIP CHANGE AND WORK GROUP BEHAVIOR, 1969, Ithaca, New York: Cornell University Press. The same book also contains information on how production scheduling and task-cycle variables impinge on group life.

14    See Paterson, T. T., MORALE IN WAR AND WORK, 1955, London, England; Max Parrish & Company, Ltd. for a classic, realistic case study that illustrates most of the above points.

15    Horan, Marcia, "Training the hard-core unemployed: A literature review, 19681976." Unpublished paper, N.Y.S.S.I.L.R., Cornell University.

16    Brown, F. "Flyers game-playing not limited to hockey," AP Analysis, ITHACA JOURNAL, November 28, 1979

17    While the various components in the motivational arsenal have the benefit of empirical supporting evidence in the literature, the kinds of linkages that I'm about to draw by and large do not; the research and experimentation remain to be conducted.

SOME ADDITIONAL LITERATURE FOR THE INTERESTED READER:

-    Latham, G., "The role of goal setting in human resource management," RESEARCH IN PERSONNEL AND HUMAN RESOURCE MANAGEMENT, 1983, 1, 169-199.

-    Reber, R. and Wallin, J., "The effects of training, goal-setting, and knowledge of results on safe behavior: a component analysis," ACADEMY OF MANAGEMENT JOURNAL, 1984, 27, 544-560.

-    Schaeffer, Dorothy, "Dealing with the incompatibility between competition/cooperation," SUPERVISION, 1987, 49 (July), 14-17.

-    Tubbs, M., "Goal-setting: a meta-analytic examination of the empirical evidence," JOURNAL OF APPLIED PSYCHOLOGY, 1986, 71, 474-483. (Technical)

# CHAPTER 8

## RECOGNITION AND REWARDS: COMMONLY USED ADMINISTRATIVE STRATEGIES FOR MOTIVATION

Reprinted with special permission of
King Features Syndicate, Inc.

[This approach has produced a lot of
motivational mileage for commercial airlines - NR]

This chapter is concerned with three mechanisms that form the nucleus of most major work organizations' reward systems. Usually these include pay systems, the use of promotions to managerial positions, and performance appraisal techniques. The motivational effectiveness of these and other techniques depends upon the extent to which they are designed to fit what is known about individual and group motivation. The previous chapter, for example, makes several points about the motivational dynamics and interplay of goal setting, knowledge of results, reinforcement, and success and failure. Administrative reward systems should be geared to these processes if they are to be maximally effective.

Unfortunately, some organizations' leaders commit themselves to reward system features for ideological reasons rather than on the basis of what is known about human motivation. Thus, a chief executive officer may insist that pay increases be based on "merit," even when many of the employees involved are performing in very unskilled occupations where there is practically no performance variation among individuals. Under such circumstances the managerial concept of "merit," which may be highly relevant for executives and other professionals, has little meaning to the rank and file. Perhaps even more important, the reward systems used in work organizations seldom are designed to take into account the ever-changing interplay of group processes. The inevitable result is some amount of friction and many lost opportunities to enhance performance through teamwork. Let us pursue the matter further.

## MONEY AS A MOTIVATOR[1]

There is considerable confusion or disagreement about the motivation potential of money among those who have read various accounts of the behavioral science research literature on this topic. The discrepancies arise in part because of the apparently conflicting studies of employee reactions to financial rewards. Many employee job satisfaction studies, for example, show that salary, wages, or income rank third, fourth, fifth, or even lower in "importance" to the worker's job satisfaction. Such factors as job duties, opportunity for promotion and "my supervisor" often are ranked by employees in opinion surveys as more important than money.

**Money talks** - Some research, however, has shown much different results. For example, a study in a rural factory a few years ago clearly indicated that this particular employee population was very money conscious and responded strongly and willingly to money as an incentive.[2] Many participants in properly administered incentive systems, including executives, production workers, sales persons paid on commission, truck and taxi drivers, will readily corroborate the fact that "money talks."

**Money isn't everything** - On the other hand, numerous employees, especially women, do not utilize their employer's job bidding system when internal company job vacancies are announced. They prefer to stay with their friends rather than transfer to another department, even at a higher rate of pay. Additionally, we all have seen newspaper or TV accounts of sweepstake, football pool, or lottery winners who, despite winning enormous sums, have returned to their original humdrum jobs after a brief vacation. When asked why they returned instead of living off investments, they usually reply, "I missed my friends." In other words, these people discovered that money isn't everything.

**Research methods can be the reason for the discrepancy** - How does one reconcile the conflicting views, "money talks" versus "money isn't everything?" Sometimes this can be explained by methodological factors affecting data collection; various studies are conducted with different research methods, on different populations and at different times. For example, when asked how important money is in comparison with other socially acceptable rewards, some individuals may downgrade money in their replies so as to "look good" to the interviewer. Researchers using less direct techniques may get different results.

**Times change, as do peoples' needs** - The economic context of the time period when such questions are asked also is important. A person may change his or her ranking of money during an inflationary period. Finally, diverse population segments operate at different levels of need and therefore attach different weights to the importance of money.

Many managers and human resource professionals during the last two decades have adopted a perspective that money is no longer as important a motivator as it used to be. They appear to believe that there are other, more significant (or 'healthier') ways to motivate people, and have turned their attention to those. This school of thought tends to consider the nature of the employee's task and the employer's administrative philosophy to be the more significant motivational wellsprings.

**Money is still important** - For many American workers, motivational strategies geared to task redesign, participative management models, and the like have limited potential because these employees are preoccupied, necessarily, with survival and security needs. They don't make enough money to develop a cushion, and are more likely to invest extra energy in second and even third jobs, if available, to supplement their incomes, than they are to invest extra energy in behalf of their primary employer. And, if they can't handle or obtain a second job themselves, their spouse in many cases takes a job which creates competing energy demands on couples and families. Many such people are more likely to be interested in overtime pay than in job enrichment. Government reports published every year on average earnings by American employees show that money is in short supply for many.[3]

**Comparisons are a key element** - On balance it is safe to say that money is an extremely significant factor in the overall job satisfaction-career planning picture, but its importance and motivating potential varies among people, and may change from one time period to another for individuals. It also is safe to say that absolute salary or wage levels are often less important than comparative levels.[4] That is, most of us look for clues and information that will tell us whether we are earning what we think we "should" in comparison with certain other people. Comparisons are made with our peers in the same or similar occupations. A dietician will compare his earnings with those of other dieticians rather than with executives and is likely to become agitated if he finds himself making less than his colleagues. Very negative results also occur when supervisors discover inadequate differentials between their own and their subordinates' earnings.

## HOW GROUPS FILTER THE MONEY MOTIVE

From the standpoint of motivation in the processes of group development, performance, maintenance and renewal, comparative pay levels among the members of a work group is a critical matter. If pay differentials develop among the members, they must be based on considerations that the group members themselves perceive to be logical and fair. If pay differentials are not allowed to develop, alternative methods must be found to reward above average performers who are achievement oriented, and controls must be applied to low performers. Otherwise the members may become hostile to each other or to the organization, and teamwork will suffer.

**People and groups do not necessarily maximize** - Many organizations use specially designed financial incentive systems to meet the need for differential rewards, especially in manufacturing and sales. Contrary to conventional belief, experience and research show that employees do not necessarily try to maximize their incentive earnings. Rather, they develop group norms which reflect trade offs. They trade immediate income for job security, stability of interpersonal relationships, and protection of their friends from arbitrary actions by management. Many manual workers who have physically demanding jobs that are incentive rated sacrifice income in favor of energy conservation--if they were to work "flat out" every day to maximize their short-term income, they would jeopardize their long-term life span: aging takes its toll. They also would have little energy left for their families and hobbies.

**Job security is a tradeoff** - Group restriction of performance develops for rational reasons even if short-term income is lost. Employees have found through past experience with incentive systems that there are two danger levels. First, when too many employees receive high bonuses, piece rates or incentives, some managements change the performance standards so that one has to work harder to receive the same pay. Or, management decides it can lay off some workers and still get the desired level of total production from the remainder. Second, when production rates dip too low below base rate, individuals may be fired or at least harassed for incompetence or not trying.[5] Thus, a cohesive group will probably stabilize productivity around a rate that is as high as it can go (or as high as the consensus of group opinion thinks it can go) without either jeopardizing income security or calling attention to the slowest worker in the group.

While many employees restrict their output under incentive plans, they do care about money up to a certain point. That is, they increase their output in order to make more money if doing so does not have side effects which conflict with achieving other aims important to them. Work groups often set informal production (or sales) norms, and the well-integrated member of a group receives social rewards for maintaining personal performance around this level. (Note: Such norms also develop in organizations having less direct financial incentive systems. For example, college professors who publish "too much" sometimes are subtly pressured to slow down by their less productive colleagues. And, students have been known to pressure their "grade grubbing" colleagues to "take it easier" and not "raise the curve.") Setting and maintaining standards, therefore, is an on-going, not occasional concern.

**A payoff for teamwork frequently is missing** - Restriction of output is not the only drawback of the financial incentive systems typically used in American industry. Sometimes unintended dysfunctional consequences arise because the system stimulates competitive dirty tricks. If there is no <u>group</u> payoff component in the system, for example, salesmen may "forget" to leave telephone message slips for each other, and may steal each other's customers.

Since most people appear to work in groups, it seems to me that the compensation system should reflect that fact. The reality, however, is the opposite. Specifically, jobs are classified according to one or another system of standard factors, and price ranges are established in relation to surveys of other employers. This is very helpful for accounting purposes, and keeps things orderly. It also facilitates budgeting and cost control. Unfortunately, such an approach has limited motivational potential, and does not even begin to address the concept of teamwork.

**Perhaps professional baseball offers a useful model** - While no pay system is likely to be foolproof, let us examine how professional baseball players are remunerated. There are several factors that contribute to a player's income from his employer:

- Base salary--usually determined by "going market rates" for the average player in each specialty, e.g., catcher or outfielder, but also influenced by the player's past performance and his specialty;

- Individual one-shot bonuses--for an outstanding performance such as a "no-hit" game by a pitcher;

- Seasonal bonuses agreed in advance by contract and which links the size of the total pay package to the player's performance statistics, e.g., batting average or a pitcher's earned run average; and

- Team bonuses that are shared (usually equally) by the players -- for overall group performance such as finishing a season high in the league or winning a championship. **The players decide as a group how to divide up these extra earnings.**

This system appears to provide equitable treatment, incorporates what we know about reinforcement theory, rewards individual effort, provides recognition for outstanding achievements, and encourages group cohesion and teamwork (although jealousies can and do arise from time to time). The same cannot be said for typical pay systems in industry, health care, government or higher education.

**Change is needed** - As one social psychologist observed, after reviewing a number of research studies, "If we wish to minimize 'process losses,' our payoff system should be tailored to match the task; it should induce the right person to do the right thing at the right time."[6] Implementation of this principle requires new approaches to task analysis, a commitment to frequent monitoring, and far better planned reward systems than exist in most work organizations today. Such a strategy also would require very close matching of employee selection and assignment practices with task and reward system design because of their dynamic interplay. Such coordination holds great promise for enhancing the productivity both of individuals and groups, but it requires extensive modification of typical compensation systems.

## ORGANIZATION-WIDE INCENTIVE SYSTEMS

Many private corporations have adopted such "rewards" as year-end bonuses, Christmas turkeys, or profit-sharing payments in the belief that such rewards enhance employee motivation. While all of these approaches have certain common underlying assumptions, let us focus, for illustrative purposes, on profit sharing. (Note: My intent here is to deal with principles of incentive administration, not profit sharing per se; profit sharing is simply being used as a widely known phenomenon to illustrate some points.)

**No losers** - Profit-sharing plans, like Christmas turkey bonuses, historically have been designed to produce a payoff for everyone in an organization. Such a positive approach to rewarding employees seems to be sensible, at least on paper, especially in a profit, money-conscious society. Indeed, according to questionnaire results in a large number of management development courses I have conducted, many managers believe such systems develop feelings of personal responsibility for the firm's profits among rank-and-file employees, increase employee's interest in the firm's progress, and develop cooperative attitudes among employees. On the other hand, a number of organizations that used one or another type of profit sharing plan with great anticipation abandoned it after a few years, mainly because they found it became "just another fringe benefit" with no real motivating power.[7] In the long run, they frequently fizzled. We will have to appeal to some of the motivation principles treated in the preceding chapter to get a better understanding of the reasons behind the employee's indifferent attitude toward end-of-the-year profit-sharing bonuses.

**Why they often fizzle: unclear link between behavior and reward** - For one thing, it is difficult for the employee to see the link between his or her behavior and the reward from such plans. Thus, while the behavior-incentive link is relatively easy for the employee to observe under individual incentive systems, and only somewhat more difficult to see under group piecework plans, the link is quite obscure in overall organization profit-sharing plans. Increased effort is clearly reflected in increased reward under individual piecework plans.   Overall organizational profits are dependent upon many factors in addition to on-the-job behavior including state of the market, sales efficiency, government contract spending and the particular method the top management chooses to use in computing profits.   Most employees are well aware of these factors.   Thus the employee often does not know which specific behavior to repeat and which to avoid in order to get the next bonus. The behavior-reward linkage is even harder to perceive as the organization's size increases.

Various incentive plans also can be compared on the basis of the time that elapses before the employee is rewarded for producing the desired behavior.   Profit-sharing plans are generally handled in once-a-year bonus payments.   The long time lag makes it difficult for the employee to develop any feeling of making progress toward a goal. Compare this to the short time lag found in most individual and group incentive plans where rewards usually are distributed weekly or monthly.   Rewards (or punishments) are more effective if received soon after the desired (or undesired) behavior occurs.   The short time frame and frequency of reward reinforce the linkage.

**Probability of success in the past has been too high** - Finally, profit-sharing plans tend to be introduced when the organization has a recent history of making profit and a strong likelihood of continuing high profits.   Consequently, employees find that the end-of year bonus will be forthcoming whether they increase their effort and cooperativeness or not. They perceive a 100 percent chance that they will receive a reward whatever they may do. Many people are more strongly motivated when the odds of success approximate a 50-50 chance; if the odds are either 0 or 100 percent, motivation to invest effort will be low.

In more recent years, however, bonus plans linked to corporate annual performance apparently have been proliferating regardless of the above arguments. One gets the impression that corporate executives are either inadequately informed about incentive principles, or are using the bonus system as a way of retaining key people rather than motivating high performance standards. They also seem to be sending a message that "We're all in the same boat; if the corporation does well, we all will benefit. Otherwise, don't expect much of an income adjustment." Many people, line managers included, interpret this as pressure to "do more for less." The result frequently is *demotivation...*, especially if no profit-sharing bonus is forthcoming at the end of a year and merit increases are limited.

## SOME UNINTENDED CONSEQUENCES OF FINANCIAL REWARD SYSTEMS: THREE MINI-CASES

As the old saying goes, sometimes "the best laid plans" go awry. The reader can learn something of value from flaws in the following financially based motivational systems that I have encountered or been told about in my work.

**Faulty output measurement** - One flaw involves a major silverware-dinnerware manufacturing organization. Most of this company's production workers are paid on an incentive basis--the more they produce, the greater their earnings. Worker productivity is measured by weight. For example, the weight of a tablespoon in a certain pattern is known. To facilitate handling and moving, completed silverware is placed in wooden boxes provided by the management and the boxes are weighed. The poundage is credited to the worker (or group) and incentive earnings are calculated accordingly.

The workers pick from a stockpile any one of many so-called "standard" wooden boxes to use. Significantly, they often pick the oldest, greasiest boxes (which sometimes fall apart as silverware is moved to subsequent in-plant locations). Why? The greasy boxes, because wood absorbs grease, are two to three pounds heavier than the new ones; therefore the worker receives higher pay. Employees, in other words, sometimes look for ways to "beat the system."

**Administrative inconsistency** - The same organization suffers from a more serious problem, conflict between younger and older members of the production work force over which persons should get which piecework (incentive) assignments. Some piece rates, because of the usual range of error in time-study techniques, are "looser" than others and therefore are a "better deal" for the worker. The older workers, because of their seniority, tend to get a disproportionate share of these, while younger workers get "tighter" ones. The younger workers also are assigned a disproportionate share of the hourly paid jobs carrying no incentive rewards. The older workers, while well aware of their younger colleagues' growing family financial needs and greater physical capacity to do fast, repetitive work, have consistently resisted any re-distribution of the assignments. A major reason for this resistance is that the company's retirement system links the magnitude of a person's pension to the last five years of total earnings immediately prior to retirement. *Thus the organization's retirement and performance-based incentive systems are operating at cross-purposes.*

**Unforseen emergencies** - A third flaw arose in a well-known Scandinavian ocean shipping firm when it opened a multi-million dollar modern dock facility in London, England.[8] The dock was designed to load and unload palletized (prepacked) cargo with forklift trucks instead of on the backs of stevedores and with cranes. Special merchant ships were designed to facilitate this process, and the dockers were trained in advance of the opening. Moreover, they received very substantial pay increases in return for their agreement to accept certain new work procedures, some of which were designed to cut overtime pay costs. Premium overtime pay had become a major cost factor over the years.

A problem arose when one of three docker crews unloading one of three equal holds (cargo compartments) in a ship was far from finished at 5 p.m., while the other two crews were finished. (All three had started at the same time.) Given the river traffic waiting to come in, it was necessary to complete the unloading that day. So, which group do you suppose received the overtime assignment with extra pay? One of the faster crews? Wrong! The slow one. After that happened two or three times, all the groups began holding back during the day so they could work overtime at a high hourly rate, despite a basic wage rate that had almost doubled when the new facility opened.

The lesson of the above three cases is threefold:

- People often operate out of self-interest;

- Reward systems require constant surveillance and frequent change. They are not in the same category of other management control systems that often can remain stable for long periods of time; and

- Proper measurement of performance is essential if incentive systems are to work as intended.

## PROMOTION TO SUPERVISOR AS A MOTIVATOR: A MIXED BAG

Organizations have many incentives at their disposal to influence employees. One often discussed among middle and high level managers is "the opportunity for promotion" to supervisory level positions. The prospect of such promotions, however, has little incentive value for large numbers of rank-and-file employees both in blue-collar and white collar ranks. Employees have learned from personal observation and the grapevine that one ordinarily does not "work one's way up from the bottom." Outstanding performance is neither a necessary nor sufficient qualification used by management for deciding who should be promoted to a better job or to a first-level supervisory position.

**Merit is not the only promotion criterion** - Employees often observe that average performers many times get promoted before outstanding performers, if the former has more seniority and a better attendance record. This does not mean that merit does not count, but in low-level production, service, and many clerical operations, both union and non-union, long-service employees generally are considered to be the most knowledgeable people available for positions of supervisory responsibility. Therefore, if they are at least average performers, they often are more likely to be promoted than short-service fireballs because theoretically they know more about their co-workers, the organization and its administrative systems and policies, the task, and its customers in many cases. This procedure also reduces charges of favoritism, although social policy and recent legislation regarding minority groups and women have introduced some new dimensions to this problem.

**Low "net profits" discourage candidates** - Many employees also calculate low Net Profits in connection with future promotions to supervisory positions. Long hours of work (which are required of supervisors and managers), loss of overtime pay (in many cases), increased pressure from top management, and the probability of becoming unpopular with former friends all contribute to this. The Cost of Failure also can be high if a person loses seniority upon returning to his or her former job after failing in a supervisory position. Additionally, one may have to absorb ridicule from relatives and former friends.

**Climbing the ladder is becoming more difficult** - Many managers still share the old belief that unskilled manual and service workers with no college degree can move up the ladder to the top of the organization, provided they are intelligent. This success story theme was more true thirty years ago than it is today. Most sizable work organizations today either implicitly or overtly assume that a college education is essential in considering a person for a position on the higher rungs of the "management ladder." Moreover, they frequently recruit from outside when filling high level vacancies. Therefore, the intelligent unskilled employee finds it necessary to compete with a substantial number of equally intelligent employees for the infrequent "promotions from within," and that promotion above the lowest management levels without a college degree is unlikely. The technological explosion, so evident in many organizations today, is aggravating this trend. Promotion opportunities also are being greatly restricted by many corporations' restructuring and downsizing designs. They have cut out of the structure huge numbers of middle management jobs thereby sharply reducing future promotion potential among supervisors and rank-and-file. See Chapter 11.

On balance, then, many employees make much different estimates on the factors Net Profit, Perceived Probability of Success, and Confidence in Calculations in connection with their promotion potential as an incentive than would be made by people who already are managers. The latter have found that it is possible to get a promotion, whereas the rank-and-file see unfavorable odds.

**Social policy also is a factor** - Governmental policy with respect to racial, ethnic and sex bias in employment also relates to the use of promotions as motivators. Rather than risk the loss of government contracts or potentially expensive and time consuming law suits, some organizations have downgraded seniority, task knowledge, educational qualifications, aptitude tests and experience in favor of numerical quota strategies. In brief, because of corrective public policy and employer resource priorities, women, blacks, and other minorities receive preferential treatment in some organizations when promotion opportunities arise. Whatever their social merit may be, these new policies (because they are not task-related) serve to reduce even further the motivational potential of future promotions as an energizer among many rank-and-file employees who previously were expecting them.

**Promotion to supervisor as a motivator is losing its punch** - My major point in including promotion into managerial ranks as a potential motivator is to illustrate that its utility for this purpose is a mixed bag. If low level promotions are to be based on past job performance alone, those getting them might very well lack leadership and administrative qualities necessary for supervisors. If promotions are to be based on an assessment of aptitudes for supervision and leadership, thorough research must be done to develop the assessment system so as to satisfy the standards of the Federal Government (and of the psychological profession). If the promotions are to be based on the premise that experience with the task and organization is paramount, then seniority offers a way out--except many executives don't like this idea even if they act on it. In any event, if the prospect of future promotion is to serve as a motivator for employee task behavior, it will be necessary to administer these rewards in the same, psychologically meaningful ways necessary for any other incentive.

**Going further up the ladder and a fairness issue** - Promotion to first line supervision from the ranks is not the only type of promotion we should consider. *Further promotions for those already in management positions also are important.* Managers frequently are promoted on the basis of bottom line achievements <u>by</u> their <u>subordinates</u>. However, if recognition earned by many in a team effort is granted only to the leader or one outstanding member, the remainder will likely become resentful, especially if the recognition is handled badly. Let's consider an example from outside the business world. A Gannet News Service writer, who once reviewed statistics on the distribution of medals to US military personnel, pointed out the following:

"In that [Korean] war, officers made up 15 per cent of those fighting. But they won almost 40 per cent of the Silver Stars, 35 per cent of the Bronze Stars... and nearly half of the Distinguished Service Crosses, the second highest decoration. While officers were getting all these decorations for valor, enlisted men were taking 93 per cent of the Purple Hearts."[9]

This practice produces psychologically unhealthy working environments and discourages motivation among the rank-and-file. Understanding this principle, such outstanding athletes as O. J. Simpson and Pete Vukovich, on award winning occasions, were careful to distribute public praise to their teammates "without whose support" they couldn't have won the awards. Vukovich actually suggested cutting the 1982 Cy Young Trophy for the best American League baseball pitcher into 24 parts and giving one to each of his teammates. These men wanted to assure the *continuing* support of their teammates in the years ahead. A wise manager acts on the same principle. Many chief executives who receive annual salaries in excess of a million dollars while "holding the line" on rank-and-file compensation appear to have forgotten this principle. Indeed, a few years ago The General Motors Corporation awarded executives cash bonuses while at the same time it discontinued profit-sharing payments to union workers.

## PERFORMANCE APPRAISAL AS A MOTIVATIONAL TOOL: SOMETHING IS MISSING

Performance appraisal as a topic can arouse a great deal of heated argument, some of which stems from differing definitions of terms. Most company's "performance appraisal" systems actually encompass two processes, not one. First, there is the review of task performance for some specified time period. It answers the question, "How did the individual do?" during that period. The second purpose has to do with planning and development, e.g., "What have we learned about this employee that bears on his or her future in the organization?" Normally this is a relatively long term concern. Of course short term performance and long term future and promotability issues are related, but for purposes of analysis it is well to clarify the focus. The discussion below is aimed at the review of the current or recent performance component.

**Techniques and forms are less important than how they are used** - Hundreds of performance appraisal articles have appeared in practitioner, professional and trade journals. Numerous chapters on the subject in traditional text-books, various entire volumes devoted to this subject,[10] and a review of more than 200 empirical studies also have been published.[11] Regardless of the extensive work behind these publications, a major purpose of performance appraisal in my opinion has been neglected. Many practitioners have been preoccupied with procedural details and the development of forms,[12] rather than with motivational process.

**New directions are needed** - Performance appraisal, as a feedback method, should contribute to the arousal of energy potential, the stimulation of energy expenditure, the channeling of that energy toward appropriate goals, and the maintenance of the energy expenditure level on appropriate schedules. *It also should encourage teamwork and effective group process.* Generally speaking, the performance review processes that I have observed serve neither purpose well. That is, they do not strongly facilitate either individual motivation or teamwork.

If performance appraisal is to be a viable motivational tool for enhancing task performance and teamwork, several attributes will have to be built into the system:

- A basic psychological process involved in motivating people and groups is knowledge of results. The same psychological process is needed in performance reviews. Psychologically meaningful performance reviews require that data be available on goals, measurable progress toward those goals, and the behaviors or strategies that either enhance or hinder progress toward the goals. Typically such data are conspicuous by their absence, although MBO systems are a step in this direction;

- Performance reviews must reflect realistic behaviors that have clear linkages to job success and goal achievement. Because such linkages are not the same for all departments, different parts of the organization may require different approaches. The process, to some extent, will have to be decentralized and geared to the different needs of specific units and groups in the organization, in addition to the organizations' general needs;

- The system should be applied only to occupational groups for whom performance review is relevant. Large numbers of jobs are of such a nature that little performance variability exists among the people doing them. In such cases performance appraisal is superfluous at best, and possibly downright insulting if it gets focused on people's personalities, as it all too often does;

- Performance feedback and associated rewards must be administered on a sensible psychological reinforcement schedule;

- The usual practice of annual performance review should be replaced by more frequent reviews which will motivate people because of their relevance, not irritate them because of their irrelevance.

And, if whole organizations can shut down for as much as several days to "take inventory" of stock, why not shut down periodically to "take inventory" of human resources and performance? The practice in some organizations of gearing performance appraisal to each employee's anniversary date, while spreading out the administrative burden across the year, bears little relationship to the achievement of group goals. The timing is wrong.

## THE PERFORMANCE APPRAISAL - SALARY LINK

Typical current organizational practice, professional admonitions to the contrary not withstanding, is to link performance appraisal results to wage and salary administration. Wage and salary administration is linked closely to overall budgetary operations, and budgeting operations usually rest on an annual model. Therefore it is no surprise that performance reviews frequently are made according to accounting schedule requirements instead of in accord with principles of psychological reinforcement theory. Effective motivation requires flexibility.

Why not press for an innovation? For example, the annual budget could include discretionary amounts for bonuses. These amounts could be allocated to departments and awarded on a decentralized basis, to groups and individuals on a timely reward schedule if an appropriate, job-related accomplishment shows they deserve it, at any time during the year. Money is a powerful potential motivator, but only if it is used as part of a psychologically sound reward system which, in turn, needs to be integrated with the organization's overall strategic plan.

## THE SHAPE OF THE CURVE

A few words also might be said about the distribution of performance appraisal scores or "grades." It has long been recognized that some performance raters are more or less lenient than others when judging employee performance, just as some teachers and professors are more or less lenient than others when assigning grades. Thus, one department or group in an organization may receive a high average performance rating and show a highly skewed distribution while another shows a normal distribution and a lower average. Human resources professionals, through rater training, try to reduce leniency tendencies and improve the quality of measurement.

**Forced ratings** - Some corporate executives try to reduce leniency when appraisal results are tied to salary increases, because lenient ratings produce a higher corporate wage bill in such systems. They do this by specifying the maximum percentage who can receive highly favorable ratings, or by requiring extensive documentation for such ratings. Since documentation is a nuisance, this practice tends to discourage extremely favorable ratings. In fact, the whole process sometimes is perceived as a farce and does not produce the desired motivational results.

**Changing the standards** - One company I know of tried to tighten up performance standards by pressing employees and managers to set "high goals" (sometimes called "stretch" goals). Then, when they achieved such a goal, they received a rating of only "fully satisfactory" or "meets expectations." Unfortunately in that company, achieving a demanding goal is not good enough - a higher rating such as "outstanding" or "excellent" is required to get a merit pay increase! Experience with this system, then, encourages employees to establish less than fully demanding goals so that they may look good upon exceeding them. The creation of artificially high standards by tinkering with the performance appraisal rating categories does not begin to tackle the motivation issues.

**Social pressure** - Many academic deans try to reduce lenient grade distributions in universities because they wish to protect academic standards and maintain the integrity of the grading system. They do this by publishing and circulating grade distributions to the Faculty, for each of several courses, so that comparisons resulting in conformity pressure will result.

**Stage of group development should drive the system** - Both the human resources specialist and the executive, to say nothing of the dean, are missing an important point when taking their respective actions. If performance appraisal (or student grading) is to be used as a motivational tool, both the nature of the feedback (knowledge of results) provided to individuals and groups and its timing are of critical importance. A team or department in a developmental stage may need lenient and more frequent reviews for reasons of encouragement. Another that is stagnating might need a low set of ratings to shake it out of complacency, or out of a temporary lull. Relatedly, remember the school years when they were typically divided into semesters that each included three six-week grading periods? Many of the better teachers utilized the grade distribution differently in the first, second and third marking periods to influence student motivation, on both an individual and group basis. By starting low and gradually easing the curve they subtly influenced goal setting and were able to feed back signs of progress. Implicitly they recognized that energy mobilization is not constant, and that the length of time required for an activity is important in scheduling incentive administration. Task groups require different performance objectives at different stages of their development.[13]

## IMPLICATIONS FOR MANAGING THROUGH GROUPS

**Teamwork requires encouragement** - Previous chapters illustrate how the ongoing life of a work group reflects a complex and continuous process of mutual accommodation among the members, between the members and the task requirements, and between the group and its larger environment. That is why this book's subject matter refers to "group dynamics:" nothing remains the same for very long. Unfortunately, the social-psychological realities of groups and their members often do not match their employers' emphasis on consistency and control. The organization-wide systems frequently are not geared to the process of getting the right person to do the right thing at the right time, at the work group level. Nor are they geared to the concept of teamwork.

Indeed, there may well be limits on the extent to which motivational principles derived from psychology can be applied in work organizations; *but the full potential for such application has not been reached. Much more experimentation is possible.* For example, in using money as a motivator, organizations could allocate some amount of money for group accomplishments as a supplement to individual accomplishments. Cooperative behavior does not always occur without encouragement. And, money is not necessarily the only reward available in this context. Merchandise and paid vacation trips often are used for this purpose in sales units; why not in other functional units as well? Days off work also could be used as a reward. As it stands now, organizations typically treat vacation time as a fixed quantity or grant it strictly in relation to years of service. Why not allow additional vacation time to be earned based on individual *and group* accomplishments?

Actually, several employers have been experimenting lately with merchandise, trips and time off as rewards. Anything from free TV sets to designer watches and diamond necklaces, to say nothing of trips to Hawaii, have been awarded to employees deemed worthy. Group performance awards also are being made. The symbolic value of these rewards for productivity and ideas has more motivational punch for some people than cash, which is here today and may be spent by tonight. Some recipients, moreover, "show off" their gifts to their families and friends, thereby providing some public relations value to their employers. The merchandise and trips, by the way, reportedly cost employers less than salary adjustments.[14]

**Group feedback is as important as individual feedback** - To capitalize on what is known about groups and team building, and to use group-based reward systems effectively, requires that performance appraisal methodology be tailored to group activities and needs. Managers must provide feedback to the total group, not just to the individual members. Appraisal forms therefore should include significant items dealing with teamwork and group process dimensions that facilitate cooperative goal achievement. Moreover, the typical individual appraisal interview, which is a one-on-one boss and subordinate interaction, will need to be supplemented by group meetings where all the members jointly review the data and discuss their implications, just as professional football teams do when the game films come in for review.

**Words in brief episodes are not enough** - One implication of this and prior chapters is that the dispensing of praise and rebukes, however timely and well-administered the doses may be, does not constitute an adequate motivational strategy. Effective team building and motivation require much more than words.

**Decentralization of the system also is needed** - Finally, improved application of psychology to work group process in organizational settings requires some significant departures from customary administrative approaches. Perhaps the key requirement is for more decentralization than most organizations have ever entertained. The ideas reviewed in this chapter certainly imply, for example, that managers and their work groups will need much more freedom of action than they presently have. While it is true that in the early days of industrialization overly powerful first-line supervisors often abused their subordinates, we live in a different era today. At the very least the first line will need more autonomy; appropriate selection, training and monitoring systems should keep the abuses at a low level. Indeed, as a later chapter reveals in detail, some organizations have tried extreme forms of task group autonomy with great success.

## ENDNOTES

1    In keeping with my limited purpose, the topic of money is not dealt with exhaustively here. For a more thorough exposition see Lawler, E., PAY AND ORGANIZATION DEVELOPMENT, 1983, Reading, MA: Addison-Wesley.

2    Rosen, N., LEADERSHIP CHANGE AND WORK GROUP DYNAMICS, 1969, Ithaca, New York: Cornell University Press, 57.

3    U.S. Department of Labor, Bureau of Labor Statistics, EMPLOYMENT AND EARNINGS Reports.

4    Patchen, M., THE CHOICE OF WAGE COMPARISONS, 1961, Englewood Cliffs, New Jersey: Prentice-Hall, 104-106.

5    Many employers use financial incentives improperly, either from an ethical or psychological viewpoint. For well-written and more thorough expositions of the topic, see Whyte, W. F., "Skinnerian theory in organizations," PSYCHOLOGY TODAY, April 1972, 67+, and Lawler, E., cited above.

6    Steiner, I., GROUP PROCESS AND PRODUCTIVITY, 1972, New York: Academic Press, 161. He proposes a number of interesting hypotheses on the design of reward systems that may interest serious students of group process.

7   Such cases were described on the front pages of the WALL STREET JOURNAL in December, 1970, or January, 1971. THE MIAMI HERALD, on the other hand, reported an Associated Press item from Maryville, Tennessee in 1968; the new owner-president, who was the former manager of the White Star Bus Lines, couldn't afford to give his employees their annual Christmas bonus after investing all his money in purchasing the firm. Therefore, they gave him one; each of the 27 employees volunteered one or more days of free time in 1969! The new owner said he was flabbergasted.

8   I am indebted to Dr. Peter Jackson, an English psychologist, for acquainting me with this case.

9   O'Brien, T., Ithaca JOURNAL, March 3, 1973.

10  Whistler, T. L. and Harper, Shirley F., (Eds.), PERFORMANCE APPRAISAL: RESEARCH AND PRACTICE, 1962, New York: Holt, Rinehart and Winston; King, Patricia, PERFORMANCE PLANNING AND APPRAISAL, 1984, New York: McGraw-Hill; Lefton, R. and others, EFFECTIVE MOTIVATION THROUGH PERFORMANCE APPRAISAL, 1977, New York: Wiley Interscience.

11  Landy, F. J. and Farr, J. L., "Performance rating," PSYCHOLOGICAL BULLETIN, 1980, 87 (1), 72-107.

12  Landy and Farr, cited above, concluded from their extensive review that only about 4% to 8% of the variance in ratings can be explained by format. They suggested a moratorium on format-related research. Amen!

13  See Cameron, Kim and Quinn, R., "Organizational life cycles and the criteria of effectiveness," 1980, unpublished mimeo, Graduate School of Public Affairs, SUNY, Albany, for evidence supporting this position.

14  Miller, Anita and Springen, Karen, "Forget cash, give me the TV," NEWSWEEK, October 31, 1988, 58. See, also, Waldman, S. and Roberts, Betsy, "Grading merit pay," NEWSWEEK, November 14, 1988, 45-46, for a lucid description of compensation gimmics, managerial practices, and performance appraisal deficiencies.

SOME ADDITIONAL LITERATURE FOR THE INTERESTED READER:

-   Feldman, J., "Instrumentation and training for performance appraisal: a perceptual-cognitive viewpoint," RESEARCH IN PERSONNEL AND HUMAN RESOURCE MANAGEMENT, 1986, 4, 45-99.

-   Geber, Beverly, "New carrots for new workers," TRAINING, 1987, 24, (Feb), 80.

-   Heneman, H. III, "Pay satisfaction," RESEARCH IN PERSONNEL AND HUMAN RESOURCE MANAGEMENT, 1985, 3, 115-139.

-   Solomon, Barbara, "When incentives add punch to production-line pay (Steelcase, Inc.)," PERSONNEL, 1985, 62, (Sept), 4-6.

## CHAPTER 9

## TASK ATTRIBUTES, CHALLENGE AND GROUP DEVELOPMENT

One by-product of modern technologies and organization forms is dull, unchallenging, highly repetitive work (even entire careers), not only in the stereotyped automobile factory, but also in insurance company offices, banks, large law offices, hospital business offices and labs, department stores, post offices, and almost any

## LAFF - A - DAY

"Think you can handle it?"

other type of organization where people work for a living. Most have departments that would easily qualify as "paperwork factories." The behavioral science literature, professional management journals, and the popular press are replete with accounts, indictments, and admonishments to "do better." Most of the literature either explicitly or implicitly assumes that the root of this problem lies in certain core elements of advanced industrial technology. These include division of tasks into single components (work simplification), specialization of assignments, repetitiveness, and, often, machine pacing of work. It is further assumed that tasks so characterized are almost universally boring, unchallenging, detrimental to motivation, and even a cause of mental health problems. This chapter examines such matters and certain proposed solutions, and some of their implications for managing groups at work.

## EXAMPLES OF PRESUMABLY MEANINGLESS WORK

Several years ago a psychologist employed by a large, internationally known pharmaceutical company discovered a quality control department where 70 women were employed as inspectors.[1] The women sat on stools visually inspecting, daily, twenty million capsules moving on mechanized conveyor belts. They manually removed any defective capsules, e.g., plastic ends improperly assembled, dents, etc. The psychologist questioned whether this repetitive, dull job was fit for humans to perform, and suggested a project. Could pigeons be trained  to inspect the capsules and remove defective ones by pecking with their beaks on keys that would activate appropriate mechanical equipment?

**Pigeons can do it** - As it happened, the experienced experimental psychologist had no difficulty in training a pigeon to do this job, and to do it well![2] The practical implications of this accomplishment subsequently were discussed by upper echelons of management. It now appeared that a few trained pigeons could replace 70 human inspectors, and without grievances, absenteeism, and psychosomatic disease to boot! (They also would have been far less expensive than today's robots.) The idea was rejected, however, presumably on the grounds that if the consumer public ever found out--as it might, once competitors began spreading the word--sales would suffer; who wants to buy capsules that have been inspected by pigeons? The most significant point of the whole experiment appears to have been lost in the aftermath. At least 70 people in that plant continued to do work that could have been done as well or better by trained pigeons.

**Inspectors get headaches** - Throughout the world of work there are hundreds of thousands of people doing jobs which trained pigeons probably could do, or which can be performed by trained chimpanzees at any rate. Susan Phillips, a tart inspector for the Scribbans Kemp Bakery, which turns out 1.5 million cakes, tarts, and confections daily, provides an English example. According to an Associated Press dispatch in 1967, Susan allegedly had been watching (inspecting) 90,000 tarts per hour for three years on a moving conveyor belt. She complained of headaches. Her case became the trigger for an unauthorized strike of 750 employees when her request for transfer to another department was refused by management.

**Jobs for the mentally retarded** - A classical "meaningless" work case occurred in an upstate New York shirt factory converted to the manufacturing of military uniforms during World War II. Because of a serious wartime labor shortage, the management began an experiment; the company tried out a few young women from a nearby institution for mentally retarded girls. They turned out to be "model" employees as sewing machine operators.[3] This suggests that the jobs involved were more suitable for the mentally retarded than for normally intelligent individuals.

Somewhat more poetic was the claim that prison riots at Durham Jail in England during early 1968 were caused, at least in part, by a "meaning of work" issue. The male prisoners maintained that making shirts was an "effeminate" activity and wanted something else to do. Accounts may be found in the London TIMES in March, 1968.

The mentally retarded women described above were given an unusual opportunity. Instead of wasting away doing really meaningless things in a sheltered environment, they were doing productive work in a factory and contributing to the nation's war effort. For them, this was not only meaningful but also enabled them to take a normal role in a normal employment setting. This raises a disturbing dilemma--for some people simple minded, highly specialized, repetitive tasks are a form of dehumanized hell. For some other people, such tasks offer a ticket to personal freedom, dignity and self-respect, and may even be challenging.

**Some people aren't bored** - Consider the case of a young man discovered through an industrial research study conducted in a large English publishing firm. He held an extraordinarily routine job (chimpanzee level) as the operator of a paper cutting machine. When the management learned from research psychologists that this man had a genius level IQ, the company offered him a promotion to a much more challenging position. He refused, because the eight-hour day on the routine job gave him all the money he needed, plus lots of time to think about his hobby--building small computers in his home at night.[4] The moral of the story is, not all employees want more demanding jobs (although some variety and change of pace probably is welcome to most).

**The evidence is mixed** - Although there has been a consistent human relations theme in the literature for at least three decades, complaining about specialized, simplified and machine-paced work--the research evidence on the motivational implications of such work has been anything but persuasive. One researcher on the basis of interviews with a large number of assembly line workers reported, "...in a clear-cut refutation of the idea that mechanical pacing is inherently distasteful to most workers...about 84% of the sample (interviewed) said that they preferred the belt line... This study...does...raise doubts about the validity of the theory that assembly line workers are repelled by the very nature of their jobs."[5] Another empirical study of assembly line workers produced the following conclusion: "...monotony or boredom did not emerge as an important source of dissatisfaction or frustration among operators in spite of the highly repetitive nature of the work... Apparently it was possible to achieve considerable satisfaction from the job itself while at the same time thinking about many other things." This study found, additionally, that task specialization and the self-perception of expertise that it stimulated *"was a source of pride and satisfaction--not monotony."*[6] (Emphasis mine.)

The two previously cited studies were conducted fifteen or more years ago. A review conducted by one of my advanced graduate students of more than thirty articles (mostly research studies) published in the late 1960s and through 1976 concludes: "While several significant advances in the understanding of the effects of job redesign have occurred in the last few years, many important questions remain unanswered... At the present time everything from work teams (formation of) to participative management to the use of new tools and equipment is lumped under the general heading of job-enrichment... Certainly more...studies must be conducted before we can draw any firm conclusions about job design (as a motivator)."[7] I've read most of the same studies and agree with him.

**Job redesign doesn't always work** - One writer in the 1970s summarized a wide variety of industrial change programs in which organizations, in this instance factories, tried various alternatives to the traditional model of simplification, specialization and assembly flow lines.[8] The author reports several types of action experiments, conducted primarily in England and Europe, as follows:

> *Rearrangement or replacement of assembly line work*; thirty-four cases in which assembly line production systems were substantially modified and often replaced;
>
> *Workers given additional responsibility*; thirteen cases of job redesign where the major intent was to increase responsibilities of individual workers or groups. This strategy includes the addition of inspecting one's own work, completing orders rather than working on only a portion, and similar modest changes;
>
> *Job-rotation*; eight cases where organizations decided to give workers the opportunity to work at more than one discrete job during the course of a day;
>
> *New responsibility for additional and different kinds of work*; five cases where worker jobs were significantly expanded so that more skill was required--e.g., machine maintenance, set-up and tool setting;
>
> *Control of work speed*; several cases in the above four categories also provided the workers with opportunities for greater control over their own work speed; and
>
> *Self-organization*; fourteen cases where workers were released from the usual organizational influence and given either the opportunity to assemble, through group activity, complete product units or were given responsibility for operating a work area, including machines. Planning, problem-solving and job design features also were sometimes left in the worker's domain. [See "autonomous work groups" in Chapter 10.]

Among other things, the reviewer of this work points out, "*A surprising number of job-restructuring exercises were resisted by workers and (therefore) in some cases changes had to be abandoned or modified...*"[9] (Emphasis mine.) Related problems with pay differentials among group members (which disturbed status hierarchies) and wage administration sometimes arose in these change programs, as well. He also noted that the need for supervisors was obviated in many cases and that there also were pronounced reductions in the need for staff and technical support.  It would seem, therefore, that the humanistic job redesign strategy can potentially result in non-humanistic cost-cutting.  Finally and quite significantly, the reviewer reports that in very few cases had changes been evaluated in any detail.

## UNANSWERED, OR PARTIALLY ANSWERED QUESTIONS

The fundamental question remains, what is the motivational potential in job redesign methods?  How important is the "task itself" as contrasted with other motivational factors in the employment setting?  Are the task factors known as work simplification, division of labor, repetitiveness and machine pacing, characteristically found in factories but also found in offices, the only significant ones?  Or, are there other task dimensions of equal or greater importance in building viable teams?  Let us see.

**Boredom is not the only issue** - The Wall Street Journal, in July of 1971, published accounts of several interviews that one of its staff writers conducted with individuals holding what most readers of this book would consider repugnant jobs.  Included, among others, were:

- Elmer Novak, a *coal miner* who does carpentry work 1,000 feet below the earth's surface while standing in water several inches deep and inhaling coal dust every day;

- Alfred Hardy, *an iron foundry worker* who cleans and prepares blast furnaces on the night shift.  His work requires him to crawl in and out of filthy furnaces and exposes him to extreme heat, smoke, and burnt resin residue in the air;

- Manuel Decena, *a hog processor in a meat packing plant* where he butchers a hog every 45 seconds.  He moves around through a mixture of blood, excrement and entrails of butchered hogs, and listens to their screams before they die;

- Leitch Brice, *a token seller in the New York City subway system.*  He works in an underground booth in an unsavory neighborhood station.  Four times in eleven years he has looked down gun barrels during holdups. His booth shakes as trains pass through the station, which is extremely hot in summer and cold in winter. Some people have thrown cherry bombs at his booth; others have tried to spit on him through the window;

- Mr. Trimarchi, *a uniformed patrolman who works in the Queens Midtown Tunnel* in New York. He spends four hours a day in a small glass booth inside the tunnel where he "watches" cars drive by. His function is to use the phone in case an emergency occurs in the tunnel. Automotive exhaust fumes readily leak into his booth;

- Dorothy Mitchell, a widowed, elderly sewing machine operator in a garment factory. She sews about 1,500 linings into 1,500 coats every day; and

- Mr. Conyers, an automobile assembly line worker who was bitter about repetitiveness, boredom, and feeling like just another "number."

## ANALYSIS OF MEANINGLESS WORK INTERVIEWS

The interviews, the full contents of which are quite vivid, reveal that dull, repetitive jobs are not the only problem. Dehumanization also can occur for other reasons:

- Filthy, if not disgusting working conditions
- Foul air
- Idleness
- Extreme noise
- Confinement

- Mistreatment by clients or the public
- Social isolation
- Extreme heat or cold
- Threat to life
- Dampness

Contrary to what we might expect, some of those interviewed expressed pride in what they do, like the income, and remained in these jobs because they offer an escape from poverty. For someone having less than a 12th grade education, coupled with probable lack of skills and heavy family responsibilities, there are few other honest ways for them to make $8,500 to $10,000 per year (in 1971). This applies to Novak the miner, Hardy the foundry worker, and Decena the hog processor.

Having a high school diploma or more education may be a key factor. Conyers, the auto worker, is a high school graduate. By any reasonable objective standards, he had it good compared with Novak, Hardy and Decena. He worked in a modern plant, was covered by a union contract negotiated by one of the nation's more progressive unions, and, according to the original newspaper article, lived in a decent home. However, he was the only one of those four men doing any real complaining. Conyers said, "At first, there's some learning. But once you know how, that's all there is. You can't do any better. You can only be satisfactory." Conyers seems to have a frustrated achievement need.

Mr. Brice, the subway token seller, is a special case:

- He worked in cages--please note that people spit and throw things at caged animals in zoos, too. One wonders who should be inside the cages;

- He was in virtual social isolation from colleagues throughout the work day;

- The New York City subway, as an environment in which to work, would produce fear in almost anybody both in 1971 and now; and

- The organization for which he worked can hardly be considered enlightened.

Brice and Mr. Hardy, the coal miner, have something in common--they both worked underground, and both had occupationally related diseases; Hardy an incipient case of the black lung and Brice anxiety and fear of being killed by a gunman. But Hardy's job required some carpentry knowledge, use of tools *and was recognized by colleagues as important because the wall supports he built in the mine shafts prevented cave-ins.* Brice's job could be performed by a child, or a trained chimpanzee, and is denigrated by much of the public that he serves. Clearly sheer repetitiveness and work simplification are not the issues here. The whole job is senseless--unless you have no alternative way to make an honest living.

Trimarchi worked in cages, too, but only for four hours each day; he also worked outside the tunnel for two hours each day and got one hour on rest break. Despite his complaints, he appeared to have it good compared to all the others:

- Very little physical effort;

- Only four hours of onerous duty per day; and

- His "cage," encased in thick glass, protected him from abusive passersby.

The fumes and temperature extremes were bad, but no worse than what the foundry worker, steel worker and meat packer had to live with, and in their cages for eight or nine hours each day instead of four. And he got over $10,000 per year for this work, which could have been performed by TV cameras;[10] in fact TV cameras have replaced this type of job in many tunnels.

The basic problem in Trimarchi's case is that the work itself seems meaningless, but not because of specialization, work simplification and mechanized mass-production technology. He watched unseeingly and alone as thousands of cars went by each day. He probably didn't have to use the emergency phone more than a few times in a month. At least Conyers, the auto worker, who also watched an endless line of cars each day, was helping to build a useful product. Trimarchi was doing practically nothing--and knew it. But, he and others continue to do it, for the money...

Decena the hog processor enjoyed his job--even though it involved assembly-line technology--even though he was wallowing in blood and guts--even though it stank--and despite the animals' fearful sounds. Some would surmise that Decena was not a well man. I'd say he was a realist making the most of what he had, physical strength and a sixth grade education.

Mrs. Mitchell, the elderly sewing machine operator who learned how from her immigrant mother, is a very special case. She liked what she was doing--and was so good at it that she could maintain a lively conversation all the while with her coworkers. (She processed, on her sewing machine, one coat every one and one-half minutes, on the average.) As a widow, whose children are grown, would she have been better off sitting around someone's house all day? In what way should her job have been enriched?

**Is job enrichment a garbage can issue?** - One other person ought to be mentioned here. Mr. Walter Pavesi once received a $5,000 "Outstanding Service Award" for his accomplishments in the New York City Sanitation Department. When interviewed about his career with the Sanitation Department, which included time on a garbage truck crew, Pavesi said, "In the old days guys would say, 'Hey, who likes to stand in garbage?' But I always saw flowers grow out of that stuff... *I used to tell the guys, 'dig in like you love it.*'"[11] (Emphasis mine.) Mr. Pavesi, who ultimately rose through the ranks and became Chief of Staff for the Sanitation Department, apparently knew how to provide psychological job enrichment.

Examination and comparison of the above jobs and people suggests that the presumed core characteristics of advanced industrialization and technology--work simplification, task specialization, repetitiveness and machine pacing--are neither necessary nor sufficient to produce job dissatisfaction and worker alienation. One must also take into account other factors such as the environment in which the task is performed, the purpose being served by the task, the potential opportunity the task offers for displaying courage, physical strength or toughness, and the background of the person doing the task, because these factors strongly affect how the individual will perceive the job and his or her alternatives. In short, *task challenge is influenced by many possible factors.*

Please understand that I am not advocating the unrestrained use of work simplification carried to ridiculous extremes and the perpetuation of noxious work environments. My message is that the "nature of the task" is in the eye of the beholder, and that effective management requires sensitivity to this fact. There is no need to automate so-called meaningless work out of existence if it is not necessarily meaningless and if it provides support for people who have no realistic options.

## TASK IMPACT ON GROUPS[12]

Thus far I have focused on selected aspects of technology as they relate to human motivation. The emphasis has been on the individual. However, the "nature of the task" also has important implications for groups. Consider, in this regard, what you know about rugby, the English version of football. Rugby players love to wallow around in filth (mud) and derive great pride in being part of a team effort where all one's teammates are exposed to physical harm. (They wear no pads or helmets.) Army paratroop squads thrive on danger, as do special kickoff teams in American professional football. Executive teams in the business world often thrive because of the high financial stakes and other risks involved in their competitive industries. Certain task factors, then, help weld all of these groups together. It is appropriate, therefore, to examine such variables systematically and consider how they apply to the processes of group development, performance, maintenance and renewal. Some of the task variables that influence group life are discussed below.

**Pressure for Accuracy** - This variable can range from low to high. It is affected by the cost of mistakes, opportunities for mistakes to occur, and allowable tolerance levels. Day-to-day accuracy pressures are especially great in work units such as hematology labs in hospitals, and aircraft control towers. Such units offer frequent opportunities for costly mistakes to occur. What's more, they have close tolerance limits; their accuracy pressures come from both employer and various government agencies, and may involve questions of life and death;

**Pressure for Speed** - Work units differ greatly on this variable. In some operations, such as a chaotic printing department constantly bombarded by clients with unrealistic deadlines, time pressures are a way of life. In others, they matter less;

**Decision-Making Autonomy** - This variable has to do with how much range of personal or group decision-making opportunity the members of the work unit have, as determined by the nature and procedure of the task requirements. (How and what to do, and when to do things.) The degree of autonomy normally is determined by the way the task is "engineered" or structured, *and by the manager's "style;"*

**Member Interaction Opportunity** - This variable concerns the degree of opportunity a task allows for individual work unit members to interact and communicate with one another. It is affected by many things--pressure for speed, physical distance between employee work stations, noise level, whether machines require their operators to remain in one spot, telephone coverage requirements, and so on. For example, individual members of high speed assembly line groups are usually isolated from each other and prevented from interacting and talking because of noise, space between work stations, and the amount of attention their equipment requires, especially in the case of mechanized assembly lines;

**Task Significance** - The value placed by the group on its end product or service, which is affected by their managers' views, the views of colleagues in other groups within the organization, and quite possibly the general public;

**External Interaction Opportunity** - Some work groups, because of the nature of their mission, space limitations, geography or other factors, are cut off from opportunities to interact with other groups in their organization. Examples include nuclear submarine crews on a long sea cruise, many regional sales units, and overseas branch offices. All of these are isolated as total units from their parent organizations. Members of a regional sales force may at the same time be isolated from each other as individuals (low internal interaction opportunity).

**Task Complexity** - This refers to the number of possible combinations of operations about which decisions must be made before a given product, process, or service is completed. It incorporates the demand for problem-solving behavior and reduction of the unknown;

**Cycle Length** - Is a function of the number of operations required to complete a given product, process, or service and the time period normally required;

**Cycle Regularity** - Refers to the repeated routine or repetitiveness of the operations employed. Are they repeated time after time with no variation, or are changes encountered?; and

**Interdependence requirements** - the extent to which the nature of the task requires each group member to carry out his specialized assignments at specific times and to coordinate his actions with other team members, in sequence.

The by-product of all these task variables is a motivational phenomenon I call task challenge. Challenge in task refers to the motivating potential inherent in performing the group's function; in brief, it is a hypothetical measure of the group's *shared sense of achievement and excitement* in performing its job. This sense of achievement and excitement grows out of the group process through which the combined task characteristics described above are translated into a willingness to act in concert with other group members. That process is described in earlier chapters where conformity and consensus dynamics are discussed.

The degree of challenge generated by the combination of task characteristics in different groups varies from group to group and from time to time. Also it has a direct bearing on group viability. Thus the greater the challenge involved (as experienced by the group members), the more closely the members should work together, the more they should identify with the group and set themselves apart from less exciting groups, and so on. It's like pitting space exploration against processing expense account reports; the sheer excitement of the one task will draw the group members together.

## THE INFLUENCE OF TIME ON
## THE NATURE OF A GROUP'S TASK - A MODEL

**Some likely relationships** - Let us turn now to Figure 6, which illustrates the inter-relationships of the above and other variables. It also shows how they are linked to group viability. I have already defined several of the variables in the diagram. Most of the others are self-explanatory.[13]

The Time Filter that encompasses "Mental Concentration Requirements" and "Member Interaction Opportunity" in the upper portion of the diagram represents the likely impact of time, learning, and practice on how these variables operate. For example, speed pressure may create a strong need for mental concentration early in a group's history. But, over a period of time the members may well gain skill and become impervious to speed requirements - they adapt to them - in which case they may be able to relax more often, concentrate less intensively on the task, and interact with one another more, like Mrs. Mitchell, the sewing machine operator. Time can have a similar effect on several other variables in the upper portion of the diagram as the group develops skill, and either learns to adapt or else finds ways to circumvent the obstacles, thus increasing their interaction opportunities.

The Time Filter in the lower portion of the diagram affects several task characteristics that impact "Challenge." For example, as a group starts up operations, its members may accept inadequate tools and equipment as part of their challenge in getting the job done. In time, however, if such inadequate tools and equipment

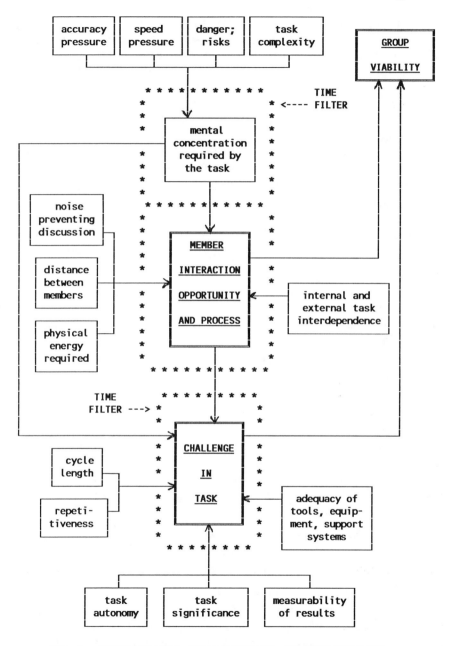

FIG. 6.   NATURE OF TASK, GROUP VIABILITY, AND TASK CHALLENGE
AS INFLUENCED BY THE PASSAGE OF TIME:  A MODEL
(Adapted from Rosen, N., SUPERVISION: A BEHAVIORAL VIEW,
Columbus, Ohio; Grid, Inc., 1973, with modifications.)

are not upgraded, they are likely to begin questioning "management's" motives and abilities; the inadequate tools and equipment will no longer be perceived as a challenge but rather as an unnecessary liability. To maintain the challenge level, such tools and equipment will have to be replaced with better ones. This can be overdone, however; if the new tools and equipment are too good, they may change the nature of the job, making it too easy and reducing the challenge inherent in the task unless new goals are set. One wonders, for example, whether challenge and group viability are lost when a highly effective work group (let's say a university faculty I once knew) moves out of dismal, uncomfortable quarters into a spanking new modern facility including all the comforts of home. In such instances there may be a tendency to perceive these new comforts as well-deserved perquisites earned by *past* performance. This "well-deserved" perception can then lull a group into some amount of complacency.

**Figure 6 suggests several hypothetical statements.** First, the greater the <u>noise</u> <u>level</u> surrounding the task and the greater the physical distances between work stations in a group, the less opportunity for members to interact, until such time as they develop sign language or acquire signalling devices, develop message delivery systems through outsiders, or learn to schedule their "break time" appropriately.

Second, the greater the task demands for the expenditure of sheer physical effort, the fewer the opportunities for members to interact with each other. This probably is an escalating relationship which will not appear unless conditions are extreme. Moreover, it, too, is modified by time because people and groups may raise their adaptation level and get accustomed to the high energy requirement.

Third, the greater the level of *mental concentration* required by the task, the less opportunity for interpersonal interaction among members, although time and adaptation should weaken this relationship also;

Fourth, the greater the task demands for *interdependence* (i.e., sequenced collaboration), the more opportunity for interaction among members. Time may modify this relationship, too. Of course, if personalities clash, high task interdependence can produce lots of friction and the group's process will probably suffer; and

Fifth, high *accuracy and speed pressures* in the task play complicated roles which may cancel each other out. On the one hand, they increase requirements for mental concentration which in turn decrease opportunity for interaction. This, in turn, depresses group viability. On the other hand, a combination of accuracy, speed, danger, task complexity and mental concentration requirements also has an impact on the challenge in the task. The right amount of such pressures will enhance the challenge; too little will detract from it, while too much will discourage the group. Observation of professional football teams and crowd behavior in the final two minutes of close games will illustrate these relationships.

**The inverted "U" again** - Several variables in the diagram bear what is probably an "inverted U" relationship to the challenge dimension.[14] That is, up to a point, increases in these variables will lead to increases in task challenge. Beyond that point further increases will become overwhelming; task challenge will give way to discouragement. This is probably true for physical energy required, cycle length, cycle regularity, task complexity, technological autonomy, and even interdependence. For example, up to a point, increasing interdependence among group members will add to the challenge of performing a task. If you don't believe it, watch what happens to most serious music students when they are put into a band or an orchestra and told to get ready for a group concert as compared to solo performances. A similar phenomenon occurs when two tennis players accustomed to playing singles combine to play doubles as a team. Beyond some theoretical breaking point, however, I believe that too much interdependence will backfire in larger groups because the members won't be able to handle such close, carefully timed relationships on a sustained basis, and the task will lose its appeal. Interdependence in smaller groups also can be a problem if some of the members lack needed skill.

Finally, *all of these relationships will be affected by the passage of time.* Early in a group's formative stages technological autonomy for the members may be unnecessary if the challenge level is high for other reasons. However, as the group gains skill at working together and acquires task experience over time, it may learn to cope so well that the task will lose some of its challenge. At this point it may be necessary to grant the group increased autonomy, replace some of its members, or change some aspect of the task. Similar arguments can be made about the other relationships shown in the lower portion of Figure 6.

"Task significance" is a dimension worth special attention - The remarkable appeal to people of all ages of Peace Corps service several years ago should not be overlooked. There is still a vast, relatively untapped reservoir of potential energy lying within the American public. Making miles and miles of plastic tubing each day, pouring concrete, excavating building sites, processing claims forms, painting one car after another, or checking passengers in at airline airport desks are activities not seen as having great social or historical significance. People do these jobs, usually without a great deal of enthusiasm. Yes, motivational techniques discussed earlier can liven things up. But the people who do such jobs are among those who *spontaneously invest enormous energy, around the clock*, to help rescue infants who have fallen into wells, help save beached whales, clean sea birds damaged by oil slicks, and to assist people victimized by natural disasters. Employers and industrial psychologists might consider, therefore, how low task significance on the job may be compensated for by involving employees in corporate community relations programs. (See my discussion of "Model T" in Chapter Eleven.)

## SOME IMPLICATIONS FOR MANAGERS

Task impact varies over time - The developmental stage of any given group encompasses task variables which influence challenge and group viability. The importance of the task dimensions varies over time. Fig. 6 reveals several "buttons" that a manager can push to create or re-create some excitement, or at least reduce boredom. A manager, in many situations, can influence mental concentration requirements, member interaction opportunity, and task challenge by direct actions and through the use of persuasive skills. In those cases where fixed technologies permit little freedom to act on these variables, other organizational solutions must be found. These include such tactics as the use of relief personnel to reduce energy requirements, organizing parties and other social activities to enhance member interaction, experimenting with group performance quotas, providing uniforms and special recognition awards to foster individual identification with the group's mission, holding periodic group meetings or "retreats," and so on. Ways also must be found to persuade the members of the importance of the group's contribution to the overall organization's mission. *The manager is the key to making these things happen.*

**Challenge is multi-faceted** - If the several relationships proposed above are real, it follows that job enrichment, job enlargement, and job rotation are only a limited sub-set of motivational tools that can impact task challenge.  There are many other variables that can be operated upon to produce similar results, although in the process one must seek to maintain group cohesion.  It is altogether feasible, as was pointed out in Chapter One (the Indian textile mill experiment), that a group of individuals will be interested in and challenged by an interdependent, specialized assembly operation where each worker contributes a small, even though simple, part of the total group product if the group is well organized, and appropriately rewarded and led.  Some job redesign strategies might destroy such a group.

Group cohesion has been identified in this book as the central variable around which other facets of group life revolve.  Cohesion in groups represents a developmental process that can be encouraged or discouraged and changes over time.  Most groups begin as collections; to become viable teams that will effectively pursue organizational goals, they must be as carefully tended as an Englishman's rose garden.  Most viable groups don't "just happen."

**Time leads to change** - The degree of challenge in the group's task and operating conditions is a major influence on the development and maintenance of group cohesion.  However, time also influences this relationship.  What begins as a challenging assignment may later become dull and routine as a group develops skill and experience.  Conversely, what begins as uninteresting drudgery may evolve into a challenging group task once the members learn what to do and start receiving rewards.  Changes will be necessary to maintain the excitement; otherwise the group may deteriorate.

**Task redesign is not the only answer** - Because of these relationships, reliance upon typical job enrichment, job enlargement, and job rotation strategies is too limited a strategy for achieving long-range impact on task challenge.  Many variables other than task variables are potentially useful.

For example, goal-setting can affect challenge and group cohesion, and participation in goal setting is likely to increase the motivation of members to work for the attainment of group goals.

Knowledge of task results and planned intergroup competition also have been discussed previously as major potential influences on motivation. They also influence task challenge and cohesion. Moreover, task success or failure influence work group cohesion just as they influence individual self-confidence, job satisfaction, and desire to stay on the job. Given what we know about knowledge of results, such relationships are likely to be strongest in those circumstances where there are clearly observable performance standards against which groups can compare themselves over time.

In brief, task variables combine with a variety of reward system variables and with the different needs of individuals. In combination these variables influence the mobilization of effort.

**The manager must help shape perceptions** - The process by which task and reward system factors combine with the different needs of individuals is influenced by the internal pressures of group dynamics that produce shared perceptions, attitudes, and standards, as described in earlier chapters. *A major part of any manager's job is to influence how these factors combine, and build and maintain consensus around the entire process.* To repeat, the ongoing life of a work group reflects a complex and continuous process of mutual accommodation among the members (who change), between the members and task requirements (which also change), and between the group and its changing external environment. Static reward systems and over-reliance on traditional ways of doing things will not produce optimal results. To be an effective team leader, a manager must be responsive to the needs for change and command an arsenal of techniques that can be brought to bear as needed.

With such an arsenal in mind, I have included, as Appendix A in this book, a potentially useful tool for managers and other group leaders. It is called "The Group Effectiveness Inventory." This is a fairly short, extensively used questionnaire from which a leader and work group can derive benefit. Read it through, and ask yourself how you think most of your group members would answer the questions. Then, make copies of it and ask your subordinates or colleagues to fill it out and return it to you anonymously. I'll guarantee that you will "get an education" in the process.

ENDNOTES

1    Verhave, T., "The pigeon as quality control inspector," AMERICAN PSYCHOLOGIST, February 1966, 109-115.

2    See Mednick, S., LEARNING, 1964, Englewood Cliffs, NJ: Prentice-Hall, Chapter 3, for an understandable explanation of how this is done.

3    Brennan, M., THE MAKING OF A MORON, 1953, New York: Sheed and Ward, 13-18. Discussed in Argyris, C., PERSONALITY AND ORGANIZATION, 1957, New York: Harper and Bros., 67.

4    My thanks to N. Georgiades, an English psychologist who was involved with the project, for telling me of this incident.

5    Killbridge, M. D., "Do workers prefer larger jobs?" PERSONNEL, 1960, 37, 45-48.

6    Turner, A. N. and Miclette, A. L., "Sources of satisfaction in repetitive work," OCCUPATIONAL PSYCHOLOGY, 1962, 36, 215-231.

7    Tucker, C. E., "Job design," Unpublished mimeo, 1976, OB Department, New York School of Industrial and Labor Relations, Cornell University. See also, Hulin, C. and Blood, M., "Job enlargement, individual differences and worker responses, "PSYCHOLOGICAL BULLETIN, 1968, 69, 41-55.

8    Wild, R., WORK ORGANIZATION, A STUDY OF MANUAL WORK AND MASS PRODUCTION, 1975, London: John Wiley & Sons.

9    Wild, R., cited above, 68.

10    It is already clear that the routine, repetitive jobs performed in many employment settings can readily be replaced entirely by modern technology. Slot machines, TV monitoring devices and change-making machines are becoming commonplace. Industrial robots also are becoming an integral part of industry. Ridgely Hunt of the Chicago TRIBUNE Service wrote an article in 1975 on robots, which are used primarily for materials handling and simple repetitive tasks. He described them as basically stupid, but they can "...do a lot of dirty, dangerous and degrading jobs. Undeterred by heat, dust, or noxious fumes, they can seize red-hot parts and...remember more than 1000 instructions." He further states that they don't come to work tired or drunk, they don't get sick or quit (an overstatement as they will break down once in a while--NR) and they never go on strike or demand a raise. (They also are immune to boredom--NR) See, Albus, J. S. and Evans, J. M., Jr., "Robot systems," SCIENTIFIC AMERICAN, February 1976, 77-86 for a serious discussion of robots. Further updates on robots appear in TIME MAGAZINE, December 8, 1980, 72-83, and in NEWSWEEK, April 23, 1979, 80-81. See also, FORTUNE, December 17, 1979.

11    Sanitation Department Outstanding Service Award article, NY TIMES, sometime during the period 9/74-6/75...

12    The following section represents an elaboration of a basic model I proposed several years ago. See Rosen, N., SUPERVISION: A BEHAVIORAL VIEW, 1973, Columbus, Ohio: Grid, Inc., 159-166.

13    Both the Figure itself and the hypothetical statements offered here reflect a combination of my interpretation of the behavioral science literature and my direct observations of hundreds of task groups in action. The nature of the relationships

is not yet supported in all cases by acceptable research evidence. Some of the variables may carry different labels in other publications, and the choice of "group viability" as the critical dependent variable is mine. Other professionals, research, and practical application will have to tell us whether these "models" are substantially correct. Hackman, R. and Oldham, G., "Motivation through the design of work: test of a theory," JOURNAL OF ORGANIZATIONAL BEHAVIOR AND HUMAN PERFORMANCE, 1976, (16), 250-279, offer another model which includes some of the same concepts used here. While their purpose differs from mine, the reader interested in a fuller perspective on job characteristics and work motivation will find their article to be worthwhile. See also, Pierce, J. L. and Dunham, R. B., "Task design: a literature review," ACADEMY OF MANAGEMENT REVIEW, October 1976, 83-97.

14    Some professionals might object to my positing these relationships as curvilinear. Most of us work with linear models and tend to find linear relationships in our studies. Linearity in the case of these variables, however, does not make sense to me and when observed probably is explained by range restriction resulting from cross-sectional research limitations.

SOME ADDITIONAL LITERATURE FOR THE INTERESTED READER:

-    Campion, M. and Thayer, P., "Job design: approaches, outcomes, and trade-offs," ORGANIZATIONAL DYNAMICS, 1987, 15 (3), 66-79.

-    Hackman, R., GROUPS THAT WORK, In Press, San Francisco: Jossey-Bass.

# CHAPTER 10

## PARTICIPATION IN DECISION MAKING (PDM): HOW AND WHY IT WORKS, AND SOME CAVEATS

While behavioral scientists have long advocated heavier reliance on worker participation in organizational governance, pressures in this direction have accelerated in recent years. Universities, schools, corporations, government agencies and the armed forces have experienced substantial rank and file pressure for a greater say in how the organization should be operated. The use of Quality Circles and similar organizational change programs - including productivity improvement and customer focus programs - in U.S. organizations is a response to this pressure.[1] Even trade unions have been confronted by the same internal pressure; many of them have had their members reject contracts negotiated in their behalf by their elected leaders.

### PDM AS A GROUP PROCESS LUBRICANT

As indicated in Chapter 6, there are three major categories of frustration sources for most employed people:

- The continual need to balance and make tradeoffs between the employer's requirements and the employees' needs in their private off-the-job lives;

- The task and its immediate context; and

- The larger organization, including its rules, regulations, and control mechanisms.

Much frustration emanating from these sources can be greatly relieved through the application of participative management techniques. The implicit assumption is that self-government reduces friction, encourages people to act as responsible adults and therefore enhances motivation, i.e., energy mobilization.

Grass-roots participation moves decision making closer to the people directly involved and who are the most knowledgeable. In this sense, it has advantages analogous to those involved in decentralization of an organization, or in reducing the number of management levels. This potentially enhances the quality of planning and reduces the chances that important variables will be ignored. *When applied to task groups, properly managed participation can reduce productivity losses from faulty group process.*

**Many impressive claims have been made** about the value of participation in various organizational settings. The empirical evidence supporting the claims, aside from laboratory studies in university settings, is less persuasive. Nonetheless, there is support. I examine some of that evidence later in this chapter before drawing conclusions regarding the potential for industrial democracy.

The following is a list of potential benefits flowing from participation in decision-making (PDM); the list summarizes both supported and unsupported claims in the literature:

- Improved productivity and quality of performance;

- Development of human resources;

- Greater commitment to organization and group goals, and improved team spirit, cooperation and teamwork;

- Increased group cohesion;

- Reduced turnover and absenteeism;

- More widespread knowledge of goals among employees;

- Higher level goals;

- More widespread knowledge of own and others' job responsibilities;

- Eased adaptation to change- technological and others;

- Better quality decisions;

- Improved fit between work demands and conflicting demands in private life;

- Reduced conflict between units of an organization.

- Higher job satisfaction

## SOME DESCRIPTIVE DIMENSIONS OF PDM

There are three major dimensions of the participation topic that are explored in the following pages:

- The extent to which employee participation arrangements are formalized;

- The "area of freedom" permitted the participants regarding topics and decisions; and

- The motivational processes involved, including such matters as goal setting and team building factors.

**The extent or range of formalized PDM arrangements** in an organization can be conceived as lying on a scale. At the low end of the formalization scale we have casual arrangements such as unplanned, sporadic discussion and consultation among managers, technicians and workers. Moving up the formalization scale we next find temporary task forces, committees and "quality circles." Then we find autonomous work groups, e.g., departments, largely responsible for their own segment of organizational activities. Still higher on the formalization scale are unions, collective bargaining, and labor-management committees. Near the extremely formal end of the continuum are worker councils and junior boards of directors. Participation can occur in all of these forms.

**The "area of freedom" permitted the participants** is a separate dimension, not necessarily related to formalization. It refers to the scope or extent of power, normally reserved exclusively for management, that is made available for rank-and-file sharing.[2] A restricted area of freedom encompasses such benign agenda items as vacation scheduling, location of soft-drink machines, and other cosmetic matters. As the area of freedom expands the participants acquire influence over safety and health problems and then move beyond to task-related agenda items--who should do what and when, procedural modification, and reward system considerations. A fully expanded area of freedom involves worker participation in significant decisions about major resources, on an overall organizational basis and reflecting large monetary considerations, e.g., whether to build a new factory or buy out a competitor.

This participation dimension is separable from formalization. For example, a highly formalized worker council or junior board of directors may have a narrow area of freedom--and be restricted by and large to cosmetic or benign agenda items. The same often is true of union locals. Alternatively, a very informal discussion and consultation based arrangement can get into very broad areas of freedom and deal with highly significant, valuable resources. One wonders if there is such a thing as an optimal combination of these dimensions.

Readers wishing to pursue the formal institutional aspects of PDM, such as joint labor-management productivity committees, are referred to a publication that includes numerous citations.[3] My own reading of the literature dealing with these formal bodies suggests that as participation mechanisms, they don't work effectively because they deal with agenda items that are too far removed from the employees' world of relevance and knowledge. That is why I have chosen to emphasize in the following pages other approaches to participation, with special emphasis on motivational processes.

## PARTICIPATION IN GOAL SETTING-- RESEARCH RESULTS

Many professionals and managers believe that participation in goal setting logically should increase the motivation of members to work for the attainment of group goals. When members share in goal formation, group goals are more likely to reflect their individual motives. Consequently, a better understanding of individual behaviors and group actions required for goal attainment and greater acceptance of the goal are likely to be fostered. Considerable experimental laboratory research supports this view.

On the other hand, classical organization theory and traditional management philosophy stipulate that goals are to be set by the organization and its managers; subordinates are then expected to strive for them in return for their pay. Some research studies conducted in organizational settings have compared <u>participative</u> goal setting effectiveness with <u>assigned</u> goal setting effectiveness. Reviewers of this work concluded that the results are not consistent. They point out that although most of the studies found some evidence supporting participative goal setting, *"a significant difference is found only under certain conditions or with certain types of employees."*[4] (Emphasis mine.)

<u>The key finding</u> is that the effects of employee participation in goal setting depend upon the conditions under which it is done, and the types of personnel involved. History also plays a part; *if employees have observed that the goals they have helped set in the past have not been acted upon by their managers, they are unlikely to work vigorously toward goals set in the future despite their own participation.*

## SELF-MANAGED WORK GROUPS

My earlier discussion of job redesign indicated that many organizations, especially in Europe and England, have attempted job redesign by developing so-called "autonomous work groups." The autonomous work group model combines job redesign with participation in decision-making. As a motivational model, then, it bridges the previous chapter with this one. Let us review some of the popularized accounts of experiments with this model before examining it more conceptually.

**The Scandinavian experience** - The NEW YORK TIMES, on November 11, 1974, reported an experiment under the headline, "Work Democracy Tested at Scandinavian Plants." Through a series of meetings, about half of the Norwegian Hunsfos Paper Mill's 1,000 employees became part of an experiment with so-called autonomous work groups. These groups were more or less given permission to change the traditional ways of doing things in their hierarchal organization. The group members learned each other's jobs, engaged in goal-setting, decided themselves how to rotate among the various jobs, set their own vacation schedules, made their own arrangements for raw material supply, and assumed responsibility for quality control in their groups. *They were given training to facilitate these changes, and the pay system was revised to reflect their new skills.* In some groups the members also voted to eliminate the job of foreman - self-management being the result.

The president of the company reported that production rose during the experiment, but interpreted the results cautiously because better equipment had also been installed during the same time period. The president also estimated that labor turnover had been cut in half. The union's chief shop steward reported greater friendship and increased job involvement among the workers.

The same article also described a similar experiment in a Norwegian maritime shipping company. An experimental ship was set up *in which traditional hierarchy was replaced by an autonomous work group strategy.* The TIMES explained that everyone ate together and went for training to the same classrooms [status levelling--NR]. Crew members also learned about all parts of the ship and one another's jobs. The whole crew rotated work assignments, including the dirtiest jobs. All of this represents a really major departure from traditional practice on board ships. Other, similar experiments have been conducted on a large scale by Volvo, a well-known Swedish auto maker.[5] Their reported results are consistent with others. (Both projects were guided by trained behavioral scientists.)

**Some experience in the USA** - An American experiment along the above lines was described in an AP article printed by the ITHACA JOURNAL on June 15, 1976. In this case a new Alcoa plant was set up on the basis of "self-government." *It had no foremen, no unions and was run by worker "teams" who decided what had to be done and did it.* The teams had seven to twelve members, internally assigned work to their members and even "dealt with personality problems, right down to hiring and firing, all on company time." One of the plant's managers reported that over a period of time some of the workers' decisions were worse than his would have been and some were better; "On balance," he said, "the result is about the same." The reader should note that the 280 workers in this new plant were selected from among 5,000 applicants. The plant personnel man told the AP reporter that only those applicants willing to rotate assignments, doing both skilled and menial work, were hired. "We were looking for people who would feel comfortable in an unstructured situation in small groups," he said. "We turned down highly skilled electricians, with 30 years' experience, who weren't interested in learning to be mechanics."

BUSINESS WEEK reported still another such experiment on June 20, 1973. According to this account, Non-Linear Systems, Inc., of California, tried to increase productivity and reduce worker discontent by giving the worker more of a say in how to run his job. Among other things, the company eliminated assembly lines and the traditionally disliked requirement of punching a time clock upon arrival and departure each day. The assembly lines were replaced by independent production units or teams, each comprised of six or seven workers. *Each team was free to organize itself in the way it considered best* to produce electrical measuring instruments. Decision-making powers at lower levels were increased--all departments assumed more autonomy and kept their own financial records. For "some time" (almost five years) remarkable changes developed. Production reportedly jumped 30%, workers increased their skills, the job of quality control inspector was eliminated, and customer complaints on quality dropped by 70%.

**Interpretation is unclear** - In examining the above popularized accounts of selected "participation in decision making" experiments in industry, all of which have at their core the autonomous work group concept, the attentive reader probably has noted that the experimental treatments are loosely defined. In other words, there is much more going on than simply increased decision making by workers. These articles also mention job enlargement or enrichment, job rotation, special training, increased pay or otherwise changed pay systems, goal setting, removal of time clocks, member replacements, leveling of status distinctions, decentralization of authority, removal of quality control inspectors, and even removal of the formal leader known as the foreman. All of these changes make it impossible to interpret the results--which change was responsible for what outcomes? Was it participation that produced favorable consequences, or something else? The scientifically oriented psychologist experiences great discomfort when dealing with such literature. However, managers who want to accomplish something may very well conclude, I think reasonably, that participation and autonomous groups are worth trying.

**Some things come out in the wash** - One of the best studies of an autonomous work group variation was conducted in a hospital laundry.[6] Participation was carefully introduced, with the full cooperation of the foreman and his superiors. The foreman, *who received training prior to the experiment*, abandoned his traditional leadership style and agreed to be a participative facilitator who would lead discussions and encourage the laundry workers to propose agenda items and seek group solutions. He also kept detailed notes throughout the experiment.

The foreman's notes indicate that 28 meetings were held in the first 15 months. The meetings averaged 30-40 minutes each. One hundred and forty-seven (147) employee suggestions were discussed in these meetings; innumerable others were discussed informally on the laundry floor between meetings. The 147 suggestions were content analyzed and counted by the researchers, as follows:

90 suggestions--work-flow-process and methods

44 suggestions--minor equipment modifications

11 suggestions--hours of work and working conditions

2 suggestions--safety

The great majority of these employee suggestions were aimed at work methods and equipment--one gets the impression that the experience led the laundry workers to think like engineers and efficiency experts!

According to the researchers, who present quantitative supporting data, productivity increased, attitudes improved and absence declined markedly. Control groups were used for comparison purposes, as were prior data on the laundry itself.

**Interpretation again is not clean** - Refreshingly, and to their credit, the authors point out that their experiment does not necessarily *prove* the value of participation in decision making. Possibly the technological and procedural changes that arose from the group discussion process would have produced comparable results had they been introduced through more conventional methods.

I think the key to their entire success experience is the first action taken as a result of the first group meeting, that is, to change the laundry's scheduled work hours; they proposed to come to work two hours earlier each day and leave two hours earlier. *The hospital administration, by permitting this change, legitimated and reinforced the participation strategy.*

Indeed, the changed work schedule itself could have been the sole cause of the subsequent improved attitudes, attendance record and performance! This schedule change, in other words, may have made it much easier for the workers to reconcile their private, off-duty life requirements with their employer's needs, thus increasing their energy potential.

Or, by starting two hours earlier each day, the laundry workers may have made it possible to "get ahead" of the demands placed on them for clean uniforms and linens by the rest of the organization. Such a head-start each day would relieve pressure and conflict, and greatly improve the quality of their work life. It is also possible that the "innumerable" ideas that came up on the laundry floor, during regular work hours and between group meetings, produced the favorable outcomes.

The reader can decide how to interpret such findings. My personal belief is that "autonomous work group" methods have demonstrable value and considerable justification from research evidence, although the evidence is not as tight as we would like.

## WHY SELF-MANAGEMENT SEEMS TO WORK

While many laboratory experiments and probably all longitudinal field experiments provide equivocal results regarding what causes what, the group discussion and decision-making process underlying the autonomous work group strategy has considerable support from empirical evidence. This evidence has come from studies of goal setting, group problem solving, attitude change, performance appraisal interviews, and other related processes.

The question common to all these applications of human interaction seems to be, what makes the process work? A complete review of this body of research is beyond the scope of this book, but a few major points derived from it are in order. The following summary is based primarily on group research, which reflects the emphasis in the literature.[7]

First, the *significance of the agenda and related decisions for the people involved* in the participative process appears to be a major (if not the major) factor in the success of group discussion and decision methods. This refers to the "area of freedom" dimension discussed earlier; *narrow or broad by outsiders' standards, the agenda must be viewed as legitimate and significant by the participants.* This probably explains why "autonomous groups" and "Quality Circles" seem to work out well in many organizations, at least in the short run. In these cases participation focuses on the immediate task level, where the group members have relevant knowledge and skills, and probably higher motivation because of the agenda's personal relevance.[8]

Second, the sheer fact of participating, *actually being asked to help, rewards ego needs and gives many people a sense of importance.* The process, in other words, arouses latent energy potential.

Third, decisions reached through group methods are group products. As such, they are "bigger" than the individuals involved, and often *give the participants the feeling of contributing to a team effort,* thereby producing pride and a sense of accomplishment. In other words, despite the fact that they may be doing fractionated, simplified, repetitive or menial work, individuals who identify with a group can and do personally experience the feelings of task control and accomplishment as an outgrowth of the behavior and accomplishments of their peers and the group as a whole. The autonomy need can be satisfied at the group as well as at the individual level.

Fourth, the group discussion/decision process *sensitizes the participants to the emerging norm or consensus.* That clarity makes the norm meaningful to them. And, if the process requires a decision, rather than simply discussion and consultation, *members have to sharpen their individual thinking and develop their own level of commitment on the issues.* The evidence suggests that group discussion/decision making pushes people in this direction.

Fifth, *the decision process, when ended by requiring a public commitment from the participants, binds the group together* and can have lasting effects on the members' subsequent behavior. For example, dock workers in England raise their hands following discussion meetings, to show their commitment to the outcome. Japanese workers have a "lingi" for this purpose. Some evidence suggests that effective results of participation are more likely if the participants perceive a high level of group agreement on the decision reached. However, public commitment tactics, such as hand raising, conceivably can backfire if called for prematurely.

Sixth, effective, long-lasting results are more likely when the discussion and decision process produces *a clearly stated action plan.*

Finally, there is some evidence, largely based upon creative laboratory experiments, that groups comprised of dissimilar members produce better quality decisions than do more homogeneous groups.[9] *The same line of experimentation also supports the need for group leader training to produce skills necessary to make the discussion and decision process work.*

## UNRESOLVED ISSUES

There appear to be at least two unresolved issues connected to the research evidence. First, *it is not yet clear whether the process can work as effectively or consistently in a typical, hierarchal setting as it does in a peer-group setting.* For example, the presence of a supervisor or manager having higher status than the members may inhibit the process. (See next section on Quality Circles.) There is evidence suggesting this can be overcome through leader training, but it must be remembered that most of the literature supporting group decision making is based on a peer group experimental model. It may be significant, in this connection, that in the Norwegian autonomous work group experiment described earlier, the workers voted to eliminate the job of foreman. One reason for this decision could have been a desire to remove a status distinction problem that was inhibiting their group process.

The <u>second</u> unresolved issue is *whether group discussion and decision making methods are even necessary.* There is limited evidence suggesting that people can be brought to a decision point by other methods, and if they also have reason to believe that their position is supported by others, the necessary subsequent actions can occur.[10] Theoretically, then, it may be possible to achieve consensus and group support through a non-coercive, one-on-one discussion process that includes both consultation and persuasion, rather than through group meetings. Not only can managers utilize individual consultation but they can also delegate this activity to a subordinate or two. Information, attitudes, preferences and advice can be obtained during coffee breaks, over the phone, at work stations without disrupting work flow, after hours and so on. This process need not necessarily be undemocratic.

**Is there enough time?** - The one-on-one strategy is much more prevalent in organizational life than one might think, and group meetings often are too time consuming and disruptive of work activities to be of long-term appeal as a strategy. The Vice President of Hunsfos, the Norwegian paper mill, for example, mentioned that in a single year approximately 300 meetings were necessary in their experiment with worker participation. He said, "You can't keep having 300 meetings on this thing every year."[11] In other words, democracy is time consuming, and time is not an elastic resource in most organizations.

My own professional experience as a "coach" for a number of temporary problem-solving task-forces and other management teams in several organizations has clearly shown me the practical limits of participative group discussion/decision methods on a long-term basis. Patients' needs, machinery processes, and client demands do not cease whenever a work group wants them to. Group discussion and decision making time requirements, in my judgment, can't be imposed in on-going organizations except on an occasional basis or in training sessions when the trainees' jobs are covered by someone else. There is no question in my mind, however, that these participative methods, when properly used, can be highly effective. The potential benefits, though, must be weighed against the time requirements. *More than likely the group meeting strategy improves the prospects for productive one-on-one consultation between meetings, such as occurred in the hospital laundry experiment. It also sets the stage for trust in further one-on-one consultations.*

## RESISTANCE TO PARTICIPATION

Many people seem to believe that resistance to employee participation in decision making stems primarily from reluctant, obstinate, or autocratic managers.  While it is true that those who occupy powerful positions in any organization (corporation, trade union, university, or hospital, for example) tend to protect their prerogatives, *managers are by no means the only obstacles to the application of democratic methods in the work place.*

**Experience outside the USA** - Several writers, for example, have indicated that the rank and file itself can be reluctant to get involved.  Thus, it has been reported that the Israelis have tried, unsuccessfully, trade union ownership of the enterprise, worker representation on boards, and joint production committees. Despite the participation, the old problems of output restriction and apathy remained.  Even extensive training of foremen and workers failed to arouse employee interest in participation. (Similar phenomena have been observed in the case of Yugoslavian worker councils.)  According to one observer of the Israeli scene, workers are capable of making some useful technical contributions based on their work experience, but this is most likely to occur at the department or shop level.[12]

**Some experience in the USA** - Studies in the USA remind us once again that the relevance of the agenda to the participants' needs and backgrounds has overriding motivational importance. High level agenda items dealing with overall organizational planning, administration and finance, are unlikely to interest most rank and file employees.  Research on student participation in university administration supports this view.  Survey data from three college campuses show that "students want to participate in those matters that most affect the individual student personally and directly; intellectual programs, off-campus housing, class cut policy, library policy, vacation policy, safety...."[13]  Two others after reviewing some relevant industrial research conclude, *"It is...our contention that for participation to be successful it must occur at a level, and in decisions, where individuals are willing, feel the need, and are able to participate."*[14]  (Emphasis mine.)  In brief, employee reluctance to participate can sometimes be explained by the fact that the wrong agenda and the wrong forum are proposed.  Of course, there are other reasons, too, which are discussed below.

**Key occupational groups can be obstructionists** - There also are non-managerial personnel in most organizations who resist participation by other organization members because they already have gained considerable power and influence for themselves which they don't wish to share. For example, one research team identified in factories "certain machine maintenance personnel" who are "experts in their own right, are regarded as 'different' and of high status both by their colleagues and management, and hold a critical position in the manufacturing process of industry."[15] In my experience, every organization has such a high status group somewhere. It usually is comprised on average of the brightest, best trained and best paid people in the organization. Some even make more money than their supervisors. They usually are the key factor in delivering the organization's product or service and have earned the right to run their own ship. (They also tend to dominate, as a minority group, the unions they belong to.) Some examples include salaried doctors in hospitals, airline pilots, and university professors. Participative programs for employee (and student) decision making must reckon with such groups in addition to predictable management resistance. The concept of "democracy" can conflict with self-interest in some surprising settings.

**Trust is an important ingredient** - Another source of rank-and-file resistance to participation lies in their often observed mistrust of the process. Many employees seem to feel that they will be taken advantage of by managers and technical people who have more expertise than they have. This is more than an attitudinal problem--such exploitation can in fact occur, and has been demonstrated experimentally by a Dutch social psychologist who previously had observed the phenomenon in employee-management councils. He found that "more participation enabled the more powerful [experts, in this case] to use their influence [expertise] more effectively."[16] This experiment at one and the same time:

- provides a solid rationale for organizations to utilize participative methods; and

- supports rank-and-file suspicions that they may be exploited in the process!

However, if one accepts the view that in the end the organization's viability serves all the parties' interests, the manipulation problem may be moot.

## WHO THE "PARTICIPATORS" ARE - COMMON DENOMINATORS

The expertise problem mentioned above raises a related question that seems to influence both managers and rank-and-file. That is, who are those who want more participation--are they competent, mature individuals, or merely ignorant agitators who should be suppressed? My knowledge of relevant literature is limited to three sources: two research studies based on students and a few studies of trade union members summarized in a literature review. One study compares active and inactive members of the same sororities in college. The results show that the active members, on average, were 20 percentile points higher than the inactives on rank in high school graduating class and on a well-standardized intelligence test.[17] The study also reveals that the active sorority members engaged in more extra-curricular activities and belonged to more organizations than did their less active sorority sister peers. Another research study conducted in a university setting found that those desiring more participation tend to be the better students academically.[18]

Parallel findings are reported on union members. By comparison with their inactive or less active colleagues, "the active union member tends to be higher...in pay, skill, seniority, and job status in general." (Three of these dimensions are likely to have some correlation with intelligence--NR.) Further, the active member "seems to derive satisfaction from social interaction, from doing things with people." He also is "more likely...to belong to other formal organizations, besides the union, for example, fraternal groups, veterans organizations and sports teams."[19] It appears that active sorority members and active trade union members have a lot in common. And, what they have in common probably is very similar to what effective managers have in common, as well!

While the above evidence is hardly conclusive, on balance it suggests that the desire for participation is not necessarily limited to ignorant agitators. And, *employers who recruit intelligent, active people should not be surprised when such people become restless in rigid, autocratic systems of administration.* Indeed, Japanese managers of Mazda's auto manufacturing plant in Flint Rock, Michigan apparently have difficulty understanding why American workers "have to be sold on an idea." These managers reportedly enjoyed unquestioning obedience from their workers in Japan,[20] which makes one wonder why participative methods work in that country.

## QUALITY CIRCLES AND WHY MANY SEEM TO WORK

A flurry of attention to the concept of "Quality Circles" (QC) was apparent in recent years until the lessons learned went down the tubes as many American companies were restructured and downsized. Both scholarly observers and practitioners seem to believe that *properly designed and administered* QC programs are a great boon to organizational effectiveness. I have little doubt that many attempts at this type of program have failed, however, because they were not properly designed or because they lacked either senior management backing, expert guidance, or both.

**The Japanese did not invent the principles** - Widely attributed to Japanese management ingenuity, the QC concept actually owes its development to the early (1930s) human relations experimentation at the Western Electric Company's Hawthorne Works, in the USA, and to subsequent theoretical and research contributions by the Lewinian "school" of group dynamics in the United States and the Tavistock Institute in England and Europe. The QC concept, in brief, represents a systematic application of what long has been known about group behavior and employee motivation. While many US and European organizations have been using various aspects of the knowledge base for at least three decades, the Japanese were quicker to accept and apply widely, patiently and systematically what is known.

**Quality circles defined** - A QC is a small (8-12) group of employees formed on a voluntary basis to diagnose "quality" problems and propose solutions. (Their agendas, however, are not necessarily limited to "quality" issues alone.) QCs may be found in manufacturing and service organizations; the type of organization is not a constraint. The members are recruited around task interests they have in common, and may or may not belong to the same department. In organizations where the QC model "catches on," numerous such groups evolve over a period of time and become a mini-organization within the larger one. That is, a QC network develops, consisting of a QC Coordinator, a QC Training Coordinator, a Facilitator (consultant), several trained QC Leaders, and several QC groups.

The QC network in such cases apparently becomes a social structure that provides rewarding experiences that the traditional departmental structure of the host organization does not provide.

*In other words, such networks are effective because they incorporate sound motivational practices.* Let us see how this is so.

**Each QC is kept small** - This enhances feelings of belonging, and makes it easier for members to participate in group discussion. (The negative effects of large group size were discussed earlier.);

**Membership in a QC usually is voluntary** - This avoids a common problem found in other participative management programs - not everyone wants to participate, and the classic QC strategy recognizes this. Moreover, since there is evidence that participators (in general) tend to be more intelligent than average, and tend to have more social contacts than non-participators (see earlier section of this chapter), the QC model by emphasizing voluntarism builds on strength;

**The QC agenda focuses on problems in the immediate task domain and is action oriented** - This approach capitalizes on what many observers of PDM programs have said over the years. Participation works best when the agenda is relevant to the employees' experience and interests, and when the "area of freedom" is meaningful;

**QC members work together as peers** - even though different status levels in the larger organization are represented in the group. Additionally, technical experts are used only when the group calls upon them, after doing much of its own diagnostic work. These two practices, status levelling and controlling expert dominance, counteract motivational problems encountered in other, more limited PDM programs, which were mentioned earlier in this chapter;

**Strong management support for the program is visible and operational** - This is accomplished in several ways. First, in some organizations two management meetings on QCs and their functions are held every year. Second, each QC has direct access to higher level management decision making groups for purposes of making presentations and recommendations. Third, each QC meets on a regular schedule throughout the year (at least every other week), during regular hours. Finally, considerable expense is incurred visibly in extensive training for QC members and their leaders. It has long been recognized that no PDM strategy works in the absence of strong managerial support; the QC model builds such support into the process;

**Relevant training that is both functional and developmental is a major ingredient of the model** - This is consistent with a long-held belief of organization change specialists. QC training for group leaders and their members includes group process instruction (to maximize understanding of how groups function), presentation skills (so that meetings with management decision-makers will be productive and not embarrassing), and analytical skills (how to analyze data, test hypotheses) and others. This has to be translated as "job enrichment" for many QC members and represents for them a challenging addition to their more routine job duties;

**The immediate supervisor does not bear the entire burden** - This is a departure from more traditional approaches to PDM. The supervisor is trained to be supportive, but a special leader for each QC is appointed and trained, and quite often is someone other than the formal supervisor or manager of the work unit in which the Circle is embedded. Thus, the supervisor or manager can continue to do what is necessary to keep the total organizational unit functioning, while the QC goes into depth on specific issues and problems. *The effect is to spread leadership opportunity and development without destroying the credibility and utility of the first line supervisor*, a problem that has cropped up in several autonomous work group experiments. This QC strategy also tends to minimize the problem of status interference because the special leader acts as a buffer between the QC group and the relevant supervisor; and

**The QC model provides a "support group" for managers** - Those managers willing to take the risk, i.e., all having QCs operating in their part of the organization, get together at regular intervals to discuss what has been going on, how they can be helpful, and presumably re-affirm their faith in the process. Since such managers, especially in the early phase of a QC program, are likely to be in the minority among the host organization's managers, the support group has important motivational implications for them.

The need for such support was first illustrated empirically in the 1950s by a study of the effects on supervisors of human relations training in a large U.S. corporation; most of the positive gains in the training program dissipated after the supervisors returned to their regular jobs and work environment.[21] The reason usually advanced for this unfortunate decrement is that support from peers and higher management levels was absent. The QC model includes "booster shots" through the support group to reinforce the initial "inoculation."

**The QC concept makes sense in the USA** - It should be clear from the above that the QC model makes motivational sense and that it has been designed with great insight into group dynamics. It also should be clear that despite comments from some observers to the contrary, *the QC model has demonstrable relevance in North America; the potential success of the model does not depend upon the influence of Japanese cultural background factors.* More likely its success depends upon patience and careful planning; it can't happen overnight.

## THE RESCHEDULING OF WORKING HOURS

Widespread trial and error experiments have occurred in many organizations through which traditional work hour systems were rescheduled in various ways. By and large, these experiments do not meet scientific research standards, but they have produced some impressive insights that have serious and significant implications for management. They tell us a great deal about employee priorities, and suggest an alternative to job redesign; that is, they suggest that there may be as much value in redesigning the standard 8 hour day, 5 day work week as in redesigning basic task procedures.

**The four-day work week** - Work hour rescheduling experiments have tried two basic strategies. The first of these is popularly called the "four-day, forty-hour work week." This strategy merely compresses the typical forty-hour, five-day work week into a four-day time period in which employees work ten hours a day and earn a three-day weekend.

The four-day, forty-hour week, while attractive to some, has by no means met with overwhelming success and in many instances has been dropped after a trial period. Much of the disappointment with it grows out of the discovery, by many individuals, that this work schedule actually increased their difficulties in adapting to the competing demands of work role and their private lives.

**Flexitime as an example of PDM** - The second strategy is called "flexitime." Unlike the four-day, forty-hour work week, this strategy has produced widespread although not unanimous enthusiasm almost everywhere it has been tried. The almost overwhelming positive response to flexitime indicates that many organizations have struck a valuable motivational well-spring. Aside from the obvious advantages to employees who under this system can lead more adaptive lives, there is something even more basic going on here in motivational terms. Specifically, *the flexitime strategy actually is a form of participative management.*

**Trust is at the core** - The employee is offered in these systems partial control over a major resource--time. Within limits they can adjust their own work hours. *This suggests to employees that the management trusts their judgment and assumes that they are mature individuals.* Such a strategy provides a degree of autonomy and operates upon assumptions that are quite consistent with the views of many social scientists and management theorists. In one stroke, this strategy enables employees to better adapt personal and their employer's needs to each other, relieve boredom, and participate in some significant decision making on an agenda item that has real importance to them as individuals.[22] Employers who haven't tried it appear to be missing a valuable opportunity.

## FLEXITIME ADVANTAGES TO EMPLOYEES - IN PRINCIPLE

**Flexitime reduces frustration** - It is readily apparent that if employees can select within limits what time they will come to work in the morning, what time they will go home, and in some cases, what time they will take their required lunch period, can "put some extra time in the bank" to be used later, and can even vary their schedule from day to day, they are in a position to plan their own "boredom" breaks and alleviate the effects of task technology. They also are in a position to adapt to a variety of life's needs that they otherwise have difficulties with.

**For example** - Working parents can more readily handle such things as medical appointments for children, conferences with school teachers, or visits to their home by installation and repair personnel. Employees under such plans also are free to take advantage of mid-day shopping opportunities, and may find it easier to hold a second, part-time job, or contribute some of their time and energy to a deserving community service organization. In addition, they gain time to deal with the administrative bureaucracy in their employer's organization, can handle banking matters during the day without cutting into their personal time, arrange to meet friends or relatives for lunch, and make it on time to an after work training or educational course. Some of these activities are linked to money--flexible working hours help some people reduce certain kinds of expenses, by permitting attendance at department store sales, and can help some earn extra money by easing time conflicts around extra jobs and vocational training.

## WHAT EXPERIENCED FLEXITIME EMPLOYEES SAY

Two years after its inception, the German flexitime pioneer sent questionnaires to almost two thousand of its three thousand employees. A large response rate was reported and of those responding 65% said that their working conditions were better as a result of the program, while 27% said that they were the same. Married, single, salaried and wage category personnel all reacted with the same degree of favorableness.

Fifty-five per cent of the respondents reported either a "better balance between work and private life" or "easier travel." This certainly supports a major view developed in this book--when theorizing about or planning the enhancement of employee motivation, the task itself is by no means the only significant factor. The German study indicated that 21% reported a "better fit between work rhythm and work load." This relates to a major and often overlooked aspect of motivational process. *Flexitime offers an opportunity for employees to adapt their energy investments to the schedule variations that occur in their work loads, some of which are required by client or customer needs.*

## FLEXITIME BENEFITS TO THE EMPLOYER

Various studies have been conducted in numerous American settings where flexitime has been tried. There is considerable consistency in the highly favorable findings. *Dramatic improvements have almost always been reported in regard to absenteeism, labor turnover and overtime requirements.* In general, attitudes have been highly favorable and most respondents prefer the freedom it affords. Some organizations have even reported improved productivity as a result of flexitime, but most who have examined this question report that flexitime has achieved a number of other improvements without affecting productivity one way or another.

A major advantage that some firms have found is that it has helped them recruit new employees. Apparently the word spreads quickly in the community when an organization goes on flexitime and increases its attractiveness to potential employees.

## REASONS WHY FLEXITIME WORKS

One follow-up account of a flexitime experiment explains the success of the system in motivational terms, as follows:

- Flexible working hour systems are not a major threat to management prerogatives, as other forms of participative management frequently are;

- The employees involved in flexible hour systems receive immediate short-term benefits and timely reinforcement for their decisions; and

- Flexitime is not forced upon any individual. That is, a worker who likes his present work hour schedule is not required to change it. This means that individual differences are fully allowed for by such systems whereas in the case of job enrichment everybody has to go along.[23]

Another article points out that flexible working hours tend to blur status distinctions between white collar and blue collar workers.[24] Whatever the reasons for its success, the remarkable early track record of the flexitime strategy certainly requires the attention of managers.

## SOME CAVEATS ABOUT FLEXITIME

**Task variables can be a constraint** - The reader should not conclude that flexitime offers a motivational panacea. It is likely that flexitime could be difficult to utilize in work groups that are organized along team lines where the members' jobs are specialized and interdependent. In such cases the decision making on working hours can not be entirely individualized unless "back-ups" are available to step in and help out for short periods of time while one of the regular specialized employees is off duty. In any event, the decision making in such cases would have to be done at the group level rather than entirely at the individual level.

**Some trade unions are opposed** - Finally, it has been noted that in the United States there is some apparent opposition to flexitime systems by leaders of organized labor. According to this account, "Labor union spokesmen argue that under some circumstances flexitime will increase the amount of time given by the employee for the same weekly wage; reduce the employee's monthly earnings while increasing the intensity ɔf his work; and encourage longer hours of work."[25]

Whatever the merits of the trade unionists' arguments, the response of participants in flexitime systems seems to indicate that the rank-and-file want it. I think it is a major step forward and will have significant beneficial effects on the mobilization of energy in work organizations and on the personal well-being of employees and their families. Happily, it also appears to be a very democratically based technique. Unions will find ways to adapt; I would guess that their own office employees have enjoyed an informal flexitime system for many years, not to mention the officers themselves.

## IMPLICATIONS OF PDM FOR TEAM BUILDING

It is apparent from this chapter that participation in decision making, while not a panacea for the employee relations ills of formal work organizations, has a lot to offer. Future research is likely to show that different amounts and types of participation will be more effective than others depending upon a work groups' (or entire organizations') stage of evolutionary development.

**PDM can be looked at as a technique for enhancing group process** - namely, the process by which decisions are made about who in the group should do what, when, where, and how. If examined in that context, it should be apparent that task complexity and the experience and skill levels of the group members are relevant considerations.

**Stage of group development is an important consideration** - A new group just starting out, if it is staffed by inexperienced "rookies" learning a new complex operation, is not likely to benefit from a PDM strategy and will have to rely on its leader and others for structure. Once into a comfortable performance stage of development, however, the collective knowledge of the by now very knowledgeable members is a valuable resource that more than likely goes well beyond the leader's own insights. At this point in its evolutionary history, a group may find PDM to be worthwhile, then, not only as a motivational strategy to combat complacency, but also as a way to enhance task procedures - good ideas are good ideas no matter where they come from.

**Powerful attitudes must be dealt with** - By now it must be clear to the reader that we are dealing with an emotional and ideological issue which has disturbing parallels in the broader fields of government, political science and international relations. Many of the participation issues characterizing managerial discussions of this subject in work organizations have appeared in other settings. For example, the colonial powers, when they finally realized the trends confronting them around the world, eventually faced such questions as; How much democracy? How soon? How should it be introduced? How do we insure the continued presence of competent leadership and administration? How do we stimulate widespread, grass-roots participation? Who will provide the technical competence needed to keep essential services going while the untrained masses are taking over and learning what to do? What institutional arrangements are best for developing priorities and resolving conflicts? What should we do with our experienced colonial governors and administrators who oppose turning over the reins, or are ill-equipped by reason of personality to deal with the necessities of power sharing? There are no simple answers and no easy solutions. But regardless of corporate restructuring and increased competition, managerial resistance to PDM in all forms represents a misguided policy.

## ENDNOTES

1    See "Talking in circles improves quality," INDUSTRY WEEK, February 14, 1977, 62-64 and Yager, E., "Examining the quality control circle," PERSONNEL JOURNAL, October 1979, 682-684 and 709.

2    Norman R. F. Maier coined the expression "area of freedom" in the 1950s and it's still a viable one.

3    Gold, Charlotte, "Employer-employee committees and worker participation," KEY ISSUES: background reports on current topics and trends in labor-management relations, November 20, 1976, New York State School of Industrial and Labor Relations, Cornell University, Ithaca, New York.

4       Latham, G. and Yukl, G., "A review of research on the application of goal setting
        in organizations," ADMINISTRATIVE SCIENCE QUARTERLY, 1976, 18 (4),
        840. See, also, Vroom, V. and Yetton, P. LEADERSHIP AND DECISION
        MAKING, 1973, Pittsburgh: University of Pittsburgh Press.

5       Gyllenhammer, P., PEOPLE AT WORK, 1977, Reading, Mass.: Addison-Wesley.

6       Bragg, J. E. and Andrews, I. R., "Participative decision making: an experimental
        study in a hospital," JOURNAL OF APPLIED BEHAVIORAL SCIENCE, 1973, 9
        (6), 727-735.

7       This summary is adapted, with added interpretation and commentary, from a
        detailed discussion by Katz, D. and Kahn, R. in THE SOCIAL PSYCHOLOGY OF
        ORGANIZATIONS, 1966, New York: John Wiley & Sons, 393-406.

8       This point is explicated clearly and in depth in Bucklow, Maxine, "A new role for
        the work group," ADMINISTRATIVE SCIENCE QUARTERLY, 1966, 11, 59-79.
        Bucklow describes the historical origins of the autonomous work group concept and
        the supporting work done by various Tavistock Institute staff. She also shows why
        this strategy is more likely to work than worker-management councils, joint boards
        and the like. Several European experiences with such formal bodies have been
        disappointing--probably because the agenda items were removed from the workers'
        area of relevance and ability.

9       Hoffman, L. R. and Maier, N. R. F., "Quality and acceptance of problem solutions
        by members of homogeneous and heterogeneous groups," JOURNAL OF ABNOR-
        MAL AND SOCIAL PSYCHOLOGY, 1961, 62, (3), 401-407.

10      Katz and Kahn, cited earlier, 402-403.

11      Salpukas, A., NEW YORK TIMES, November 11, 1974.

12      Derber, M., "Worker participation in Israeli management," INDUSTRIAL RELA-
        TIONS, 3, 1963, 51-72.

13      Golden, Patricia and Rosen, N., "Student attitudes toward participation in univer-
        sity administration: an empirical study related to managerial prerogatives,"
        JOURNAL OF COLLEGE STUDENT PERSONNEL, November, 1966, 329.

14      Hespe, G. and Wall, T., "The demand for participation among employees," HU-
        MAN RELATIONS, 1976, 29, 426.

15      Hespe and Wall, cited above, 422.

16      Mulder, M., "Power equalization through participation," ADMINISTRATIVE
        SCIENCE QUARTERLY, 1971, 16, 31-38.

17      Willerman, B., "Relations of motivation and skill to active and passive participation
        in the group," JOURNAL OF APPLIED PSYCHOLOGY, 1953, 37, 387-390.

18      Golden, Patricia, M. and Rosen, N., cited earlier, 328.

19      Tannenbaum, A. S., "Unions," in March, J. (Ed.), HANDBOOK OF ORGANIZA-
        TIONS, 1965, Chicago: Rand-McNally & Co., 746-747.

20      "Mazda struggling with U.S. experiment," MIAMI HERALD, August 27, 1988, 4D.

21   Fleishman, E., "Leadership climate, human relations training, and supervisory behavior," PERSONNEL PSYCHOLOGY, 1953, 6, 205-222.

22   Full details may be found in Bolton, J. H., FLEXIBLE WORKING HOURS, 1971, Wembley, U.K.: Anbar Publications, Ltd.

23   Elbing, A. O., Gadon, H. and Gordon, J. R. M., "Flexible working hours: it's about time," HARVARD BUSINESS REVIEW, 1974, Vol. 52, 18-20.

24   Hedges, J. N., "Questions and answers on flexitime," SUPERVISORY MANAGE-MENT, 1974, Vol. 19, 9-15.   Some sophisticated research on the subject has been reported by Golembiewski, R. T. and others, "Factor analysis of some flexitime effects:   attitudinal and behavioral consequences of a structural intervention," ACADEMY OF MANAGEMENT JOURNAL, 1975, Vol. 18, 500-509.

25   Owen, J. D., "Flextime: some problems and solutions," INDUSTRIAL AND LABOR RELATIONS REVIEW, 1977, Vol. 30, No. 2, 156.

SOME ADDITIONAL LITERATURE FOR THE INTERESTED READER:

-   Hammer, Tove, "New developments in profit sharing, gainsharing, and employee ownership," Chap. 12 in Campbell, J. and Campbell, R. [Eds.], PRODUCTIVITY IN ORGANIZATIONS, 1988, Vol. II, San Francisco: Jossey-Bass.

-   Lawler, E., HIGH INVOLVEMENT MANAGEMENT, 1986, San Francisco: Jossey-Bass.

-   Ronen, Simcha, ALTERNATIVE WORK SCHEDULES: SELECTING, IMPLEMENT-ING, AND EVALUATING, 1984, New York: Dow Jones-Irwin.

FUN 'N' GAMES with COCHRAN!

"Don't think of it as being cut. Think of it as a pragmatic business decision in a highly competitive industry."

## REASONS FOR STAGNATION REVISITED

As pointed out in Chapter One, a task group can stagnate or deteriorate for a variety of reasons:

- Development of inflexibility and non-responsiveness to its environment due to an overdose of internal conformity pressure; in executive groups this often is the result of being overly dependent upon either an exceptionally talented or a highly domineering leader for a long period of time;

- Complacency following a period of success, often triggered or accompanied by a sense of reduced challenge;

- Loss of a key member;

- The group's mission loses significance to the larger organization;

- The group, or some of its members (including its manager), come to believe they are not being appropriately rewarded for their contributions;

- One or more newcomers to the group disturb the status structure that was previously established;

- Age related skill or motivation deterioration results in a tapering off of performance;

- A bad relationship develops between the group's manager and the one at the next level up;

- Individual member life cycle changes, for example, parenthood, produce competing interests which detract from commitments to the group;

- Previously planted seeds of factionalism find time or impetus to develop, especially if the group is having difficulty meeting its objectives under competitive circumstances; and

- Many other possible scenarios.

Sometimes two or more of these phenomena occur simultaneously, which aggravates the problem.

Symptoms of group deterioration abound, but are not always readily measurable in precise terms. Common observations of group deterioration include such statements as, "They've lost their edge," "They're tired," "They're not hungry anymore," "They have come to know each other too well," or "They need some shaking up." Absenteeism often increases, along with internal bickering and scapegoating. Performance indicators, if available, also either level off or actually deteriorate.

*When a group that has performed well historically suddenly develops serious problems, it probably means that its motivation and talents have been squeezed for too long, that its maintenance has been neglected, and that it's too late for simple, one shot solutions.* The same can be said of total organizations.

**Prevention is the best approach** - Renewal of a group is far less of a problem in organizations that, as a matter of principle, invest continuously in development of their people - rank and file, supervisors, and managers alike - and in recruiting new blood simultaneously. They avoid hardening of the organizational arteries by deliberately maintaining a reasonable amount of internal churn on a continuing basis. The short term costs of such a policy are offset by major dividends in the long run, just as physical plant maintenance on a continuing basis delays long term capital investment requirements. However, just as physical plant maintenance frequently is neglected, so is group maintenance.

**Eventually renewal becomes inevitable** - Even in well maintained groups, there comes a time when maintenance will no longer suffice. Major renewal efforts become necessary. A sustained and significant change effort must be mounted in such cases. Let us consider some methods used.

## GROUP RENEWAL TACTICS

American employers do not lack tactics for dealing with stagnating task groups, although in my judgment they frequently do not apply them on a sustained basis with creativity and according to a systematic strategy. Here are a number of typically used tactics, listed in ascending order of their severity:

JAW BONING - Exhortation campaigns are launched by management to encourage the declining group to get its act together and do its corporate duty. These campaigns include anything from pep talks and increased use of team meetings, to "retreats;"

SHUFFLE THE PLAYERS - Some members' job duties are juggled around to try and find a better task-person fit and possibly generate renewed challenge;

TIGHTEN THE SCREWS - The performance review and reward system are applied with renewed vigor to stem the slide. More demanding goals are set, and the business planning system is tightened up to remind people that they are part of a larger scheme. Financial incentives also may be adjusted to provide encouragement or punish those presumed to be slacking off;

BRING IN SOME ALLIES - Pressures are orchestrated and amplified from other groups within the organization, for example the accounting or quality control departments, or from customers and clients, to get the declining group to "shape up;"

INCREASE ATTENTION FROM HIGHER UP - The group's reporting relationship to the larger organization is changed.  Either a different more senior manager takes responsibility for it, or the current more senior manager escalates the amount of his time and attention for the group.  This sometimes is merely symbolic, but often produces very different interpersonal chemistry between the group's immediate manager and his or her higher level manager;

MAKE LIFE DIFFICULT - If none of the above gets the desired results, management sometimes decides to make life tougher for the group.  <u>Harassment</u> <u>begins</u> - work loads are increased, informal ground rules on time off and other perquisites change, and lunch hour and coffee break periods are more strictly enforced.  Specialists (both internal and external consultants) appear on the scene to examine the situation and sometimes impose deliberately unreasonable demands to make life uncomfortable.  Their assumption is that "deadwood" will quit when life at work gets rough;

ESCALATE THREAT LEVEL - Rumors begin about possible reorganization, and threats may be made to transfer individual members to other, less desirable jobs or locations;

CUT OFF ITS HEAD - The group's manager is replaced, either as a knee-jerk reaction in the belief that this will "shake the group out of its doldrums," or as the result of a logical analysis that suggests a new style of leadership is needed; actually, this often is used as a <u>first</u> step toward renewal and usually doesn't get the job done effectively;

THE "D & D" TREATMENT - One or more key members other than the manager are <u>d</u>emoted or <u>d</u>ispatched, either because they have become "trouble makers" or because their skill or motivational deterioration are seen as the cause of the group's problem.   This also can reflect a management belief that by making an example of key members they will demonstrate to the rest just how serious the problem is;

REORGANIZE - The group's structure and individual member job definitions are significantly changed, and another group quite possibly is merged with it to create a "new chemistry;" or, in the most extreme situations;

BLOODBATH - Widespread member replacements occur, through significant numbers of layoffs, transfers, and new hiring. This often is accompanied by a massive infusion of new technology. In extreme cases the entire group may be dissolved and its functions assumed by others.

**A plan is needed** - Most of the above group renewal tactics reflect a trial and error, "quick-fix," controlling or directive approach that is not especially attuned to what is known about group behavior and attitudes. For example, in many instances it makes more sense to renew a group through a combination of job enrichment, work hour rescheduling, consultancy intervention focused on facilitation, and training. Or, the autonomous, self-managed task group concept described in Chapter Ten might offer an effective solution for a group needing new challenges. In any event, the options are many but often are applied one or two at a time without benefit of a thorough diagnosis and plan, and usually not until serious problems have already developed. Team rebuilding requires both a diagnosis and strategy. There are no viable "quick fixes" for groups in need of renewal because the variables are numerous and their relationships are complex.

The model presented in Chapter One and discussed in subsequent chapters shows the appropriate directions. Systematic management attention will be needed to the group's mission, staffing patterns, leadership and training requirements, the reward system, group process, task design, and relations with other groups in the organization. Attention to the group's physical plant layout and its spectators may also be needed. Effective renewal cannot be a hit-or-miss exercise.

## PART TWO:  RENEWING THE ORGANIZATION

Sometimes it is instructive to step back from one's immediate focus, in this instance the renewal of task groups, and consider the larger context, renewal of the organization and American industry. To set the stage for my conclusions, I shall make a brief excursion into the past, beginning in the 1940s...

## TWO MANAGERIAL IRONIES OF WORLD WAR II

During World War II the most powerful manufacturing machine the world had ever seen was developed in the USA despite two important facts:

First, the labor force was comprised of a hastily assembled, rag-tag collection of:

- Inexperienced women who had never before worked in a factory;

- Men deemed unfit for military service either because of physical disabilities or advanced age; and

- Thousands of undereducated, previously underemployed black people who moved into the industrial cities from rural locations.

Second, a unique symbolic reward was relied upon heavily. The Army-Navy "E" for Excellence, proudly displayed by its recipients on flag poles, was awarded by the Federal government to whole factories as a total group reward.

The fact is, major employers during World War II, especially manufacturers, had it easy; the motivation to work was provided by a compelling sense of national purpose. Almost everybody wanted to win the war, and hard work combined with personal sacrifice was the agreed route. In addition:

- There was an industry-trade union-government-education partnership;

- School children conducted massive scrap metal and paper drives;

- Clothing was collected for our Russian and British allies;

- Government savings bond drives were frequently conducted, with heavy support from celebrities;

- Hollywood produced many morale building movies; and

- We even elected a President to a third and then a fourth term!

In brief, common enemies brought us together as a unified nation. Attitude change programs, quality circles, participative management, and numerous other innovations in management practices which have emerged in more recent years were not necessary.

All hell broke loose in American industry after the war. The number of strikes and man days lost to strikes skyrocketed and unionism flourished. The economic and career interests of returning veterans wanting to reclaim their old jobs clashed with those of women and black people who wanted to keep them. Fortunately an expanding economy and the GI Bill of Rights that produced financial support for skills training and college educations helped contain the conflict.

## ENTER THE HUMAN RELATIONS MOVEMENT

In the midst of the post-war strife, the human relations movement came into its own. The modern roots of this philosophy, i.e., the well-spring for McGregor's Theory Y (reviewed below) that many managers by now know about, lie in the Hawthorne Plant-Western Electric studies of work group relations (done in the 1930s) and in Kurt Lewin's classic wartime research on attitude change. These studies were augmented by significant leadership and motivation research conducted during and shortly after the war, much of which was funded by the military.[1]

While much of this work was being debated in the 1950s and '60s, and being ignored or rejected by most American managers, the Japanese came to town...and took it all home with them. They have made far more effective use of it than we have.

Let's examine Theories X and Y; they capture the heart of the post World War II human relations movement and carry it all the way into the late 1970s.

## A REVIEW OF THEORIES X AND Y

According to McGregor, a Theory X manager is one who assumes that the average adult is, *by nature*:

- Indolent and not ambitious
- Indifferent to organizational needs and goals
- Aversive to responsibility
- Selfish

- Resistant to change
- Gullible
- Not very intelligent
- A child grown large

Conversely, a Theory Y manager is one who assumes that the average adult has potential, *by nature* to:

- Develop, learn and share with others
- Behave in accord with organizational goals

- Assume increasing responsibilities
- Work collaboratively with others

[Note: See Appendix B for my version of an updated XY Theory of Management - NR.]

Isn't it interesting that the United States Army, a *military* organization, obviously has taken the human relations research and the views of its major proponents more seriously than many business organizations? Note the nationwide TV recruiting advertisements used by the US Army - *"Be all that you can be,"* coupled with the emphasis on becoming part of a team - *"When the tank wins the whole team wins, not just one person."* Apparently it works; they've used the ads for quite some time, since Selective Service ended and Army service became voluntary. To some extent the growing shortage of young people for entry level jobs in industry is aggravated by the military's successful recruiting practices.

The military are not the only organizations capitalizing on what has evolved from the behavioral sciences. Many corporations also have learned some valuable lessons. For example, Motorola's extensive advertising campaign in the nation's press during the early to mid 1980s emphasized their quality circle program. And the Digital Equipment Corporation, IBM's major competitor, placed a half page recruitment ad in the New York TIMES on September 27, 1987 featuring their internal emphasis on "team spirit" and the "excitement" of working with their dynamic groups. Hewlett-Packard TV ads ("What if?") in late 1987 and early 1988 emphasized employees who have new ideas and are committed to putting them to work, 24 hours a day, 365 days per year.

## ENTER THEORY Z

William Ouchi's book on Theory Z management[2] in 1981 created a great deal of public interest, and deservedly so. His account of Japanese companies' human relations practices coupled with his observations of various American companies led him to propose a new model of effective organizations, one that builds on Theory Y and goes beyond it. His views have much in common with Peters and Waterman who published IN SEARCH OF EXCELLENCE a year later.[3] All three writers discovered, via direct observations and interviews in several of America's most successful corporations, some general principles that the behavioral scientists had been documenting since the 1930s.

Theory Z is a reformulation of McGregor's Theory Y, but at an organizational level of analysis rather than at the individual level. Ouchi explains that *Theory Z organizations are built around managers who believe in and practice Theory Y management.* According to his extensive observations, such organizations are characterized by:

- Long term employment stability for their employees;

- Considerable career mobility across internal unit boundaries;

- Information mechanisms that are treated as servants, not masters;

- Egalitarian atmosphere; trust and commitment are relied upon rather than hierarchy and monitoring;

- A commitment to teamwork;

- Widespread participation in decision making, coupled with extensive training in participation skills; and

- A managerial philosophy in which profit is not regarded as an end in itself; rather as a reward to the firm if it continues to provide true value to its customers, to help its employees grow, and to behave responsibly as a corporate citizen

The earlier human relations, leadership, attitude, and small group research, most of which was highly consistent with the above elements of Theory Z management, spawned many management development and supervisory training packages. As they proliferated, more and more companies bought and used them during the 1950s, 60s and 70s. Quality Circles and "OD" programs also came on the scene and generated a lot of attention, not to mention the growth of sensitivity training (T-groups) for managers. In addition, the nation's press joined the party. Numerous supportive articles appeared over the years in publications like NEWSWEEK, FORTUNE, and the WALL STREET JOURNAL. Finally, behavioral science departments and programs proliferated rapidly in university business schools that produce large numbers of corporate managers.

## THE RETURN TO THE ABCs OF MANAGEMENT

Regardless of all this enlightened input to American industry, and despite the fact that Peters and Waterman and Theory Z information were being widely read and discussed with the inescapable implication that teamwork pays, the crunch came. Beginning in the late 1970s and early 1980s a counter-revolution called a "shake-out" emerged, partly for economic reasons and partly because many corporate leaders had come to believe that the American worker had become smug, complacent, indifferent, or even indolent. Many boards and senior executives decided to go back to or re-emphasize the ABC's of management. What are the ABC's of management ?

**A** ccountability of the <u>individual</u>

**B** ottom line fixation

**C** ost control at any cost (including general layoffs and a "youth movement" in the managerial structure)

The euphemistic descriptive terms associated with the ABC's are "re-structuring" and "downsizing," bland enough in tone, but devastating in their effects on teamwork. Accompanying the ABC's we are seeing:

- A renewed emphasis on tightening up performance appraisal systems and practices;

- A surging interest in strategic planning, usually accompanied by heavy reliance on highly detailed quantitative measures;

- Increased emphasis on linking organizational, unit, and individual goals;

- Lots of effort to design "pay for _individual_ performance" systems;

- Increasing use of high technology, often further diminishing employment prospects for the educationally handicapped;

- Exhortation programs

- Widespread recruiting to attract new, younger people with "better" or more recent training; and

- Sharply reduced budgets for training and development.

Except for the last one, the above are roughly parallel to the "hit-or-miss," controlling tactics used for renewing groups, which are reviewed in Part I of this chapter.

## THE ABCs IN CUBA AND RUSSIA, TWO THEORY X NATIONS

**Dealing with bad motivation in Cuba** - I find it interesting that the Communist Cuban government, according to the NY Times in 1969, began a drive to remedy the "indifference and indolence" (note the similarity of these terms, and others used below, to the frequent criticisms of American employees in the late 70s and early 80s) that it admitted had seriously affected production and services. The principal objective was to combat absenteeism and other forms of labor indiscipline, shoddy work, low productivity, disorganization, and carelessness with equipment. Granma, the official Cuban newspaper, said that to tighten its control over the country's 2.8 million workers, the government was directing all its agencies to prepare a complete labor record for each Cuban worker. The dossiers were to include a worker's personal data and a periodic evaluation of his performance... In other words, they adopted a government operated performance appraisal system!

**Pay for performance, in Russia** - Also in 1969, the NY Times reported that the Soviet Communist Party endorsed a plan that encouraged factory managers in selected locations to dismiss surplus workers and to use the resulting savings to increase the pay of remaining employees! - a "pay for performance" policy extreme not unlike what many American Corporations have been doing lately.

**Soviet planning systems stifle innovation** - Labor problems in Cuba persist according to occasional newspaper accounts, and the

Soviet Union's problems with their 5-year plans, alcoholism, low productivity, and lack of innovation continue to get attention of journalists and others who read Soviet newspapers. Indeed, former Communist Party Chairman Andropov, in 1983, publicly remonstrated with government and industry leaders about the need for more "discipline" throughout the entire "chain of development, supply, and production."

More recently (MIAMI HERALD, July 1987) the head of the Soviet Academy of Sciences Economics Department, a man according to the Associated Press who is very close to Party Chairman Gorbachev, levelled scathing public criticism at various Russian-built consumer products. Gas guzzling, unsafe, polluting autos, and TV sets suffering from spontaneous combustion in people's homes were his prime targets. *He maintained that the need to meet assigned production targets often makes Soviet managers unwilling to interrupt the flow of production to modernize or innovate.* Has this not also been true in the US, not only in production operations but also in office, service, and even educational and research environments?

**"Renewal" in the Soviet Union** - The Russians recently modified their emphasis on planning and controls, according to a UPI dispatch in late December 1987. Newspaper articles pointed out that as of January 1, 1988, Soviet companies that produce 60% of their industrial output were to be cut loose from central controls and required to make a profit, or face layoffs and plant closings. Workers are to learn a "new concept - to be profitable." One of Chairman Gorbachev's economic advisers pointed out that there are three parts of their labor force not supporting the new approach: "...managers who do not want to relinquish their power, lazy workers who prefer being told what to do rather than think for themselves, and millions of people who do not earn their wages but who while the day away with tea breaks." He calls the latter group "factory magpies." Numerous strikes and protests occurred within a few days of the government's announcements.

## WHY THE ABCs WILL BE COSTLY IN THE LONG RUN

I am well aware that unforseen economic or competitive circumstances often require a belt-tightening response. I also agree with a business "turnaround" consultant who maintains that 80% of the business failures in this country "...are the result of mishandled internal elements."[4] In plain English, he's talking about

mismanagement.   However, just as there are numerous tactics for
renewing work groups, there also are numerous approaches to
renewing organizations.   The return of many American employers
to the ABCs of management, *especially when unsupported by other
tactics*, represents a sterile approach.   This is the same overall
strategy used by the Soviets and Cubans; more discipline and
control are the essence of a Theory X approach.   The likely aftermath, according to much accumulated research evidence and professional observation, includes:

- Fixation on the numbers as ends in themselves;

- Simmering anxiety, anger, and mistrust among employees and
  between the rank and file and management;

- An underground desire to get even;

- CYA memos-and finger pointing;

- <u>Reduced</u> risk taking;

- <u>Reduced</u> tendency to innovate;

- <u>Reduced</u> <u>teamwork</u>; and

- A large number of age discrimination cases in court.

Even some Soviet leaders and economists have come to understand
that such a strategy neither brings out the best in people nor
capitalizes on their strengths.

In many cases the ABC's have been "sold" to Americans as
necessary medicine to counteract the onslaught of foreign competition.   I'm not so sure that the prescription is the right one.   Two
companies I know of, for example, recently experienced roughly
50% reductions in employment through corporate restructuring.
Executives in both have told me many months later that as a result:

- Morale is low;

- Customers "feel" their morale problems when they call;

- Middle level managers and other employees are
  actively questioning the corporation's commitment to
  career growth, a powerful motivator;

- Job insecurity has increased among those who survived the cuts;

- Role overload and burnout are increasingly prevalent among survivors of the cuts; and

- Quality is slipping.

Motivation through fear and insecurity is <u>not</u> the best route to the innovation and risk taking that most observers seem to agree is needed in American industry.[5]

**The picture is not entirely bleak** - Many American companies are renewing themselves through a combined strategy of reducing costs <u>and</u> inducing innovation based on sound human relations practices. Organizational structures are being streamlined, but participative methods also are being employed, along with new approaches to marketing and market research; managers are learning from their employees and customers, through participative methods. They also are learning more about their competitors.[6]

## A NEW CHALLENGE ON THE HORIZON

Streamlining corporate structures by surgically removing numerous middle level managers and their jobs has become a fairly common practice in recent years, and promises to continue. This not only saves money but also is presumed to enhance communication in the organization. In addition such re-structuring is supposed to increase a company's ability to make quick adjustments to its volatile environment through faster decision making. Leaving aside the obvious personal costs to many individuals and families, such gains, if in fact realized, also will have their costs to the corporate world. Let me explain.

**Middle managers have served a purpose** - Middle level managers historically have served as a buffer between two different cultural levels in their companies - senior management above, and first-line supervisors below. In many organizations these groups come from different educational and socioeconomic backgrounds and deal with very different demands. The middle level normally has been promoted from the lower supervisory ranks, either in the organization where employed or from another.

Because of their origins, middle managers usually understand what goes on below. And, as experienced middle managers they have learned how to translate communications both up and down in the structure. Many have been successful mediators of conflict between levels, and have applied great skill in keeping lower levels of supervision satisfied that "someone up there is sympathetic" with their operating problems. They also have protected lower levels by intervening in their behalf with executives.

**Removal of middle managers will increase friction between levels** - Removal or substantial reduction of the mid-management buffer has to result in more direct contact between the executive and first-line supervisory levels. This can be good for the corporation where mid-management historically has not seen fit to communicate all it knows to higher levels. However, unpleasant surprises are likely to produce unpleasant reactions.

**Many lower level supervisors are not ready** - More contact between executives and lower levels also will bring to light the fact that large numbers of first-line supervisors are inadequately trained and developed. Many aren't ready to take on the added communication, conflict resolution, data interpretation, coordination, and decision making responsibilities created by the mid-managers' removal from the structure.

Promoted into the ranks of supervision largely because of their specific task knowledge, supervisors typically lack experience beyond the narrow functional specialties in which they have long worked. In addition, the corporate sponsored training courses they have attended too often have been narrow in scope - aimed at current, job-related needs rather than development for broader, more demanding responsibilities.

**Climbing the corporate ladder will become more difficult** - Senior executives, as they become more aware of these deficiencies through increased contact with lower level managers, in many cases will become impatient. Accordingly, first-line supervisors will find themselves increasingly cut off from promotion opportunities because of the shrinking number of mid-management positions and their own narrow backgrounds. Thus, *one of the prime motivators in American industry, opportunity to move up the corporate ladder, will be seriously eroded*, both for upwardly mobile supervisors and their ambitious subordinates. Further conflict is likely.

**The senior managers' dilemma** - Senior management, in such circumstances, will be faced by a significant dilemma - take on more responsibility themselves, or re-build the mid-management levels all over again. The latter will be the more attractive alternative to them since most senior executives already are working 55 to 70 hours a week.

But, by the time enough decision makers become attuned to this need, many or most of the mid-managers who have been bought out or forced out in recent years will have adapted to a new life. Many I know of, even if qualified to pursue new directions in corporate life, have no interest in returning to the heat of corporate kitchens.

**A shortage of management talent looms** - The bottom line of this argument, therefore, is that the nation's major corporations, who must survive in an increasingly competitive <u>international</u> economy, are about to encounter yet another problem - a massive shortage of talented, appropriately educated and broadly experienced managers. They will encounter this problem exactly when they need it the least - as they attempt to build their competitive efforts internationally. Most American managers, like their fellow countrymen, speak and read only in English, and know very little about the cultural traditions, history, religions, business practices, politics, or even geography of countries other than our own. The slimmed down executive teams emerging throughout our corporate world will not be able to acquire the necessary international knowledge and skills while simultaneously performing their normal duties. They will need help.

## DETERIORATION IN THE U.S. SOCIETY

During World War II, American industry enjoyed the luxury of a national sense of purpose that is nowhere to be observed today. We lack a strong link between corporate renewal and the needs of our society at large. By comparison with the historical period during which World War II was fought, why can't we just get on with the business of generating the same sense of national purpose? What's different now?

To begin, <u>in the work place</u> technologies are much more complex than they used to be. Building an airplane today, for example, is a far more difficult proposition than it was in the 1940s. Moreover, neither autocratic nor sexist management are nearly as acceptable as in the past, and American workers are much more sophisticated today about what constitutes "good management." Motivation today is a tougher, more complicated sell.

In the larger society, we are a mess.  Here are some social problems with us now, that were not around in the 1940s:

- Drug and alcohol abuse; AIDS

- An excessive school dropout rate

- Alarmingly high unemployment among black youth

- Birthrate decline, and increased infant mortality rate

- Aging population with inadequate health care system

- Numerous school closings

- College financial woes

- Increasing child abuse

- A growing illiteracy problem

- Loss of jobs to other countries

- Financial disaster for small farmers

- Proliferation of deadly weapons among private citizens

- Lost leadership in technology, health care, and education

- National humiliation by terrorists

- Pollution of air and water supplies

**It is entirely likely that the nation's employers are losing a lot more productivity, competitiveness (both domestic and international), and potential innovativeness to these societal problems than they are to "indolent or badly motivated employees."** For example, employees who can't read or do their arithmetic, parents of drug dependent children, people involved with or victimized by crime, and employees having serious health problems or who live with unhealthy family members enter the American work place on every shift.  Their problems come right through the corporate doors with them.  (See Chapter 5 for a review of the linkage between what goes on at work and what goes on outside.)  Severe downsizing, restructuring, and technological change tactics add fuel to the fire.  And motivational, leadership development, and team building strategies that are limited to regular working hours and the employer's physical premises, while useful, are not enough to put it out.  **Renewal of our corporations, in other words, requires simultaneous renewal of our society.**

## EDUCATION AND TRAINING IS A KEY PROBLEM AREA

According to the Wall Street JOURNAL, "In the first half of this year [1987] the New York Telephone Company gave its simple 50-minute exam in basic reading and reasoning skills to <u>twenty-one thousand</u> applicants for 780 entry level jobs. <u>Only 16 percent passed</u>." According to the same article, David Kearns, Chairman of the Xerox Corporation recently said, "Education is a bigger factor in productivity growth than increased capital, economies of scale or better allocation of resources." And, Anthony Carnavale, Chief Economist for the American Society of Training and Development, "estimates a $25 billion <u>annual</u> productivity loss to the American economy due to poorly educated workers."[7] **If that much is being lost to poor education, imagine the total when adding in losses from drugs, crime, ill health, and traffic congestion.**

## TOWARD THE DEVELOPMENT OF MODEL T

In my view there are several things that have to happen to turn American industry around.

<u>First</u>, we must realize that tightening up performance appraisal practices, reductions in staff, infusing more youth having limited experience into management, establishing pay for performance systems, computerized management information and control systems, strategic planning, and yes, even quality circles, job enrichment and autonomous work groups, regardless of their merits in specific cases, also are not a cure.

<u>Second</u>, employers must return to fundamentals. A massive infusion of job skills training for the rank-and-file, such as we saw in World War II, is needed in many companies where employees simply do not know how to do things. We <u>know</u> they can learn.

<u>Third</u>, renewed emphasis on teamwork is needed. This requires managerial involvement that can't be delegated. Unfortunately, many writers on the subject of management have been showing great enthusiasm for vastly expanded spans of control and increased reliance on electronic technology to monitor work activities. Their views do not auger well for the development of teamwork. Large spans of control lead to large work groups, unless small, informally supervised groups are developed. However, "self-managed" groups make little sense in the absence of skill and experience.

Fourth, a national effort is needed to educate and develop a new class of managers, men and women who are far more knowledgeable about the world at large than most managers we have at present. Neither a degree in engineering, nor a traditional business school degree, nor experience in a single function such as marketing or finance, no matter how extensive, is enough. We need managers who understand, in depth, the world beyond our own borders. A strategy for making this happen is needed now. The collaboration of government, educators, business leaders, and funding foundations will be required to pursue some truly innovative approaches to management development.

Finally, in the absence of a national sense of purpose which at this writing seems to be a pipe-dream, employers should work toward developing a local sense of purpose, one that takes into account that their organizations and employees are part of a community that needs help. Let me explain.

Many of our national problems have their roots in the social instabilities of our society. They are at least partly caused by the continued dissolution of social bonds and the disruption of families, organizations, and entire communities by massive population shifts. Remember what happened, in Chapter 1, to the Packing and Shipping Department when its stable group structure was destroyed? And, do you recall what happened, also in Chapter 1, when a social structure was created in the Indian textile mill? Group stability and collaboration toward the achievement of mutual goals are needed both inside and outside the work place.

## BUILDING A LOCAL SENSE OF PURPOSE - MODEL T

Employers can begin by adopting a local cause that their employees and the community can enthusiastically identify with and support. There are many candidates. However, merely shelling out some of our money for the United Way during a finite calendar period is not enough; people have to get involved. Therefore, some specific worthy agency or cause within the community should be adopted by a corporation (or separate divisions) for special attention going beyond traditional fund raising campaigns. Even the process of selecting the cause, if it includes employee participation, would start paying human relations dividends within the firm. And, if employee consensus can't be reached on a single worthy cause in the community, adopt two or three, or allocate time to each in sequence, according to a 2-3 year timetable.

The employer can then forge a <u>partnership</u> with local government, the school system, other employers, trade unions, the local media, religious and philanthropic organizations, and develop a strategic plan for pursuing the cause or causes selected. For example, the Greater Cleveland Round Table, a consortium of 70 business, civic and religious leaders, is collaborating with the local school system to fund a five million dollar "Scholarship in Escrow Program." College tuition support monies from this fund are being reserved for students who earn them through their grades in school.

To make the linkages clear between the organization's welfare and that of the larger community, employers should commit significant financial resources to the adopted cause, but in relation to corporate productivity and profits. For example, employees should be able to earn the equivalent of war bonds and stamps, or product redemption coupons, based on their productivity or contributions to corporate success, and the corporation should match these earnings, all in behalf of the chosen cause.

Customers and suppliers also can be folded into the effort. AT & T provides a partial example. Its Christmas advertising on national TV in 1987 offered the public an opportunity to buy long distance telephone time gift certificates for family and friends. One percent of the proceeds were set aside by the Company to support the "Special Olympics Fund" for the physically handicapped.

One implicit objective here is to give the substantial numbers of people who have relatively dull, unchallenging jobs something they can get warmed up about, while at the same time enhancing corporate efforts. History amply demonstrates how generous Americans can be with their time, talents, effort, and money when circumstances are sufficiently compelling and organized.

A further step is to make arrangements for individuals and groups of employees to take <u>company</u> <u>time</u> to participate "at the front;" their colleagues, as part of a teamwork campaign, will make up for the lost time. There must be a personal touch - fund raising is not enough. Knowing this, the Florida Power and Light Company, the North Carolina National Bank, the Shea and Gould Law Firm, the General Development Corporation, the Southern Bell Telephone Company, and fourteen other companies doing business in South Florida loaned a total of 38 executives to the United Way in 1987. Each apparently worked for two or more months, full time, in behalf of the United Way.[8] This is a step in the right direction, but falls short of a full employee involvement program.

Finally, achievements by employees in behalf of the community must be rewarded as if they were traditional bottom line achievements within the company. They should be attended by plenty of public acclaim. And the corporate reward system will need some new incentives thinking to back up the acclaim.

Through linking corporate and community interests, everyone has to win. A corporate Vice President of Ryder Systems, Inc. put the message very well in a newspaper interview when explaining her company's community relations efforts and expenditures: "People do not live in a vacuum. They live in their community. The community affects our employees, and our employees affect the community. [Ryder's donations of money and services] make employees very proud to work here."[9]

There is no doubt in my mind that through shared community action, employees and employers alike can develop renewed mutual trust and confidence that would carry over to the economic success of the firm and the nation's vitality. **Teamwork in the community and in the work place are mutually supportive concepts. Coupled with massive training, I call it Model T.**

In case the reader may think all of this is pie in the sky or a radical's ravings, here are some views from John Smale, Procter and Gamble's Chairman and CEO, when discussing his company's substantial involvement in community affairs: "I don't think that...any large, multinational corporation can be managed solely against the criterion of the bottom line. That's certainly the way we're measured, as managers, but that falls far short of the total responsibility companies of this size have." "...We have 13,000 employees who make their homes here. We're thoroughly involved in the city." [Cincinnati][10]

Ladies and gentlemen, managers, change agents, educators, students, whatever you are -- I am talking about a World War II level of effort, but in local communities and without bloodshed. There are plenty of people who know how and what to do, and there is much that can be accomplished, together.

## ENDNOTES

1   This research was conducted by several identifiable professional groups at The Ohio State University, the University of Michigan, Harvard University, and elsewhere. Soon after, Douglas McGregor gave us Theory X and Y and Chris Argyris contributed his related views on learning and growth. All of this was augmented by Abraham Maslow's widely publicized writings on self-actualization and David McClelland's well-known work on the need for achievement. These people gave us many of the concepts and models subsequently captured by the management training packagers. Most of the more widely used packages have their roots in these early works. The Ohio State researchers included E. Fleishman, E. Harris, H. Burtt, J. Hemphill, C. Shartle, R. Stogdill, and B. Winer. The best known University of Michigan researchers are R. Kahn, D. Katz, R. Likert, A. Zander, and D. Cartwright. R. Bales was the key small groups researcher at Harvard University, while W. F. Whyte also made significant contributions to the early human relations literature along with F. Roethlisberger and W. Dickson who participated in the famous Hawthorne Studies. M. Sherif and Carolyn Sherif, at the University of Oklahoma, did the seminal research on intergroup conflict and cooperation.

2   Ouchi, W. THEORY Z, 1981, Reading, MA: Addison-Wesley.

3   Peters, T. and Waterman, R., Jr. IN SEARCH OF EXCELLENCE, 1982, New York: Harper and Row.

4   Scherrer, P., "From warning to crisis: a turnaround primer," MANAGEMENT REVIEW, September 1988, 30-36.

5   See Kiechel, W., "How was your Christmas party?", Fortune, January 18, 1988, 159-163 for a summary of corroborating views based on other consultants' experiences.

6   See "America's leanest and meanest: companies that are rising to the challenge of tougher competition," BUSINESS WEEK, October 5, 1987, 78-88; and Waterman, R. H., THE RENEWAL FACTOR, 1987, New York: McGraw-Hill, for plenty of examples. See, also, Mohrman, Susan and Mitroff, I., BUSINESS NOT AS USUAL, 1987, San Francisco: Jossey-Bass, for a penetrating view of what it's going to take for American companies to compete in a tougher world.

7   Wall Street Journal, September 28, 1987.

8   Miami Herald, November 13, 1987.

9   Miami Herald Business Monday section, September 7, 1987.

10  Keiger, Dale, "Leadership profile series," SKY MAGAZINE, 11/87, 52-59.

# THE  TASK  GROUP

## EFFECTIVENESS  INVENTORY

By

Ned Rosen

This questionnaire reflects my work with several hundred groups in a large variety of organizations over the last 15 to 20 years.    Most of the items apply to almost any type of task group.  The Inventory, for example, can be used by a board of directors, management team, project team, temporary task force, standing committee, an accounting office staff, sales unit, production team, the staff of a hospital ward, a fund-raising team, and so on.  Some of the items may require modification or deletion depending upon the specific type of group involved.

It often is advisable to deal with the Inventory one section at a time. Each section begins with a capitalized main heading.  The main headings are Goals And Motivation, External And Internal Resources, Task Procedures And Process, Internal Climate, and Output.

The questionnaire is suitable for use by managers, human resource professionals, or lay persons having an interest in improved teamwork and group process.  While different members of a group are likely to report different viewpoints on many of the questions asked, appropriate discussion of the data can produce insights and improvement efforts.  A trained facilitator may be needed in some situations.

Respondents, anonymously, should circle the number on each item scale to reflect their best judgment. Completed questionnaires should be processed by a neutral person who can tally a frequency distribution for each item. These data are then played back at group meetings for reactions **and action planning** purposes.  The process can be repeated at agreed intervals to keep track of progress.

## GOALS AND MOTIVATION

1. Clarity of group goal(s) and priorities:

   clear 9 8 7 6 5 4 3 2 1 unclear

2. Member acceptance of group goal(s) and priorities:

   no member holdouts 9 8 7 6 5 4 3 2 1 several holdouts

3. Realism of group's goal(s) and priorities:

   realistic 9 8 7 6 5 4 3 2 1 unrealistic

4. Worth-whileness of group's goal(s):

   significant 9 8 7 6 5 4 3 2 1 trivial

5. Decisions are:

   being made 9 8 7 6 5 4 3 2 1 being avoided

6. Acceptance of decisions:

   most members agree 9 8 7 6 5 4 3 2 1 too many holdouts

7. Member interest level:

   most members                most members
   eager to help 9 8 7 6 5 4 3 2 1 disinterested

8. Amount of challenge in group's task:

   high 9 8 7 6 5 4 3 2 1 low

9. Member energy expenditure in pursuit of group's goals:

   substantial 9 8 7 6 5 4 3 2 1 limited

10. Sense of progress toward goal(s):

    lots of progress 9 8 7 6 5 4 3 2 1 little progress

11. Group's value to members as a place to acquire new skills:

    high 9 8 7 6 5 4 3 2 1 low

12. Group's value to members as a career stepping stone:

    high 9 8 7 6 5 4 3 2 1 low

## EXTERNAL AND INTERNAL RESOURCES

**13. Support for group from higher level management:**

willing                      grudging
support 9 8 7 6 5 4 3 2 1  acceptance

**14. Support from group's clients in organization:**

willing                      grudging
support  9 8 7 6 5 4 3 2 1  acceptance

**15. Skill resources in group (including leadership):**

all we need  9 8 7 6 5 4 3 2 1  inadequate

**16. Group's size:**

just right  9 8 7 6 5 4 3 2 1  too big or too small

**17. Membership mix:**

good combina-                  too similar or
tion of people  9 8 7 6 5 4 3 2 1  too different

**18. Budget:**

adequate  9 8 7 6 5 4 3 2 1  a handicap

**19. Overall time allocation to get group's work done:**

just right  9 8 7 6 5 4 3 2 1  too long <u>or</u> too short

**20. Work/meeting space:**

adequate  9 8 7 6 5 4 3 2 1  a handicap

**21. Access to electronic technology:**

adequate  9 8 7 6 5 4 3 2 1  a handicap

**22. Availability of training support:**

adequate  9 8 7 6 5 4 3 2 1  a handicap

**23. Group's reporting relationship/location within the larger organization structure:**

appropriate  9 8 7 6 5 4 3 2 1  not appropriate

# TASK PROCEDURES AND PROCESS

**24. Group's internal reporting relationships:**

appropriate  9 8 7 6 5 4 3 2 1  inappropriate

**25. Amount of task specialization in group's structure:**

just right  9 8 7 6 5 4 3 2 1  too much/too little

**26. Group's problem attack behavior;**

analytic, diagnostic,                    group jumps to
thoughtful, thorough  9 8 7 6 5 4 3 2 1  premature solutions

**27. Group's timetable for accomplishing tasks:**

established  9 8 7 6 5 4 3 2 1  not established

**28. Matching task assignments with individual member abilities:**

tasks assigned                     tasks assigned
to right members  9 8 7 6 5 4 3 2 1  to wrong members

**29. Adequacy of members' task performance:**

members meet  9 8 7 6 5 4 3 2 1  sloppy work
commitments                       and/or late

**30. Allocation of work load among members:**

fair and equitable  9 8 7 6 5 4 3 2 1  uneven

**31. Group's meeting mechanics:**

systematic  9 8 7 6 5 4 3 2 1  haphazard

**33. Member teamwork and coordination:**

high  9 8 7 6 5 4 3 2 1  low   n/a

**33. Leadership within group:**

effective  9 8 7 6 5 4 3 2 1  ineffective

**34. Ground rules on such matters as confidentiality, sign off authority, using channels, etc.:**

Established  9 8 7 6 5 4 3 2 1  not established

**35. Communications between this and other relevant groups:**

clearly established  9 8 7 6 5 4 3 2 1  not established

## INTERNAL "CLIMATE"

**36. Accessibility of members and leader to each other:**

>  high  9 8 7 6 5 4 3 2 1  low

**37. Mutual trust and confidence among members:**

>  high  9 8 7 6 5 4 3 2 1  low

**38. Members' listening behavior:**

> we listen to and                     we do not
> understand each other  9 8 7 6 5 4 3 2 1  listen well

**39. Enjoyment level:**

> members have fun  9 8 7 6 5 4 3 2 1  members do not
>       together                          enjoy each other

**40. Conflict within group:**

> constructive                      intimidating
> confrontation  9 8 7 6 5 4 3 2 1  and destructive

**41. Opportunity for member participation:**

>  encouraging climate  9 8 7 6 5 4 3 2 1  repressive climate

**42. Conformity pressures within group:**

>  strong  9 8 7 6 5 4 3 2 1  weak

**43. Professional pride of group in itself:**

>  a lot  9 8 7 6 5 4 3 2 1  very little

**44. Cohesiveness-morale of this group:**

>  high  9 8 7 6 5 4 3 2 1  low

## OUTPUTS

**45. Group's innovativeness:**

> group generates many                 group generates few
>   new ideas/methods  9 8 7 6 5 4 3 2 1  new ideas/methods

**46. Group's productive output (amount):**

>  high  9 8 7 6 5 4 3 2 1  low

**47. Quality of group's work:**

>  high  9 8 7 6 5 4 3 2 1  low

## MCGREGOR'S TWO FACTOR THEORY - REVISED *

# THEORY X$^2$

- PEOPLE ARE INFINITELY ADAPTABLE; WE CAN MOVE THEM AT WILL.
- GROUPS IN THE WORK PLACE ARE A NECESSARY EVIL; THEY SHOULD BE BROKEN UP FREQUENTLY.
- JOB SECURITY MAKES PEOPLE COMPLACENT.
- MONEY ALWAYS WAS AND STILL IS THE BEST MOTIVATOR.
- MANAGEMENT'S JOB IS TO PLAN; EMPLOYEES ARE THERE TO GET IT DONE.
- PEOPLE WORK BEST WHEN HELD INDIVIDUALLY ACCOUNTABLE.
- PAST ACCOMPLISHMENTS DON'T COUNT; TODAY IS WHAT MATTERS MOST.
- THE BOTTOM LINE IS PARAMOUNT.
- NINETY PERCENT OF OUR MERIT INCREASE MONEY SHOULD GO TO OUR TOP 10% PERFORMERS.
- THE BEST IDEAS COME FROM HIGHER UPS.
- GROUP DECISION MAKING PRODUCES MEDIOCRITY.
- THE TRAINING BUDGET IS TOO BIG.
- THE WOMAN'S PLACE IS IN THE HOME.
- STRESS REDUCTION IS STRICTLY "MIND OVER MATTER."
- YOU CAN'T TEACH AN OLD DOG NEW TRICKS.
- EMPLOYEES, EVEN GOOD ONES, SHOULDN'T BE PROMOTED RAPIDLY.
- COMMUNICATIONS SHOULD BE DRIVEN BY A "NEED TO KNOW" POLICY.
- IF THEY [EMPLOYEES] DON'T LIKE IT HERE, THEY SHOULD LEAVE.

# THEORY Y$^2$

- SUPERVISION IS AN OBSOLETE CONCEPT.
- COORDINATED TEAMWORK IS VALUABLE TO THE ORGANIZATION.
- STRATEGIC PLANNING IS AN IMPERFECT PROCESS.
- QUALITY, PRODUCTIVITY, CUSTOMER SERVICE AND EMPLOYEE SATISFACTION FEED ON EACH OTHER.
- CORPORATIONS HAVE COMMUNITY RESPONSIBILITIES BEYOND THE BOTTOM LINE.
- PEOPLE WHO FEEL SECURE IN THEIR EMPLOYMENT ARE MORE LIKELY TO INNOVATE AND TAKE RISKS.
- GETTING CLOSE TO YOUR CUSTOMERS IS A GOOD IDEA.
- GROUP DECISION MAKING PRODUCES COMMITMENT.
- THE TRAINING BUDGET SHOULD BE TRIPLED.
- EMPLOYEES SHOULD BE ENCOURAGED TO LEARN FROM THEIR MISTAKES.
- EMPLOYEES AT ALL LEVELS HAVE A LOT OF GOOD IDEAS.
- AGE IS NO BARRIER TO LEARNING.
- FULL AND OPEN COMMUNICATION IS THE BEST POLICY.
- WOMEN CAN MAKE IMPORTANT CONTRIBUTIONS TO SIGNIFICANT BUSINESS ACCOMPLISHMENTS.
- DECISIONS SHOULD BE MADE BY THOSE CLOSEST TO THE PROBLEM.
- REWARDS SHOULD BE SPREAD AROUND.

* From Rosen, Ned, TEAMWORK AND THE BOTTOM LINE: GROUPS MAKE A DIF-
FERENCE, 1989, Lawrence Erlbaum Associates, Inc.